Digital Etiquette

D1258367

by Eric Butow, Kendra Losee, and Kelly Noble Mirabella

for dummies®
A Wiley Brand

MAY - - 2022

Digital Etiquette For Dummies®

Published by: **John Wiley & Sons, Inc.**, 111 River Street, Hoboken, NJ 07030-5774, www.wiley.com

Copyright © 2022 by John Wiley & Sons, Inc., Hoboken, New Jersey

Published simultaneously in Canada

No part of this publication may be reproduced, stored in a retrieval system or transmitted in any form or by any means, electronic, mechanical, photocopying, recording, scanning or otherwise, except as permitted under Sections 107 or 108 of the 1976 United States Copyright Act, without the prior written permission of the Publisher. Requests to the Publisher for permission should be addressed to the Permissions Department, John Wiley & Sons, Inc., 111 River Street, Hoboken, NJ 07030, (201) 748-6011, fax (201) 748-6008, or online at http://www.wiley.com/go/permissions.

Trademarks: Wiley, For Dummies, the Dummies Man logo, Dummies.com, Making Everything Easier, and related trade dress are trademarks or registered trademarks of John Wiley & Sons, Inc. and may not be used without written permission. All other trademarks are the property of their respective owners. John Wiley & Sons, Inc. is not associated with any product or vendor mentioned in this book.

LIMIT OF LIABILITY/DISCLAIMER OF WARRANTY: WHILE THE PUBLISHER AND AUTHORS HAVE USED THEIR BEST EFFORTS IN PREPARING THIS WORK, THEY MAKE NO REPRESENTATIONS OR WARRANTIES WITH RESPECT TO THE ACCURACY OR COMPLETENESS OF THE CONTENTS OF THIS WORK AND SPECIFICALLY DISCLAIM ALL WARRANTIES, INCLUDING WITHOUT LIMITATION ANY IMPLIED WARRANTIES OF MERCHANTABILITY OR FITNESS FOR A PARTICULAR PURPOSE. NO WARRANTY MAY BE CREATED OR EXTENDED BY SALES REPRESENTATIVES, WRITTEN SALES MATERIALS OR PROMOTIONAL STATEMENTS FOR THIS WORK. THE FACT THAT AN ORGANIZATION, WEBSITE, OR PRODUCT IS REFERRED TO IN THIS WORK AS A CITATION AND/OR POTENTIAL SOURCE OF FURTHER INFORMATION DOES NOT MEAN THAT THE PUBLISHER AND AUTHORS ENDORSE THE INFORMATION OR SERVICES THE ORGANIZATION, WEBSITE, OR PRODUCT MAY PROVIDE OR RECOMMENDATIONS IT MAY MAKE. THIS WORK IS SOLD WITH THE UNDERSTANDING THAT THE PUBLISHER IS NOT ENGAGED IN RENDERING PROFESSIONAL SERVICES. THE ADVICE AND STRATEGIES CONTAINED HEREIN MAY NOT BE SUITABLE FOR YOUR SITUATION. YOU SHOULD CONSULT WITH A SPECIALIST WHERE APPROPRIATE. FURTHER, READERS SHOULD BE AWARE THAT WEBSITES LISTED IN THIS WORK MAY HAVE CHANGED OR DISAPPEARED BETWEEN WHEN THIS WORK WAS WRITTEN AND WHEN IT IS READ. NEITHER THE PUBLISHER NOR AUTHORS SHALL BE LIABLE FOR ANY LOSS OF PROFIT OR ANY OTHER COMMERCIAL DAMAGES, INCLUDING BUT NOT LIMITED TO SPECIAL, INCIDENTAL, CONSEQUENTIAL, OR OTHER DAMAGES.

For general information on our other products and services, please contact our Customer Care Department within the U.S. at 877-762-2974, outside the U.S. at 317-572-3993, or fax 317-572-4002. For technical support, please visit https://hub.wiley.com/community/support/dummies.

Wiley publishes in a variety of print and electronic formats and by print-on-demand. Some material included with standard print versions of this book may not be included in e-books or in print-on-demand. If this book refers to media such as a CD or DVD that is not included in the version you purchased, you may download this material at http://booksupport.wiley.com. For more information about Wiley products, visit www.wiley.com.

Library of Congress Control Number: 2022933664

ISBN: 978-1-119-86980-1; 978-1-119-87016-6 (ebk); 978-1-119-87004-3 (ebk)

SKY10033764_031622

Contents at a Glance

Table of Contents

Introduction

Well, look at you. We're proud of you for taking steps to become a responsible citizen online by learning about digital etiquette, also called *netiquette*. You wouldn't be reading an actual printed book unless you wanted to sit in a comfortable chair, set your favorite beverage on the table next to you, and soak it all in.

We have a lot of good stuff to share with you to make you a better person online — and you may be surprised that you'll see how to be a better human being here in real life. If you read this entire book, your mindset will change, and others' perceptions of you will change for the better.

About This Book

The purpose of *Digital Etiquette For Dummies* is to help you communicate effectively online. The number of pages in this book has tipped you off that doing so is easier said than done. After all, we can just say that you have to be nice to people, but there's a lot to unpack in that simple concept.

It's not just behaviors that you need to know about and refine — you also need to know about laws governing online behavior, because the wild west approach to communicating on the Internet started to disappear decades ago. That's not just true of *spam* (a friendly reminder that this kind of spam has nothing to do with the processed meat you can buy) but also of data privacy.

So we start by defining etiquette in the digital age. We talk about spam and privacy laws not just in the United States as a whole but also in individual states as well as specific countries and regions. And we talk about communicating effectively — no matter your age and no matter what forum (including social media posts and groups, virtual meetings, livestreams, and phone conversations).

Foolish Assumptions

When writing this book, we assumed that at least one of the following statements describes you:

>> You are a human being who wants to better connect with fellow human beings.

>> You have a business and you want to communicate more effectively with current and prospective customers.

>> You are committed to devoting time and energy to make yourself a better communicator.

If these assumptions are correct, this is the right book for you! We're confident that the tactics and information here can help you achieve your goals.

Icons Used in This Book

To make things easier and ensure that you don't miss important details, we have made use of various icons throughout this book. Here's what the different icons look like and mean:

TIP

The Tip icon is a small piece of expert advice that saves you time and makes your experience online more enjoyable.

REMEMBER

Because we cover a lot of details and information, every now and then we throw in the Remember icon to remind you of important details we've already covered. We know you're reading every juicy detail of the book; the Remember icon just helps resurface some of those tidbits.

TECHNICAL STUFF

Who doesn't love a little geekfest on technical jargon? Okay, a lot of people! But that's why we've pulled out these paragraphs so that you can understand the technical aspects of digital etiquette without getting overwhelmed.

WARNING

Yes, this book has a few warnings. When you see the Warning icon, please take a few extra moments to understand the effect of what we're saying.

Beyond the Book

In addition to what you're reading right now, this book comes with a free, access-anywhere Cheat Sheet that provides a handy list of digital etiquette rules as well as strategies for navigating the Internet with aplomb. To view the Cheat Sheet, simply go to www.dummies.com and type **Digital Etiquette For Dummies Cheat Sheet** in the Search box.

Where to Go from Here

The first three chapters in Part 1 introduce you to digital etiquette, including what digital etiquette is (and isn't), laws and policies, setting and respecting boundaries, and rules for everyone at all age levels, from kids to adults.

We think you should at least familiarize yourself with the concepts in the first three chapters because you need to know the concepts in Part 1 so that you can conquer digital etiquette in Part 2. If you deal with email often, you'll want to focus on Part 3. (It not only talks about email etiquette but also fills you in on what you need to know so that you don't run afoul of legal trouble in your email marketing campaigns.)

After that, we have a lot of information about virtual meetings, which were already popular before the COVID-19 pandemic propelled interest in that topic into the stratosphere. And let's not forget mobile etiquette. (Part 5 talks about not only text messaging but also how to be polite when you're talking on your phone.) If you want to focus on a specific area, the table of contents will guide you to where you want to go.

Now it's time to get started reading about what etiquette is and how to use it in your online communication. Enjoy the book!

1

Etiquette Guidelines

IN THIS PART . . .

See how etiquette has changed in the digital age

Know the online ramifications of online behavior

Recognize the importance of minding your manners

Chapter **1**

Defining Etiquette in the Digital Age

I t's easy enough to define etiquette, isn't it? Just be kind to one another.

That's all, folks — thank for reading!

Of course, you know that's not the whole story or else you wouldn't be reading this book. It's hard enough to know what etiquette is when you're dealing with other people face-to-face. But now communications devices have added many more rules for communicating not only with video cameras, which are ubiquitous on computers and phones, but also in situations where you don't even see the other person (and you may have noticed that makes people seem less considerate, to put it mildly).

Before we can talk about how to apply etiquette to the digital age in which everyone now finds themselves, we need to review some definitions. Once we do that, I'll discuss how you can apply etiquette in different situations, including social, small group, and business environments.

Coming Up with Some Definitions

Let's start with the obvious question: What is digital etiquette, anyway?

You may also have heard digital etiquette referred to by the portmanteau *netiquette* — that scrunching together of the words Inter*net* and *etiquette.* No matter which term you've heard, the same definition applies: You should follow these basic rules of behavior whenever you interact with others on the Internet or use electronic devices like smartphones. And by *Internet,* we mean all kinds of online communication, including email, forums, and social networking websites.

Netiquette

Let's start a deeper dive by talking about the term *netiquette,* which may be the most familiar to you. This term predates the modern Internet by quite a few years — 1983, specifically. This was the era when bulletin board systems, or BBSs, were the primary means of communicating online.

The acronym *BBS* doesn't ring a bell, huh? Maybe the national services CompuServe, The Source, and America Online can help you (not so fondly) remember the days when you had to save up for a faster modem — such as 56Kbps or even (gasp!) ISDN.

The two prominent dictionaries have slightly different definitions of netiquette, but it's useful to keep both in mind:

>> The *Oxford English Dictionary* defines *netiquette* as "the correct or acceptable way of communicating on the Internet."

>> Merriam-Webster (http://m-w.com) defines netiquette as "etiquette governing communication on the Internet."

REMEMBER

Netiquette rules vary, depending on the forum you're in. For example, email rules are different from when you're chatting in a live forum. We go into more detail about those differences later in this chapter.

Etiquette versus online ethics

In trying to wrap your mind around the notion of etiquette, you need to be able to distinguish between *ethics* and *etiquette.* You may have heard both terms used interchangeably when people talk about online behavior. If you think they're the same, lose that thought like you lose the TV remote.

The term *etiquette* is the code, at times unspoken, that indicates the polite way to behave in a society. *Ethics* is a set of moral principles that tells you what's good and what's bad. In a movie, you may have seen a character who you know is a bad guy but who acts politely toward everyone in the film; the perfect manners don't fool you, because you know that the bad guy is still a villain who is naturally immoral.

Some behaviors also fall under the definition of *bad* ethics, which may help explain why people confuse the terms. For example, someone who lies and cheats to get what they want, no matter whether it happens in person or online, displays behavior that belies a deeper problem — we're talking about someone who cannot think ethically.

If you want to read more about the differences between ethics and etiquette, the Pediaa site has a good overview at `https://pediaa.com/difference-between-ethics-and-etiquette`.

TIP

Seeing Which Situations Call for Etiquette

Certain rules of etiquette apply *all* the time, such as sneezing into your arm or elbow. (That's polite behavior no matter whether you're in a pandemic.) Other rules apply to specific situations, such as chatting with others in an online meeting.

How you behave ethically online can impact your ability to make a living. It's now standard procedure for an employer to examine your social media profiles before deciding whether to accept your application, let alone contact you about an interview. If you want to keep certain information private, change the privacy settings on your profiles to show them only to specific connections, such as people on your friends list.

REMEMBER

General rules of etiquette are in effect all the time, and others are specific to each situation. You *must* know the basics of good manners online, and this opening chapter offers the perfect opportunity to give you a 30,000-foot overview of how to apply etiquette online.

Before you forge ahead, stop for a moment and remember that what you do can also affect you legally. Have you ever heard anyone say, "What's on the Internet stays on the Internet"? Though it's unclear whether that statement will remain true over time, it is certainly true now. So, with your behavior recorded for others to find, do you doubt that you need online etiquette? (By the way, we delve into the legal issues of online behavior in Chapter 2.)

WARNING

Social: Chatting with others

Social situations have rules in place that you're probably familiar with, such as not saying things that you know would be hurtful to another person. Without standing physically in front of someone, though, it's easier for us to forget that we're actually talking to a real person, even if they aren't physically present.

So, whenever you're chatting with friends online, take the opportunity to review what you should be doing in social conversations — what passes for good etiquette, in other words. As you read, think about whether and how you're following these rules so that you can train yourself to chat with others more effectively.

Hold a good conversation

Just as in a face-to-face chat, learn how you can hold a back-and-forth dialogue online. If you monopolize a discussion where you're the one saying most everything, don't be surprised if you're called a *troll* — a person who is intentionally harmful to gain attention and/or cause trouble. It won't be long before people start finding ways to avoid you.

Avoid gossip at all costs

It's easy on social media to succumb to the urge to gossip, especially if the person you're gossiping about isn't included in the group of people you're talking with. Don't let yourself believe that private online groups are safe, though, because — just as with in-person gossip — online gossip finds a way to get back to the person you're talking about. Then, like all gossip, it boomerangs on you.

Engage

Social media and other forms of online communication make it easy for you to ignore everything that other people write. After all, no one knows whether you're actually paying attention, right?

If you've posted something, however, you may get some feedback on those posts from your friends and other people who can see your posts. It's good form to respond to people with a personal thank-you message or a clicked Like icon — or both.

Even if you don't want to type anything in response, clicking the Like icon next to the comment lets the commenter know that they've been recognized and that their comment is valuable. And, you may not know it, but you've improved your social standing with as little effort as a click or tap. If you see this person offline, your real-life social standing grows a little, too.

Connect positively

If you find a comment that you want to talk about, don't be afraid to express your opinion by typing your own comment in response. Before you start typing, though, shift into the right mindset and make sure that it's a healthy conversation.

In online discussions, you're likely talking to a real person. So, if you think that the conversation runs the risk of turning into an argument where both you and the other person become angry — and you both look bad to anyone else participating — consider not saying *anything*.

TIP

If you want to connect with others by taking photos of your friends, ask for permission before you tag them in your photos. Facebook, Instagram, and other social network sites allow you to tag photos so that all the friends of your friends can see the photo, too — though your friends may not appreciate it.

Think before you post

There are several good reasons not to post something objectionable or even threatening — including the quite established fact that it can land you in hot water with your friends or even with law enforcement. Have you, or has someone you know, done one of the following?

>> You shared unflattering photos of your friends and then were baffled that they were upset — at least until your friends posted unflattering photos of you and then you started to get the message.

>> You left a comment on a false story without checking with one or more credible sources, like major news organizations and/or fact-checking sites like Snopes that have a database of stories that are shown to be false or true — or a mixture of the two.

>> You posted about doing something illegal because you thought it made you look cool to your friends, but instead you got in trouble with the law. For example, someone contacted law enforcement when they saw that you bragged about drinking, driving home drunk, and arriving home without a scratch — except when you hit a couple of parked cars but managed to drive off with no trouble.

>> You've posted some confidential details that someone later used against you. For example, if you're going through a divorce and you've posted a lot of ugly details, you're shocked that the lawyer for your ex somehow found those details and is using them against you.

>> You had no responses to your complaints that it's too hot in the summer or to your photos showing that you had scrambled eggs for breakfast. That got you to thinking about what others want to see in your social media feeds and you

started making better decisions about what to post — and being more careful has reduced your stress because you feel no pressure to post every little event in your life.

WARNING

When you're impaired in some way, you're more likely to make poor judgments and decisions. That's true even if you're just checking your email and social media. Don't respond to a message if you have a hangover, if you're tired, or even if you've just awakened and you're looking at the content on your smartphone without having that first cup of coffee. The same is true if you're agitated — take some time to think about the situation and shift your mind to a place where it's feeling good and you're ready to respond like an adult. This strategy beats saying something that could damage your reputation or get you into even worse trouble.

Meeting: Behaving appropriately in a small group setting

The COVID-19 pandemic accelerated online meetings to the nth degree, and suddenly the Zoom video chat app was everywhere — even in our dreams, it seemed. But the pandemic also shined a bright light on the need to behave appropriately in small groups online.

Just like in a face-to-face meeting, online meetings require etiquette. There are things you should do and things you definitely shouldn't do. And, when acting as the leader of an online meeting, you definitely should know these rules because you may have to enforce them. Let's break it down.

Do these things

Here are things you should do in an online meeting:

» Prepare for the meeting ahead of time by eliminating distractions as much as possible and making sure (if at all possible) that you won't be interrupted.

» Arrive at the meeting a few minutes early. If you're the meeting host, you should do this anyway. And if you're not, you can wait for the host to enter the meeting while you make any last-minute preparations.

» If you're the leader of the meeting, introduce everyone in the meeting.

» Take turns and don't interrupt each other.

» Speak clearly and expect that you may have to repeat yourself because — even if your microphone works well — other participants may not have decent speakers.

>> Be yourself and remember not to focus on the box showing your face in the app window. Focus on others and engage.

>> If you can, look into your camera when you're talking. That helps others realize that you're looking at them. (It's harder to do when the webcam sits on top of a large monitor.) Don't be afraid to look away from the camera from time to time in order to look at the person you're speaking to on the screen, because that's a natural behavior.

>> Many video meeting apps have text chat so that you can type with the entire group or with a particular user. If you need to use text chat to communicate, be sure to tell everyone (or at least the leader) about it before you begin. And, if you chat privately with someone, use it sparingly so as not to distract yourself and others.

>> Dress for the occasion. If you're chatting with friends, dress how you would if you were meeting them in person. And, if you're in a business meeting, dress as you would for an in-person meeting.

>> If you're the leader of the group and the one responsible for closing the meeting, you need to be the one who closes the meeting with any reminders and by thanking everyone, perhaps individually, for attending the meeting.

REMEMBER

Dress well from head to toe for your meeting. If you have to take a bathroom break or tend to someone, such as a child or pet who wanders into your space, you have to stand up — and then participants can see what you're wearing. If you've been sitting there in your underwear, how do you think people will react? (Your eyes probably grew wider just thinking about that scenario.)

Don't do these things

Do *not* do any of these things in an online meeting:

>> **Raise your voice:** Even if you think doing so will help someone with a bad speaker hear you, no one else with good speakers wants to hear it. You or the person leading the group will have to work with the person to fix the problem — probably offline.

>> **Talk over the speakers:** If you do, expect your audio to be muted because Zoom and many other online video chat apps have that capability. Some speakers will just turn off everyone's audio unless someone raises their hand in the app.

>> **Engage in side conversations:** We talk elsewhere in this book about not having too many side conversations in the chat window, not only because it's distracting but also because people will notice that you're not paying attention to the speaker or to anyone else.

- » **Turn off your camera:** Sure, it's physically possible to turn it off if you want to carry on a side conversation, but that doesn't mean you should do it. When someone in a meeting turns off their camera, what's the first thought that pops into your head? You immediately think that person is checking out, right? If you need to turn off the camera and microphone to do something important, like go to the bathroom, let the leader of the group know as soon as possible. If you want to go grab a snack, well, you should have thought of that before the meeting began.

- » **Snack:** Speaking of snacks, it's a good idea to eat before or after the meeting so that people don't have to watch (or even hear) you. We talk about this topic in more detail later in this chapter.

- » **Multitask:** Look at the camera or the screen. If you need to check something in the meeting such as a spreadsheet to confirm some data, you can do that, but don't look on your phone when someone else is talking or you think you can just listen in. Other people can see you and they will notice. That can cost you down the road — and maybe not that far down, either.

WARNING

Don't meet while driving. That should be self-evident, but too many people do it — maybe even you.

Corporate: Behaving professionally in the workplace

Okay, you say, all this information about what you should do and what you shouldn't do is helpful stuff. But when you're in the virtual workplace, it seems that those behaviors aren't enough.

And you're right!

Now that your dopamine levels are coming back down to normal, you may naturally wonder what other professional behaviors you may want to use both in online meetings and in written text like online chats and email.

Send a virtual handshake

When you're in an online meeting, be sure to greet everyone in the meeting and tell them that you're happy to see them. If someone connects with your website by using a form that asks your company for information, send a personalized thank-you message from the appropriate person. The owner or CEO qualifies, don't you think?

TIP

If you have no form, consider adding a *chatbot* (a program that simulates and processes human conversation, in other words) to your website so that people can ask basic questions and the chatbot's artificial intelligence, or AI, can provide friendly answers. Plenty of chatbots are available, and you may have heard of some of them, like Netomi (`www.netomi.com`) and Zendesk (`www.zendesk.com`).

Put a face to your name

You need to put a face to your name so that people can know that you're a real person. They will not only be more inclined to do business with you but will also know that your business is real.

REMEMBER

Be sure to add a face to your name on social media, too — especially on business social media sites like LinkedIn.

Know your (time) zone

When you make appointments with your business contacts online, be aware of the time zone of the other person. When you're going to meet online with someone in a different part of the world, you need to check with that person and make sure that the agreed-on time works for them. (4 P.M. in the wintertime in New York City is not 4 P.M. in London; it's 9 P.M., and you don't want to be calling then.) Though a good time for you may be the early morning hours, that may be nighttime for someone else, so be sure that the other person is a night owl.

This is true even if you're in the same country. If you're in California, which is in the Pacific time zone, and you want to meet with someone in the Eastern time zone (three hours ahead of you), be sure to set a time so that both of you are in the office and not at home, in traffic, or at lunch.

REMEMBER

The same reminder about time zones applies for email messages. If you're expecting a response right away from someone halfway around the world, you may be frustrated until you realize that you sent the message when the other person was fast asleep.

Connect during business hours

To follow up on our suggestions about time zones, be sure to stick to business hours. This has become such an issue in the workplace that Portugal established a law forbidding bosses from contacting employees outside working hours: `www.cnbc.com/2021/11/15/portugal-bans-bosses-from-contacting-employees-outside-working-hours.html`.

Yet there may be times when you need to contact someone outside of working hours because of a genuine emergency. As always, think of these scenarios ahead of time and work with your team to set the ground rules for communicating while you're at home.

Even if you're not working with a team, speak ahead of time to the person you plan to talk with so that you both can understand when you're going to contact them online by way of either Zoom, web chat, or email.

In sum, set expectations ahead of time. No one likes to have their off time interrupted and have to delay telling their kids bedtime stories because your boss or one of your team members thinks it's okay.

Don't just write — proofread

Online communication is primarily a written medium, and though you may meet using Zoom or another online video app from time to time, you don't want to do that all the time. In a corporate environment, you'll likely chat with each other via text in a collaboration app like Slack or, for better or worse, email messages.

With email, you have the benefit of not having anyone else read your message until you're ready to send it. (We won't visit the horror of accidentally pressing the Reply All icon.) The bad news is that many people — and you may be one of them — believe that they're better writers than they are. So they think they can just bang out a message and send it.

You don't have the benefit of having an editor with you, the way we do with this book, but you do have the ability to take a break, focus on another task for a little while, and then reread your message. We think (heck, we *know*) that you'll be shocked by what you find as you proofread.

Don't be surprised if you delete a lot of unnecessary words and maybe replace some of them with new ones that sound better. And you may be surprised to find that you may not want to send the message, after all — you may want instead to think about what you *really* want to say and then write a different version later. You're allowed to do that, you know.

Well, what about writing in a live chat or texting? Here's our simple advice: Keep everything short and sweet, but not so short that people may have trouble understanding you — that is, don't write acronyms and abbreviations in place of every other word!

TMI

If you grew up during the 1990s and beyond, you know what the acronym *TMI* means: too much information. Yet a lot of advice floats around the web saying that you have to be authentic because that's what people like — especially younger people.

What's the balance? Here, too, we have some simple advice. Just ask yourself one question: Does what I'm about to explain about myself further the conversation and help make my point to my co-workers and/or customers?

If you talk about how you grew frustrated by your computer's slow speed and so you developed a design for your app that solved the problem, that's a great way to make a connection. But if you talk about how terrible your life is with no purpose to it, it comes across as unprofessional and can cost you customers, your job, and maybe your business.

Business: Conducting yourself properly among colleagues

Tips about proofreading, conducting meetings, and refraining from telling your life story are all well and good, you might say, but how about day-to-day conduct? We're glad you asked, because we have four ideas for dealing with that subject. Read on.

See how other people use online communication tools

If you're using online communication tools, you have to follow some rules of the road. For example, on a social media platform, you shouldn't engage in behavior that another person finds harassing, because it will be reported to the platform's help staff and you might find yourself banned.

You should familiarize yourself with these rules, but you may want additional guidance and motivation. Try these three strategies:

>> **Look at how others communicate before you start communicating yourself, if you can.** For example, see how different people communicate in a Slack chat before you chime in so that you can get a feel for the environment and how the discussion is going. If the discussion is more formal, use more formal language. If it's more easygoing, you can switch up your communication accordingly.

> » **Look on the web to understand how other people communicated effectively in Zoom meetings or email messages or whatever other medium you're interested in.** If you're a fan of Tom Hanks, let's say, you'll have no trouble finding examples of how he communicated on the web. The same goes for how to find examples of businesspeople who communicate effectively with their customers.

> » **Talk to peers.** These people may be other business owners. They may be coworkers. They may even be managers. Whoever they are, talk with them one-on-one to find out how they connect with others in different situations.

Consider your audience

The "feel" of a conversation between you and someone else, or between a group of people, is something you should pay attention to before you engage. But there's no substitute for actually thinking ahead about the audience who will be in the discussion with you.

When you're in a professional situation, you may be speaking with a customer, with your boss, or with different coworkers online (or with *all* of them). That knowledge should give you an idea of how you should communicate from the get-go. For example, if you're with a customer, you'll be as helpful as you can be and answer every question, no matter how boring you think it is.

In a situation where you're meeting with the CEO of your company, it's a good bet that your communication should be formal and professional. If you're in a Zoom meeting, that can also mean formal business dress.

WARNING

There's no reason to talk badly about someone or a group of people in any environment, online or not. If you happen to be male and think that being online with a group of coworkers who are all men gives you the freedom to denigrate women, you may be updating your résumé sooner than you ever expected.

Remain neutral

The first popular television police show was *Dragnet*, and the protagonist, Sergeant Joe Friday, had the slogan "Just the facts, ma'am" when interviewing witnesses. (Don't believe us? Search for the term Dragnet on Facebook. Think we're old? No comment.)

When you're talking online in a professional setting, stick to the facts and be as clear as possible. Don't make any jokes or try to start an argument. No one can read someone's tone or facial expressions, though emojis online do help with that task and provide some context. Yet without other nonverbal cues, like body language, people translate messages in their own way. Some of that translation comes from how they're feeling.

You've likely encountered the end result: The other person misinterprets or becomes angry about what you said, and suddenly you're defending yourself against accusations that have come out of proverbial left field. And, of course, you *never* start sniping back, right?

Switch when you have to

You may need to switch your communication method when you find that you can't get your point across in the current medium. For example, you've probably had a long email conversation with quotes from previous messages stretching endlessly in the email window. Or maybe a conversation has devolved into an argument because neither of you understands what the other is saying. In that case, it's time to set up either a phone conversation or an online chat via an app so that you can talk with each other in person.

TIP

An online chat app may be the best way to gain some clarity because you both can see each other's faces (as well as some helpful nonverbal cues) on your webcams. These cues can help both of you understand what the other is feeling and help you create a solution.

Eating: Shielding meeting participants from your eating habits

Do you like to hear other people gobbling their food during an online meeting? (Hearing yourself eat may be bad enough.) Then consider that other people on your Microsoft Teams call may not like hearing your slurps and smacks.

Even if you turn off your microphone, they have to watch you, and we'll bet you dollars to (ahem) doughnuts that you dislike watching other people eat as much as they dislike watching you. And if you're eating and a bunch of lettuce falls out of your burger, that means you have to leave the meeting and clean up. Not very professional, don't you think?

So, if you're setting up an online meeting with Zoom, Microsoft Teams, or a similar app and everyone can see each other on their webcams, set expectations about food or drink ahead of time. Don't assume (and we know the saying about the word *assume*) that everyone will adhere to the rules. Make it clear that there will be no eating of snacks, doughnuts, or any other meal during the meeting.

TIP

Should you ban drinks during online meetings, too? That's harder to do because, in an in-person meeting, people usually bring drinks so that they avoid feeling parched, and they will push back against any directive not to have drinks. You still run the same risk of having drinks in a virtual meeting as in an in-person meeting, so be consistent — if you allow beverages in an in-person meeting, allow them in your virtual meeting, too.

Telephone: Paying attention to the conversation and your behavior

You remember the telephone, don't you? You still use it on your smartphone to *speak* with people. Many companies still rely on voice calls to interact with their customers, and even people in office settings have phones with receivers you pick up.

When you talk on the phone, you need to be aware of not only the conversation but also your behavior. This section details what we mean.

Follow this general guidance

In any call, here are some good rules to follow:

>> Answer the call within three rings.

>> If you can't answer the call within three rings, it means you're busy and letting the call go to your voicemail so that you can refer to it later.

>> Speaking of voicemail, record your greeting in your own voice that's reasonably cheerful. Be sure to tell people that you can't pick up the phone right now and ask them for any information you need, such as their name, a brief description, and/or their phone number.

>> Check your voicemail when you can, perhaps on a schedule. For example, you may want to check it once in the morning and once in the afternoon.

>> Use your speakerphone only when it's absolutely necessary — and only if you're in a quiet place.

>> When you call someone to talk, tell them the purpose of the call. If the other person doesn't agree with the purpose, you need to come to an agreement before you can start the call.

>> Speak clearly. This advice should be obvious, but it's easy to become lazy and start talking like you're in the same room with the other person — at least until they jolt you back to reality when they loudly ask, "*What?*"

- » Use proper language. This advice should also be self-evident, but you need to pay attention to it before you start using language you would use only with your friends and not in a professional setting.

- » Actively listen and take notes. By *actively listen,* we mean that you may want to repeat what someone says to ensure that you understand them. And you can type as you talk to make sure you're taking notes, though that's harder to do with a speakerphone than a headset, because the speakerphone may be close to your keyboard.

Help your customers

For customer service calls, we have more tips to share with you:

- » Immediately introduce yourself when you pick up the call. Also ask who you're speaking with.

- » Be friendly, but if you can't do that, at least be neutral — unless you want to rile your customer enough that they decide to complain and your life becomes more difficult than it already is.

- » Listen to your volume level. If you're starting to talk more loudly because the environment around you is growing louder, your customer may start to complain that you're yelling at them. So you may need to move the call to another location.

- » Before you move your call to another location, ask the other person for permission to put them on hold or to transfer a call. The reason might be the noise of your environment or the need to find more information to be able to give the customer the right answer (or to forward them to the person who has it).

REMEMBER

You may find people who have problems speaking on the phone. Maybe they detest talking by phone or they have medical issues that prevent them from talking or listening for any length of time (if at all). There may be times when you *have* to speak by phone, but in that case, respect the other person by being brief — and perhaps by sending any follow-up questions by email or text message. Or, if a person doesn't want to chat with you using a webcam on Zoom or another online chat app, many of those apps have live text chats so that you can still speak without video. Being flexible can help you gain brownie points with both customers and coworkers.

Chapter **2**

The Legal Ins and Outs of Etiquette

The wild west days of communicating online are coming to an end, and more laws are setting boundaries on what you can and can't do (on pain of imprisonment). Despite the laws on the books and more laws being considered as we write this book, there are still *other* unwritten rules of online communication — just as they are in real life — that you need to know about.

In this chapter, we talk about federal laws governing online behavior in the United States as a whole as well as state laws (including laws in our home state of California), but we promise to keep the legal jargon to a minimum.

Next, we tell you about the policies your company needs to follow to make sure you don't run afoul of any regulations. We wrap up this chapter by telling you how to respect boundaries in your communication with members of your company team and your customers.

Laying Down the (Communication) Law

In the United States, federal laws govern everyone in the country as well as state laws that augment what the feds already have in place. (If you're not in the United States, we can't go over summarize all the laws in every country for you, because you'd have a very thick book that you'd be intimidated to pick up, let alone read.)

Instead, we take the trite 30,000-foot view of the laws so that you understand how they affect you. We also include links to websites spelling out the full laws, in case you want to get into the weeds.

Looking at federal laws

The Communications Decency Act (CDA), passed in 1996, has a section numbered 230 that protects freedom of expression on the Internet. More specifically, the section provides immunity from liability for website platforms when it comes to third-party content, such as people posting on a social media platform.

What's more, Section 230 includes a Good Samaritan section, which protects operators of interactive computing services from civil liability if a service removes or moderates that third-party material, even if the speech is constitutionally protected.

Where did this section come from? Let's start with one of the earliest Internet service providers (ISPs): The World, launched way back in 1989.

TIP

The World is still online, all these decades later; you can visit the website at `https://theworld.com`.

As ISPs began to grow toward widespread use in the early 1990s, a pair of lawsuits were brought against two national ISPs — CompuServe and Prodigy — by users who felt their speech was being suppressed illegally. The question at the heart of the lawsuit? Were ISPs *publishers* or *distributors* of user content?

The CDA and Section 230 were designed to answer that question, stating categorically that ISPs were mere distributors of content and therefore had no editorial control over the content being distributed. The CDA soon found itself being challenged in the courts, however, and eventually found itself in the Supreme Court. In 1997, the Supreme Court unanimously struck down the anti-indecency provisions of the CDA but left Section 230 alone. (For more on the story, check out `www.eff.org/issues/cda230/legislative-history`.)

The end result is that Section 230 is widely hailed as the legislation that enabled the Internet and the web to grow into the indispensable communication medium we have today. And, despite recent court challenges to Section 230 (especially around technology companies' control over political discussions), several court decisions have found that the section is constitutional.

If you want to look into the various court cases in detail, the Legal Information Institute at Cornell University has both the US Code and notes on its website (`www.law.cornell.edu/uscode/text/47/230#`; see Figure 2.1).

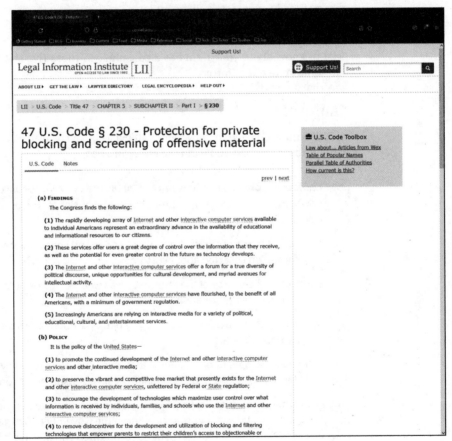

FIGURE 2-1:
Title 47,
Section 230 of the
US Code on the
Legal Information
Institute website.

Parsing the state laws

As of this writing, five states — California, Colorado, Nevada, Vermont, and Virginia — have enacted their own data privacy laws. These laws have similar language in several areas, including

» The right to access and delete personal information

» The right to opt out of the sale of personal information

» Requirements that commercial websites or online services post a privacy policy (which we talk about later in this chapter)

TECHNICAL STUFF

These state laws didn't just come into being by themselves. Legislators received help from the Uniform Law Commission (www.uniformlaws.org/home), a nonprofit organization, founded way back in 1892, to help states produce nonpartisan, uniform laws so that if you move from, say, Virginia to Vermont, you're not gobsmacked by completely different laws.

We don't want to smack your head, goblike or otherwise, so we tell you what you need to know about your rights as a consumer in these five states, starting with our home state of California.

California

In California, you need to know about an existing law as well as a proposition that was approved in 2020 and will take effect in 2023.

» **California Consumer Privacy Act of 2018:** The CCPA gives consumers a lot of power to dictate their privacy preferences to a business. The provisions include the right to

- Request that a business disclose categories and specific pieces of personal information collected about customers

- Request the source of the information as well as the business purpose for that customer information

- Request that the business delete any personal information the business may have collected

- Request to opt out of the sale of their personal information by a business (which is not allowed to discriminate against consumers for opting out)

» **California Consumer Privacy Rights Act:** Voters approved Proposition 24, the Consumer Privacy Rights Act (CPRA), in the November 2020 general election. The CPRA will go (or, depending on when you buy this book, has gone) into effect on January 1, 2023.

The CPRA expands consumer data privacy laws in three ways:

- Consumers can stop businesses from sharing their personal information.

- Consumers have the power to correct inaccurate personal information collected by a business.

- Consumers can also limit the use of sensitive personal information by businesses. That information includes race, ethnicity, religion, sexual orientation, specific health information, genetic data, and the consumer's precise geolocation.

» What's more, the CPRA authorizes the formation of the California Privacy Protection Agency to implement consumer privacy laws, enforce those laws, and levy fines. This new agency will also have to figure out how to interpret the portion of the CPRA that says businesses can't keep personal information for longer than "reasonably necessary."

» **Data Broker Registration:** California law defines a *data broker* as a business that deliberately collects and sells consumers' personal information to third parties. If you're a data broker in California, you have to register with the state attorney general's office every year.

What this means for you as a private citizen is that if you want a list of data brokers in the state, you can access the website at https://oag.ca.gov/data-brokers. The website has links to the broker submission information, the contact email address, the broker website address, as well as a link to a list of incomplete registrations.

Colorado

On July 1, 2023, the state of Colorado added the Colorado Privacy Act (CPA) to the existing Colorado Consumer Protection Act. The CPA defines terms for covered businesses, consumers, and data, notably the term *controller*, as the person or group that determines how they use customer data.

As you would expect, the CPA also includes information about consumer rights and business responsibilities about using customer data. Under the law, the state attorney general and district attorneys throughout the state have the authority to prosecute violators. (For more on the specific language of the legislation, see https://leg.colorado.gov/bills/sb21-190.)

Nevada

Nevada state law requires websites to give visitors the option to opt out of having their personal data sold to third parties. The website also must give customers the ability to contact the company to request that the company not sell their personal information that has been collected.

A company can add one or more of the following three communication methods to the website:

>> **A web page or website** that allows the user to make the request, such as on a form

>> **An email address** the user can click on to submit the request

>> **A direct phone number** to the company that allows someone to verbally submit a request

Nevada added another Internet privacy law in 2021, SB260, that narrowly defines the term *sale* when it comes to consumer data, creates new requirements for data brokers, and adds exemptions for certain entities, like consumer reporting agencies. You can view an in-depth summary on the JD Supra website at www.jdsupra.com/legalnews/nevada-gov-sisolak-signs-senate-bill-sb-5355176.

Vermont

Like laws in California and Nevada, Vermont has a law that requires data brokers to register annually. However, data brokers need to register with the Vermont secretary of state, not the attorney general. The secretary of state website at https://sos.vermont.gov/corporations/other-services/data-brokers has information about what is and what isn't a data broker, a link to a data broker search, and a link to the state's data broker law.

Virginia

The Virginia Consumer Data Protection Act, or CDPA, was passed in 2021 and goes into effect on January 1, 2023. The CDPA applies to all persons who conduct business in the state and who also meet these two criteria:

>> Control or process the personal data of at least 100,000 consumers in a calendar year

>> Derive 50 percent of gross revenue from the sale of personal data as well as control or process the personal data of at least 25,000 consumers

The JD Supra website has a good overview of what the law does, how you can prepare for it, and how to handle uncertainties about implementing the law, at www.jdsupra.com/legalnews/virginia-s-new-data-privacy-law-an-8812636.

Setting Company Policies

If your business does business online, it's common sense to have policies in place to make sure that your business is protected, no matter whether laws exist to protect you. That means you should seriously consider putting a privacy policy on your website that includes at least the following information:

>> What types of personal information your business collects

>> What information is shared with third parties, if any

>> How consumers can request changes to their information

>> How someone can opt out of having their data collected

TIP

Content management website platforms such as WordPress have built-in privacy policy builders. That may not be enough for what you need, however, so you may want to turn to attorneys or companies that specialize in crafting online policies. One low-cost option Eric uses for his business as well as his website clients' sites is Termageddon (https://termageddon.com).

But online policies aren't just about posting a privacy policy on your website and forgetting about it. You also need to specify the terms of service for your product, service, or content.

You also need to understand how to market your business online so that you don't run afoul of laws designed to eliminate junk email — what you probably know as spam. (It's no longer just a processed lunch meat or a famous *Monty Python* skit.)

Specifying your terms of service

You may find a Terms of Service document on a website (we show you an example in Figure 2-2), with a product or as part of the legal documentation you receive as part of a service you've signed up for. Most likely, you have paid scant attention to a Terms of Service document or web page because you consider it flotsam and mentally toss it aside.

If you're running a business, however, a Terms of Service web page or document is essential if you want to protect your product, service, or web content from copyright infringements as well as from legal liabilities.

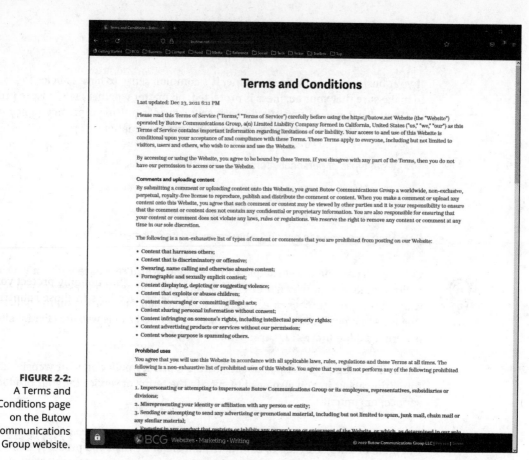

Terms and Conditions

Last updated: Dec 23, 2021 6:11 PM

Please read this Terms of Service ("Terms," "Terms of Service") carefully before using the https://butow.net Website (the "Website") operated by Butow Communications Group, a(n) Limited Liability Company formed in California, United States ("us," "we," "our") as this Terms of Service contains important information regarding limitations of our liability. Your access to and use of this Website is conditional upon your acceptance of and compliance with these Terms. These Terms apply to everyone, including but not limited to visitors, users and others, who wish to access and use the Website.

By accessing or using the Website, you agree to be bound by these Terms. If you disagree with any part of the Terms, then you do not have our permission to access or use the Website.

Comments and uploading content

By submitting a comment or uploading content onto this Website, you grant Butow Communications Group a worldwide, non-exclusive, perpetual, royalty-free license to reproduce, publish and distribute the comment or content. When you make a comment or upload any content onto this Website, you agree that such comment or content may be viewed by other parties and it is your responsibility to ensure that the comment or content does not contain any confidential or proprietary information. You are also responsible for ensuring that your content or comment does not violate any laws, rules or regulations. We reserve the right to remove any content or comment at any time in our sole discretion.

The following is a non-exhaustive list of types of content or comments that you are prohibited from posting on our Website:

- Content that harrasses others;
- Content that is discriminatory or offensive;
- Swearing, name calling and otherwise abusive content;
- Pornographic and sexually explicit content;
- Content displaying, depicting or suggesting violence;
- Content that exploits or abuses children;
- Content encouraging or committing illegal acts;
- Content sharing personal information without consent;
- Content infringing on someone's rights, including intellectual property rights;
- Content advertising products or services without our permission;
- Content whose purpose is spamming others.

Prohibited uses

You agree that you will use this Website in accordance with all applicable laws, rules, regulations and these Terms at all times. The following is a non-exhaustive list of prohibited uses of this Website. You agree that you will not perform any of the following prohibited uses:

1. Impersonating or attempting to impersonate Butow Communications Group or its employees, representatives, subsidiaries or divisions;
2. Misrepresenting your identity or affiliation with any person or entity;
3. Sending or attempting to send any advertising or promotional material, including but not limited to spam, junk mail, chain mail or any similar material;
4. Engaging in any conduct that restricts or inhibits any person's use or enjoyment of the Website, or which, as determined in our sole

BCG Websites · Marketing · Writing   © 2022 Butow Communications Group LLC | Privacy | Terms

FIGURE 2-2:
A Terms and Conditions page on the Butow Communications Group website.

REMEMBER

You may see the label Terms and Conditions referred to instead as Terms of Service (or ToS), Terms of Use, General Conditions, Legal, Notes, or the standard software document EULA (short for End User License Agreement). What's the difference between the titles Terms and Conditions, Terms of Service, and Terms of Use? Nothing. It's just a matter of preference about what you want to use. For example, if you have a product, you may want to use the title Terms of Use because the document is about the terms of using the product.

Seeing what's needed

All these terms and conditions comprise a contract in which the owner of the product, service, and/or website states the conditions of use for the product or service. For example, this document lists rules that users must follow when interacting with one another on a social media site and specifies what will happen if those rules aren't followed.

In your terms and conditions, you need to ensure that you have liability clauses and disclaimers, such as the fact that a website will likely go down from time to time. This is because a vital reason to have a Terms and Conditions document, no matter what you call it, is to cover your backside. If one or more users bring court action against you, your Terms and Conditions document is your first line of defense.

Comparing privacy policies with terms and conditions

Why do you need a privacy policy as well as a Terms and Conditions document? Aren't they the same thing?

It's true that a privacy policy and Terms and Conditions are legally binding documents. But that's where their commonality ends.

Privacy policies are legally required in most countries. They not only protect your users but also declare your compliance with the privacy laws in those countries and, in some cases, states.

Terms and conditions, on the other hand, are designed to protect you and your business. Business owners can set their rules about how their website, service, and/or product is used — within laws set by the country and perhaps the state where you do business.

Banning spam from your company toolset

Speaking of company policies, the growth of the Internet and email brought with them the unwanted email phenomenon of *spam* — the company practice of sending unwanted email messages to large numbers of people. The practice (in one form or another) dates all the way back to 1978, though the word *spam* wasn't used to describe the practice until 1993 (www.socketlabs.com/blog/know-history-spam).

The practice became so widespread and raised so many alarms by the early 2000s that the United States Congress passed the Controlling the Assault of Non-Solicited Pornography And Marketing Act in 2003. The act is better known by its acronym: CAN-SPAM. The CAN-SPAM Act established the first national standards for sending commercial email.

REMEMBER

You can tell computing spam from the lunch meat because Hormel, the food company, refers to the lunch meat as SPAM. And the term is a portmanteau — a combination of the words *spiced ham*. There's no telling how much attention, good or bad, spam producer Hormel has received from the word being used constantly in online communication.

If your company is already sending out email messages as part of its marketing strategy — or is planning to — you need to be aware of the seven guidelines underlying the CAN–SPAM Act. That's because, when it comes to taking a closer look at the "ingredients" of the CAN–SPAM Act, seven is the lucky number. Here's a breakdown of what this law means — in seven easy bullet points — for your company's email marketing strategy:

» **Don't use a misleading header for your email messages.** That is, make sure the intended recipient is the one who is receiving the message and that the person in the From box in the message is the person from your company.

» **Make sure the subject line matches the message content.** The subject line should always give the reader a good idea of what's in the message.

» **Address what the message is about up front.** That is, if your message is an ad, tell them it's an ad. Don't be misleading. Your recipients may reward your honesty.

» **Include your company's current physical postal address and your phone number.** Your recipients want to know that you're an actual business. (This is also required by law in Canada, and we'll talk about Canadian requirements later in this chapter.)

» **Give your recipients the option to unsubscribe from future emails.** And make sure that the opt-out language is clear and easily found because, if people can't find it, your company or the authorities may start to field complaints that will distract you and your team.

» **Be sure to unsubscribe people.** The CAN-SPAM Act requires that you must process unsubscribe requests for at least 30 days after you send the email, and every unsubscribe request must be processed within 10 business days.

» **Don't charge a fee or ask for any additional personal information to have them unsubscribe.** If your company uses an automated email marketing service such as Mailchimp, you can set up Mailchimp to have people fill out a short survey about why they're leaving.

WARNING

Don't have your company send messages by way of a Gmail account. Gmail addresses show recipients a) that your business has no website or b) that your business has no money to pay for a unique website domain that comes with free email addresses or c) that you don't want to make the effort to create your own accounts. One or some combination of these excuses will lead to the same destination: It looks like your email and your business aren't legitimate. And it doesn't help that professional spammers use Gmail accounts because they're free.

REMEMBER

You may have heard this one a million times already: Always monitor what people are saying and reading about your company by creating a Google Alert with your company name, having someone review your social media, and by checking websites where your company may be mentioned. (This might be a good task for a marketing intern.) Your company is responsible for complying with the CAN-SPAM Act, even if you outsource your marketing to a separate company. Keeping track of who's-saying-what can not only help improve your marketing but also put out any email marketing fires.

TIP

If you want to find more guidance about CAN-SPAM requirements and see answers to frequently asked questions, go to the source: the Federal Trade Commission (FTC). You can visit its CAN-SPAM compliance guide web page (see Figure 2-3) on the FTC website at `www.ftc.gov/tips-advice/business-center/guidance/can-spam-act-compliance-guide-business`.

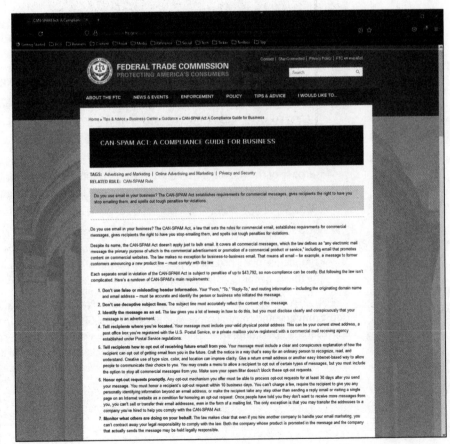

FIGURE 2-3:
The CAN-SPAM Act Compliance Guide for Business web page.

Conducting your business online

If you're a glutton for punishment and make your way through all the clauses and subclauses of the CAN–SPAM Act, you may end up thinking that there's no way you can end up doing any business online. The good news is that the FTC has anticipated your doubt and preemptively answers a lot of *frequently asked questions* — you know, FAQs. We've summarized those questions and answers for you in the following list:

» **The three information types:** The CAN-SPAM Act applies depending on the primary purpose of the email message. The FTC has three different types of information:

- *Commercial content,* which advertises or promotes a commercial product, commercial service, or website that's operated for a commercial product or service

- *Transactional or relationship content,* which is content about a transaction you've already agreed to with the other party, as well as updates sent to a customer about an ongoing transaction

- *Other content,* which doesn't fit into one of the other two categories

» If you're guessing that your email falls into the commercial category, then pass Go and collect your 200 dollars — the email is governed by the CAN-SPAM Act.

» **Combo guidelines:** What happens if your email contains both commercial content and one or both of the other two types of content? The primary purpose of the message decides: If the email Subject line and/or body of the message would cause the recipient to conclude that the message is of a commercial nature, the message falls under the CAN-SPAM Act.

» **Who's responsible?:** If your message is sent by more than one company, such as one designed to announce a partnership between you and other companies to sell products, you can have one of the other companies send the message for CAN-SPAM compliance.

The From line in the message must be from an account with that other company and must comply with all other CAN-SPAM requirements. If they don't, all the companies listed in the message will be held liable, so be sure that the other company knows CAN-SPAM backward and forward.

>> **Forward properly:** Speaking of forwarding, if you want to have a message with a link to invite readers to forward your email to a friend, the sender may be required to comply with the CAN-SPAM Act.

Has the person or company selling the product or service offered to pay the forwarder in some way, such as with a cash payment or in exchange for a benefit such as driving traffic to the forwarder's website? Then the seller is the person or company responsible for following CAN-SPAM guidelines.

If you want to view the FAQs in their entirety to gather more information and see examples, head on over to the FTC: www.ftc.gov/tips-advice/business-center/guidance/can-spam-act-compliance-guide-business.

Looking at specific industry regulations

If your industry has any specific email-sending regulations, contact the industry groups you're affiliated with to find out whether they have any guidelines. Hopefully, they post any information on their website, but if not, a quick email or phone call may identify issues you need to be aware of.

In addition to checking online communication rules in your industry, you should look at organizations dedicated to fighting villains such as malware, spam, and viruses and to creating better online communication. The Messaging, Malware and Mobile Anti-Abuse Working Group is one such organization, but because that's a mouthful, the group also goes by the abbreviation M³AAWG, which is only slightly easier to remember, let alone say. Fortunately, after you type www.m3aawg.org (see Figure 2-4) into the address bar, you can bookmark the page and forget the URL.

You know that the M³AAWG is a serious effort when you look at its list of sponsors, which includes Adobe, AT&T, Comcast, Facebook, Google, LinkedIn, and Microsoft. And the list of full members is equally impressive: It includes Apple, Cisco Systems, IBM, and Twitter.

The site includes a list of best practices as well as other tips for sending proper messages, and you don't even have to sign up to be a member — they're free to view directly from the M³AAWG website.

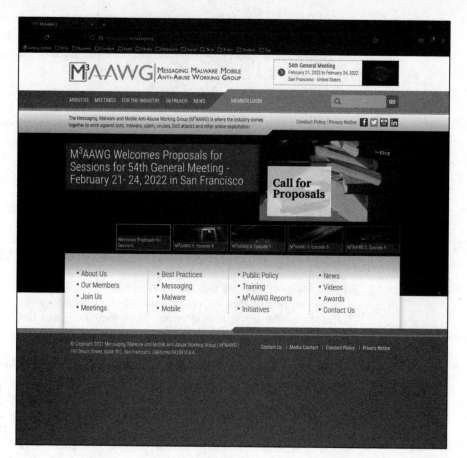

FIGURE 2-4:
The M³AAWG website includes links to best practices.

If you suspect that your email messages are being blocked by the intended recipient or you can't receive email from a specific person, a good place to find out whether that's the case is the Spamhaus Project website at www.spamhaus.org (see Figure 2-5).

The Spamhaus Project is a global organization based in Andorra, a small European country that's easy to forget (and we won't judge you). It's tucked away in the Pyrenees Mountains on the French/Spanish border. The word *spamhaus* is a made-up German expression, coined by founder Steve Linford to refer to an Internet service provider that spams or provides services to spammers.

Like M³AAWG, The Spamhaus Project has a lot of big sponsors, including Amazon Web Services, 1&1, and Rackspace. It provides a lot of free services, including the ability for you to see whether a domain name or even a specific IP address is on one of its blocklists. If you continue to receive spam, you can also see whether the sender is on the Spamhaus Project Register of Known Spam Operators database.

FIGURE 2-5:
The Spamhaus
Project website
has links to
various online
resources to help
you identify
spammers.

TIP

The Spamhaus Project also has some interesting infobits about spam, including the fact that 80 percent of spam can be traced to 100 known spam operators in the Register of Known Spam Operators.

Adhering to country and regional laws

If you live outside the United States, you likely have policies in your country (and perhaps your region) that will apply to your online marketing operations. This section covers the legislation in North America and Europe (and chances are that these laws have influenced online marketing laws where you live).

TIP

If you want to see a comprehensive list of spam legislation by country, start with the Wikipedia website article at `https://en.wikipedia.org/wiki/Email_spam_legislation_by_country`. From there, you should be able to find the legislation that applies to your country.

The European Union

You may have heard a lot about the General Data Protection Regulation, better known by its abbreviation, GDPR. The *GDPR* is a regulation touted by the GDPR website at `https://gdpr.eu` (see Figure 2-6) as being the toughest privacy-and-security law in the world.

FIGURE 2-6: The GDPR has a comprehensive website to answer your questions.

Like similar laws in the US, the GDPR lays out seven principles for protecting data:

>> Your processes must be lawful, fair, and transparent.

>> You must process data for legitimate purposes directly related to the subject of that data.

>> You should collect and process only as much data as you need for your purposes and not one bit more.

>> You must keep personal data accurate and updated.

>> You should store personally identifiable data only as long as you need for your specified purpose.

Any data processing you carry out must ensure security, integrity, and confidentiality, such as by using strong encryption.

>> The person responsible for managing the data — the *data controller*, in GDPR terminology — must be able to demonstrate GDPR compliance.

What we list here only scratches the surface. You can view the latest news about GDPR and get all your questions answered (and then some) on the GDPR website at https://gdpr.eu.

REMEMBER

If you do business in the European Union, or you plan to, you're also bound by the rules in the GDPR. So, if you're not familiar with those rules, now is a great time to put down this book and do some research. We'll be here when you return.

The United Kingdom

Brexit may be a reality, but data protection knows no borders, and so it's no surprise that UK laws are modeled closely on the GDPR. The people who put together the UK policy decided to make things easy and just refer to their policy as UK GDPR.

The Information Commissioner's Office, or ICO, is an independent body that contains information about the UK GDPR for businesses and individuals. For businesses, that means you can't just learn what the UK GDPR requires; you also need to take a self-assessment test to see whether your business is ready to adhere to the UK GDPR — no matter whether you're in the UK or you want to do business in the UK.

For consumers, this means you can learn what your rights are under the UK GDPR, including your rights to be informed, to get your data deleted, to limit how organizations use your data, and more.

All this information, as well as a complaint form, is available on the ICO at https://ico.org.uk, as shown in Figure 2-7.

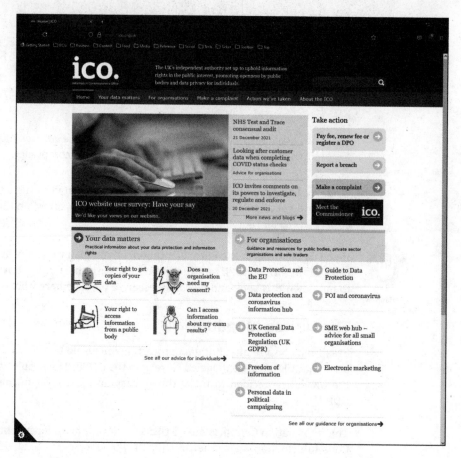

FIGURE 2-7:
The Information Commissioner's Office website offers news, advice, and common topics.

Canada

Though Canada is a country that still recognizes the UK monarch as the head of state, Canada makes its own rules — including antispam laws. Canada is straightforward, as is its wont, and calls its antispam law Canada's Anti-Spam Legislation (CASL).

The Canadian Radio-Television and Telecommunications website has a page about the CASL that you can find at `https://crtc.gc.ca/eng/internet/anti.htm`, as shown in Figure 2-8.

Like similar antispam laws, CASL regulates all electronic messages — including email and texts within, from, and to Canada — that organizations send with what the law calls *commercial activity*.

FIGURE 2-8:
You can find plenty of helpful links and information on the CASL home page.

The website has not only a lot of frequently asked questions and other helpful links but also a list of five compliance tips to follow — including a phone number you can call to ask for help. (We haven't called it ourselves, but we expect that you'll talk to a real person because it's Canada.)

Honoring Boundaries

The COVID-19 pandemic accelerated talk about setting boundaries in all communication, but especially with online communication. Health officials helped guide people in moderating their physical boundaries to keep themselves safe, such as by physically touching with a fist bump. Others suggest not touching at all because using the Vulcan hand salute from *Star Trek* as a greeting is clearly healthier (and hipper).

The most discussion about boundaries centered on understanding everyone's mental boundaries, especially with the mental stress of many people forced to change their lives and daily structure. Though the boundaries we talk about in this section have no legal force (at least here in the US, where we are), understanding and setting boundaries are helpful goals if you want to avoid any legal misadventures.

You may have read in Chapter 1 about how to communicate with people, and that's fine. In this chapter, we review some of that material, in case you don't want to go back (but you always can).

Then we talk about setting boundaries, talking with your team to set policies in your business that work for everyone (or at least reasonably so), and why you should consider centralizing your communication online. Finally, we talk about using the right medium for the message you want to send.

Communicating with people during work hours

There are plenty of rules, stated and not, that you should follow when communicating with your employees during work hours. This advice doesn't change when you connect online just because people work in different parts of the country and/or the world or because pandemic safety requires that everyone work from home.

With that said, let's quickly review the basics of communicating with people online:

» Use face-to-face communication whenever possible, and that means to get together with an online chat app such as Zoom. That's no substitute for meeting with people in person, but it still helps fulfill the human need to see the other person you're talking with.

» Listen and pay attention to what people are saying.

» Make eye contact as much as possible to show you're engaged.

» Pay attention to nonverbal messages. Online, you can't see all those messages someone else's body is telling you, but you can still learn a lot by their facial movements and even body movements, like someone moving around in their chair when they're uncomfortable.

» Participate in the conversation. Everyone in the meeting needs to contribute if it has a chance of being effective.

» Speak calmly and openly — you know, like a professional.

» Acknowledge people's time and thank them for talking with you.

So what, you ask? That's basic stuff. But working online has also required a greater understanding about boundaries during work hours. After all, when someone works from home, their entire workday isn't taken up by work. They have to manage their family (called the *real* job by some), go to appointments, and try to juggle the bowling ball, chainsaw, and dinner plates as best they can.

REMEMBER

Working remotely also makes it easier for people to violate someone else's boundaries, no matter what role they have. We talk about how to call out boundary violations later in this chapter.

Every employee and every manager is different, so you will experience policies created from your company's unique priorities, expectations, and boundaries. Those include how you will communicate with one another, such as using Zoom for online meetings and using an app like Slack for project communication.

If you're a manager who will be developing your online communication policies, you need to resolve several issues:

>> What the at-home job duties and responsibilities are

>> How you want to create work-from-home schedules

>> When and how you can contact people after work hours

>> Whether you want to give people the option of working on weekends and holidays

>> How often the communication policy needs to be changed and who's responsible for reviews and changes

You may have guessed (correctly) that you need to bring your ideas to your managers and to your employees in order to craft an overall policy. That's best done in a meeting setting — maybe even more than one meeting — where you can finalize that policy. Be sure to come prepared to every meeting and communicate to your team that you expect them to do the same.

TIP

If you want to find a remote job or you're a manager who wants to hire remotely, one good resource is We Work Remotely (https://weworkremotely.com), shown in Figure 2-9. The site has not only remote job listings but also a guide to hiring remotely that you can apply to any industry. And you can post remote jobs on the site for $299.

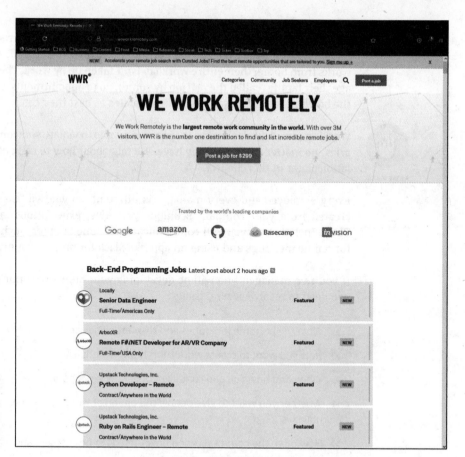

FIGURE 2-9:
The We Work
Remotely website
lists current
remote jobs on
the home page.

Communicating with employees in general

When you're communicating with employees, you find out pretty quickly that no two of them have the same two communication styles. (And, if you try to use the same styles for everyone, you may learn this lesson the hard way when employees walk out the door.)

Before you start putting together your policy, it's Business 101 to talk with each of your employees individually to learn how they like to communicate. More importantly, you need to ask them what their boundaries are — including not only scheduling boundaries, like having to take time off for an important medical appointment, but also mental boundaries.

What do we mean by mental boundaries? Here are some examples:

>> Setting your work hours, especially when working from home.

>> Blocking out time to work and other times for other responsibilities — including relaxing and enjoying other activities.

>> Not participating in (or just not holding) meetings that can be better communicated as email or Slack messages.

>> Knowing when you "get into a groove" and want to continue working to get something done without interruptions.

>> Learning what employees like and don't like to do with work. For example, if someone doesn't want to get together with other employees because they're an introvert and being social means being stressed, don't force the employee to join the others.

In sum, mental boundaries are set to make sure that your employees are the most effective and productive they can be.

TIP

You should use these tips to find out how you're spending your own mental energy so that you can set your own boundaries. If you know your boundaries, you'll be able to communicate those to your employees, too.

Letting technology lend a hand

When you're communicating online, no matter whether you're in the office or working remotely, technology can help you set those boundaries. We can't guarantee that you won't be bothered, but these solutions can help immensely:

>> Take advantage of email out-of-office messages, better known by its acronym, OOO. After you set up the OOO in your email app, whenever someone sends you a message, the email app sends the OOO message automatically. That OOO message can also include a link to the person handling your work while you're out.

>> Create an OOO voicemail greeting that will tell people you'll get back to them when you can and whom to contact in case of an urgent matter.

>> Use your online calendar to block off time to work. If someone tries to set up a meeting with you in your calendar app, they'll see that you're busy.

>> A shared calendar app can also set days and times for your normal work schedule when you're available to chat.

>> In a shared messaging app like Microsoft Teams, you can create and publish an Away message so that people will know you're unavailable when they try to reach you.

Responding to boundary crossings

Naturally, some people will cross your boundaries because they think their priorities are greater than any you might have. As a manager, you need to address this issue upfront and come to an understanding that (hopefully) everyone will adhere to. But some people will believe that you won't mind because they think it's too important or they're feeling pressure from higher-ups to get things done.

What do you do? If you're in an office setting, it can be hard if all the offices are open or have cubicles, because someone can just come by and either knock or just say hello. It's a bit easier if you're working remotely, because you can simply decline to answer the phone or you can use technology to save the day.

With that said, here are some suggestions that may help:

>> If someone tells you (or demands) something that crosses your boundaries, simply say, "That doesn't work for me." The best case scenario is that the other person will get the message and will work with you to find a solution. (Worst case? You may need to find a new job or a new employee, depending on your position.)

REMEMBER

Mister Rogers always said, "Look for the helpers." If you know you won't be available ahead of time, you should talk with one or more people you know who could help a person needing something from you. Be aware that anyone you approach with your request will likely want you to do the same for them when they're not available.

>> In your online employee collaboration app, you may want to include any notes specifying that that you'll be out of contact for a few hours during the day and invite people to find time outside that window to connect.

>> If you'll be out for longer than a few hours during the day, you should write an OOO email message.

>> You may need to set boundaries around projects as well. For example, in your company's email or employee collaboration app, you may need to write a message saying that you won't be able to work on a project until a specific date — usually, after your current project ends.

TIP

You may want to consider looking at your email messages only at certain times of the day — not only to ensure that you block out your time for other tasks but also to send the message that you're not available at everyone's beck and call.

Communicating during off-hours

Communicating in off-hours needs to be an integral part of your employee communication policy. The Human Resources Online website (`www.humanresourcesonline.net/global`) has a good overview of seven areas of an off-hours communications policy based on the policy of the Singapore Alliance for Action. We think it's good enough to share with you, so here's a quick summary of those seven areas:

>> **Objective:** State what the purpose of the policy is, such as the need to strictly limit the criteria for off-hours communication because employees deserve time away from work to be their best selves at work.

>> **Nature of work:** This section talks about the criteria required to call an employee outside of work.

>> **Expectations:** The expectations about when employees should be contacted, such as whether they're for all employees or just those employees who aren't formally on leave.

>> **Communication:** This section should include the employees who need to be contacted about a critical business issue. You need to list how you should communicate with each of those employees, such as by way of text, email, or phone call. And the policy needs to tell people what to say during the call, including the issue or problem at hand, what needs to be done, the time-frame, and the preferred ending.

>> **Employee responsibility:** This section needs to explain what the employee is responsible for, such as

   • Not contacting other employees unless absolutely necessary

   • Communicating when they will be unavailable, such as in a family emergency

   • Providing regular feedback during the crisis

>> **The HR manager's responsibility:** This section lists what the human resources (HR) department is responsible for, including

   • Communicating the policy parameters to employees — especially new employees

   • Managing any concerns and grievances about the policy

   • Determining whether employees who are unable to respond to work-related matters after-hours should be reprimanded

>> **Testing:** Once the policy is in place, have a limited-time test — such as a few months — and then have a company-wide review of the policy to see whether any changes need to be made.

You can find more information, including a template you can adapt for your own use, from the Singapore Alliance for Action at `www.humanresourcesonline.net/hr-guide-to-an-after-hours-communiation-policy`.

Centralizing Messages

One challenge of communicating with people online is the ability — or lack thereof — to centralize messages. That's why businesses are as interested in online team communication software as kids are to sugary treats. Such software keeps communication in one place so that employees can log in with their account, find the information they need, and stay connected with others. Managers can track their employees' work and progress more easily. And many apps have live audio and video meetings integrated into them.

You may have heard about some of these apps: Microsoft Teams, Slack, and Basecamp have all been in the media. You may also know names like Telegram, Trello, and ClickUp. Many of them have mobile apps, too, so people can stay connected wherever they go.

If you're in the market for team communication software for your business, where do you start? We suggest the Capterra website (`www.capterra.com/team-communication-software`) which you can use to search for team communication software.

You may get googly-eyed when you see that the number of apps in the list as of this writing is 297, but that's why we recommend Capterra as a good place to start. The idea is not to panic. You can click on the View the Capterra Shortlist option in each product entry in the list to view a grid with the top 25 products to see how they compare. If you have more specific needs, you can talk to one of Capterra's experts by phone for free so that they can create a personalized list of software for you.

Choosing the Best Medium for the Message

No matter whether you decide to use just an email app and Zoom or a centralized message app to communicate with your team, you need to know which medium to use for your message. After all, you have plenty of media to choose from, including phones for voice communication, email, text via phones or online chat apps, and even face-to-face communication remotely using Zoom or the aforementioned team communication software.

What's more, you have different audiences that you have to communicate with. Some people like communication orally by phone or in an online video meeting, but some prefer to have text in email or on their phone.

Breathe slowly, because we're here to give you the tips you need to make the right decision about which communication method is best for your situation.

Identifying the message

Start by asking what the message is about. For example:

>> Is your information time-sensitive?

>> Is the information you want to convey general or specific?

>> Is your information sensitive in any way — that is, should only specific individuals view the information?

>> Do you need to communicate with one person, a group, or the entire company?

>> Who is the person or group of people you're talking with? Your message will vary depending on whether you're talking to an employee or talking to your boss.

>> Does the message require a response?

The type of message you're sending can affect how you deliver your message.

Understanding your culture

If your company culture is about using face-to-face communication in the workplace, you should use it for every communication, if at all possible. But if your team is used to getting messages in all sorts of formats, keep doing that. Consistency is key, no matter whether you're working in the office or remotely.

Picking a delivery method

Speaking of receiving messages in different formats, you need to know what your audience wants to receive. Sometimes that's easy, if you have a culture that knows what it's getting, such as a weekly meeting on your shared communication platform. But if you have a culture where different people have different preferences, you may feel that you need a top hat, cape, and wand to make it all work.

For example, some people want to connect using email or text because they check that method most often and find meetings — online or in-person — mostly a waste of time that distracts from their work. Others need to see people's faces.

REMEMBER

On a small team, you can try to manage everyone's preferences as much as possible. If you find that you need to have a communication policy companywide, this is a great opportunity for you (or someone you delegate) to do that. Yes, you can give some autonomy to departments and small teams, but when it comes to things like communication mediums to use, that should be a company decision.

Now it's time for another "what's more" — you may want to have some messages sent in as wide a format as possible. For example, if you have a state of the company report for the year just ended, it's better to have an in-person meeting, if it's available.

If it's not, a video is the next best thing because people can see your face. A video meeting may have too many people in it for the app to handle, so a recorded video distributed on shared communication or even on a private YouTube channel may be the best option.

TIP

You should consider having a live video instead of a recorded one if your technology permits it. Though a live video means there's a better chance of having bloopers, the same is true of a live event, anyway. And a live video means you can take questions afterward, so you have an opportunity to create a deeper connection with your employees.

Chapter **3**

Minding Your Online Manners at Any Age

You know when you meet someone face-to-face that the other person's age tells you how you should communicate with them. If you're talking with your peers at work, you speak with them differently than you would with friends when you're on the town.

The height of the COVID-19 pandemic laser-focused attention on what it meant to mind your manners because there were far fewer people to talk with in person — and you didn't want to stick around for too long, anyway.

Alas and alack, viruses change over time, and everyone is still trying to figure out how to paint that nasty SARS-CoV-2 virus into a corner. As much as we hope the virus is stuck in that corner by the time you read this book, online communication is still the order of the day for people in many age groups.

The strain of the pandemic has frayed manners in person, but maybe because people are more used to talking online these days, they may feel that manners are optional because the folks they're addressing can't see them — or else said people can just turn away by turning off their web cameras, so no one in a video meeting sees them.

But this doesn't describe *you*, right? If you're reading this chapter, we're guessing that you're not so sure — and kudos to you. Don't get stars in your eyes, though, because we want you to channel your inner Miss Manners in this chapter.

We start by talking about manners for different audiences, from adults to kids, before we remind you about common manners everyone should know. And we begin by talking about how etiquette varies by audience.

Seeing How Etiquette Varies for Different Audiences

Imagine that you're in an online meeting with video, so everyone else in the meeting sees you. You start using a bit of profanity, and you think no one will mind.

Then, on one of the other cameras, you see that two children have walked in and are asking questions of their parent. The parent of that child gives a look into the camera that would melt lead.

Oops.

One definition of an adult is someone who sets a good example for others in any situation, including online communication. But how do you model that behavior?

Adults: Being up front about behavior and modeling that behavior

If you remember one rule in this book, please remember this one: Don't do things online that you would never do in a face-to-face situation.

It's even more important to remember this rule because you face more variables online when you connect over the Internet. You've probably seen examples shown repeatedly on TV news programs where kids and/or pets have barged into a meeting room where someone is attending a meeting and the unintended visitors start distracting people.

Worse, when you communicate online via text, people can't use your facial expressions and other non-verbal cues your body gives off to get the entire picture of what you are trying to say. Yes, emojis help a bit, but they can't compensate for being there in person. And, without seeing you in person, people will fill in the gaps the best way they can. You may find yourself being defensive and confused when your intended recipient doesn't take your message the way you expect.

So, you guessed it, here's a list of behaviors you should be up front about when you talk with people online.

TIP

>> **Understand the rules and community standards.** This is especially important when you're on social media websites, because they do have a lot of rules that you should know about. If you can't find those rules, just perform a quick search, such as *Facebook rules,* to help.

If the team responsible for your intranet has no rules or standards set up for communicating properly, ask them to put rules and standards on their site. You may have to formally approach your boss and put together a presentation to get it done, but it's worth the effort to prevent miscommunication that wastes everyone's time.

>> **Respect others.** If you wouldn't say something in person or in a face-to-face Zoom meeting, don't say it in a text message, either. If you disrespect people in your brain and you don't think it's a problem, that information will get out. People will react. That's when you'll find out that you have a problem.

>> **Be neutral.** When you're not sure about how someone will interpret information, keep what you're saying as close to the facts as possible. Don't inject your opinions into your argument, because someone might interpret it in any way they want.

>> **Understand when humor is warranted.** Don't use humor and sarcasm unless you know your audience well. If you're sending an email message to your team and you all know each other's communication styles, you can be freer to be yourself — but not always. For example, don't be disrespectful to anyone, even if you're on familiar terms with them. When you send messages to people you're not familiar with, are you sure they'll understand you?

>> **Don't use all caps when you talk.** You shouldn't yell at someone in person, and you shouldn't yell at someone online by using ALL CAPS.

>> **Don't use multiple exclamation points.** You can use an exclamation point sparingly when you need to make a forceful point, but don't use multiple exclamation points. You're in an online communication medium, not a comic strip.

>> **Keep personal information to a low ebb.** If you give out personal information, make sure it's related to the point you want to make. Otherwise, you don't have to volunteer anything if you don't want to — and keep in mind that, if you do share personal information, some people may try to use it against you if they feel you threaten them.

> **» Report violations.** When you see a problem arise, report it. This is especially true of posts you see on social media, but it's also true if you see private info that might badly affect others. For example, if a peer at work disrespects one or more groups of people, that will likely harm the company, so you should talk about it with your boss and/or human resources rep.

TIP

It takes constant practice to not only behave the right way but also think the right way. If you don't practice (or you fall out of practice), whatever you're thinking about will spill out without your questioning it because it seems so *natural*. And then you're the proverbial frog in a pot full of warming water. (You know, the frog that eventually gets boiled alive because the heat keeps increasing — that frog.) So, practice at every opportunity. And one day you may find yourself giddy that you slayed some inner demons at the same time.

Students: Interacting with classmates and being serious

No matter whether you have kids old enough to understand your wise parental counsel about how to interact in a virtual classroom or you're an adult student who's taking online courses, a lot of what we cover earlier in this chapter applies to your experience in the online classroom.

Obviously, there are some differences when people are talking in a live video chat as opposed to texting, using email, or using a learning management system (the industry term, not ours), such as Canvas, that allows your students to download and submit coursework as well as connect with each other.

So, when you're thinking about how to connect with your fellow students online or you want to talk with your kids about how to interact online, here's the *Cliffs Notes* version of what to remember:

> **» Put your name in your message.** Don't assume that your instructor will recognize the username in your email address or the username you use in your learning management system. (You may want to look up the old proverb about the word *assume*.)

> **» Identify the course or subject you want information about.** The answer you need depends on what you're talking about. But if you just want to know the date of the next exam, the universal response still applies online: "Read the syllabus. Cripes!"

> **» Follow the leader.** If you're communicating with your instructor or a teacher's aide — that is, anyone who outranks you in the classroom pecking order — let

that person establish the level of conversation. You don't want to send a message with profanity and acronyms that your instructor may not understand. (Okay, they'll probably understand the profanity, if not the acronyms.)

>> **Use proper grammar and punctuation.** You're using a written medium to communicate, so using proper writing skills will impress not only your instructor but also your fellow classmates. You'll also want to pay attention to your instructor about how to use acronyms and emojis. (Instructors, we talk about using them later in this chapter.)

>> **Keep your tone neutral.** You don't know how other people will react to something you type that you think is funny. And you wouldn't yell in a classroom, so don't yell online by using all caps or exclamation points.

>> **Be factual.** If you are unsure about something before you send it, check it out first. It's important to get the facts straight in an assignment, so fact-check your information before you send it on in an email or a chat message. (It may be harder to check online during a video class because you need to pay attention to what's going on.)

REMEMBER

If you're not sure about something and you're getting conflicting information from what you see in a Google search, bring up your concern with your instructor first. The instructor will give you some guidance and may thank you because now they can present this information to the rest of the class.

>> **Keep in mind that nothing is private online.** If you're talking to your children about this topic, it's something you need to say early and often: Everything on the Internet is stored somewhere. Students should keep not only their own information private but also others' information.

>> **Stay focused.** This is advice for both instructors and students. Staying focused means making brief points about the topic under discussion. If some of the points aren't clear, people will let you know and you can elaborate. Even then, keep your responses as short as possible so as not to annoy your instructor and classmates.

>> **Be as respectful online as you would be in the classroom.** The rule is simple: If you wouldn't say something to someone's face, don't say it online. Use your instructor's proper title or the title the instructor prefers. Don't trash classmates' opinions online, not just because it's the right thing to do but also because the instructor can still discipline you as though you were in a real classroom.

Teachers: Presenting information to students

If you're a teacher and you've read the previous section, you've probably also taken some notes about which topics to discuss with your students.

Eric talked with a friend of his, Anthony Barcellos, who is a math instructor at American River College in Sacramento, California. Barcellos noted that teacher/student communication is often intergenerational. "Teachers tend to have much less experience in digital communications than their students," he said.

With that in mind, the following sections present some other important things to know about communicating with students.

Be clear

Be upfront with your students about the rules. Here are some ideas to get you started:

TIP

>> **Tell students how to correctly use the chat box if you use an online chat app, like Zoom.** Students can easily just start chatting privately with others about other topics and not pay attention to you and the lesson.

If you're concerned that your students will just ignore the chat box rule, meeting apps allow you, as the meeting host, to turn off the chat box. What's more, if you're fortunate enough to have a teaching assistant or peer tutor associated with your class sessions, they can be useful in moderating the chat box while you're presenting the subject matter.

>> **Students need to use their real names.** It's part of common courtesy.

>> **Speaking of common courtesy, remind people that they should be as courteous as they would be in person.** That means the "please and thank you" rule still applies.

>> **Point out the I Agree button and any other quick-response buttons in the virtual classroom app you're using.** That way, people can respond quickly without having to type out the response.

>> **Point out the Virtual Hand icon so that your students can raise their hands and ask a question in your virtual classroom app.** If you're using a general purpose virtual chat app, like Zoom, be sure to mute everyone before the meeting starts.

>> **Let your students know that you'll start on time, just as you would in an in-person classroom.** That way, students know that they need to get rid of their distractions (like smartphones) before they arrive, log in before class

starts, and be ready to work. (We agree that it's a good sign that students are waiting for you when you log in.)

» **Tell students how you communicate, such as your email address and/or a link on your learning management system (LMS).** And be clear when students should expect a response, such as on a Monday if a student sends a message on a weekend. Barcellos also noted that you need to cross-link your communication systems so that you receive messages right away, such as forwarding LMS messages to your email inbox. (If you're not sure how to do that, call on your institution's technical support staff.) "Teachers have a responsibility to be attentive to students, and not to ignore their requests for help," he added.

REMEMBER

Barcellos says that it isn't a good idea to "dumb down" discourse with students. "Teachers have a responsibility to be clear and understandable," he asserted, "but that merely suggests avoiding overwrought vocabulary and taking care to define any technical terms that need to be used in a class. After all, learning those terms will be part of what's supposed to occur." Barcellos added that modeling formal usage pays dividends to students who master it. "Don't try to be someone other than yourself."

Use acronyms wisely

Resist the urge to use acronyms until you establish their meaning with your students. For example, if you use LOL, some people may not think it means "laugh out loud." We have heard stories of people who think LOL means "lots of love," which has caused some awkward situations.

That may be hilarious to read about, but if it happens to you in your class, it may not be so funny. So, spell out the acronym, tell the students what the acronym is, and then you can use it later. Some (or all) of your students may virtually roll their eyes (or send you the appropriate rolling-eyes emoji), but your mind will soothe your bruised ego because you don't have to clean up any confusion you may cause.

Barcellos pointed out that it's unrealistic to expect students to maintain formal writing standards on discussion boards, such as the ones you can find in learning management systems, where students interact with each other. "Let them speak in their native digital language(s)," he said. "Students will feel more welcome to express themselves and a lot more will be said."

REMEMBER

In a discussion board or an online forum about the class, you need to keep close tabs on the discussion to make sure it's appropriate to the task or assignment — as much as you can, anyway. Check the protocols adopted by your institution.

Follow the submission rules

We've broken out submitting assignments into a separate section because it warrants special attention. Many virtual classroom apps have features that allow students to submit their assignments within the app, and you have probably gnashed a few teeth as you set up the submission function for your students.

No matter whether you set up assignment submission on a virtual classroom app or require your students to submit assignments via email, be clear about how to do it. (Apps may require a second explanation in plain English by the instructor.) Ensure that students understand that they need to put their name on the assignment and add the correct Subject line.

TIP

You may want the first class assignment to be as simple as instructing students to send you a message in the app or by email (or both) with the student's name and the correct Subject line. Anything else you want the student to include in a message is up to you.

If you expect your students to submit attachments with those messages, provide specific instructions such as the type of format for documents. Common formats include Microsoft Word and Adobe's Portable Document Format (PDF).

WARNING

Make sure the formats are as pain-free to create as possible. Most students can create files in Word or Google Docs, but creating a PDF file can be tricky for some. For certain classes, like math, you may want to have students take photos of written pages with their phones and upload them.

Kids: Being flexible for kid behavior

Even if you're not a teacher, you may have contact with kids who need advice and guidance about how to communicate online. You may have kids of your own like Kelly. You may have nieces and nephews like Kendra. Or you may have a more curious situation, like Eric, where you sometimes have older daycare kids who are being kept home for safety reasons but need to connect online to keep up their studies.

The COVID-19 pandemic made schooling online a must, and kids of any age may be overwhelmed about how to take classes online. That's especially true of younger kids, and so, as the adult, you have to be flexible and answer kids' questions.

Setting up your system

Before your kids start logging in, you need to make sure that they have the right equipment beyond a computer or tablet. Kids may need headphones with a microphone included so that people can help them, but if you have a modern iPad or laptop, this may not be an issue.

You may also need to have a separate account on the computer or iPad only for school so that your kids don't find any apps or other distractions when they get bored. Just remember that you have to devise some methods for changing and keeping the passwords on your child's main account that unlocks access to all the goodies.

REMEMBER

Don't forget the basics that you would include in an in-person classroom setting, including paper, pens, and/or pencils for taking notes or for drawing things the teacher wants students to make and show others on their webcam. Check for anything else you need in the teacher's syllabus, or ask the teacher for a list of what your child needs.

Testing, testing . . .

You should also make sure the computer's Internet connection is strong. That means either a good Wi-Fi connection or an Ethernet cable. If you aren't sure about the connection, try using it to call someone else (like a relative) outside your house if you can, and see whether you find any glitches you can fix. For example, if your Wi-Fi connection keeps dropping off, connect an Ethernet cable from your computer to the modem.

Speaking of your microphone, apps also have settings to test the speaker level and the video to see how you look and sound. For example, you may need to increase the volume and change the height of the monitor so that your child can see and hear correctly.

Testing is also a great way for your child to understand how they should look on the screen and what they should do, such as look directly into the camera when they're speaking as well as try different tasks like muting the microphone for a cough.

TIP

You may want to talk with your child's teacher about holding a practice class before the real class starts. That will not only get your kid(s) comfortable with using online tools but also work out any bugs and glitches so that the first day of online class is smooth (well, smoother) for everyone.

Common Rules for Everyone

Throughout this chapter, we talk about rules for specific audiences, and we touch on some common rules. Now it's time to focus on those common rules that cover everyone in online communication, in case you haven't read these already or you just need a cool refresher.

Dress appropriately

When you write email or text messages, no one cares what you're wearing when you write it. But when you have a video meeting, everyone appreciates it when you dress for the occasion.

In business, your boss may dictate what people need to wear in meetings. That may be business casual, or it may be a suit-and-tie if you're meeting with a hot lead that you're trying to convert into a customer.

"But," you say, "I can wear a nice shirt or a suit and tie on top and my shorts or sweatpants underneath — and shoes are optional. Right?"

Consider what people in your meeting will think if you have to get up to go to the bathroom or get something to drink and you forget to turn off your camera, so they see your teddy bear jammies. Or suppose that your child is wearing something on top and absolutely nothing on the bottom because it's just too hot where you are?

Care to wager some quatloos about how long it'll be before you get yelled at? (You can also wager New Republic credits if you prefer *Star Wars* over *Star Trek*.)

So, wear a full outfit. That means real pants and real shoes. You'll not only avoid embarrassment — you'll feel more engaged and, dare we say, almost like you're there in person.

Eliminate background noise, if possible

When you're at home with kids and you don't have your own, private cave, it's frustrating to work and hold meetings when you hear a bunch of noise in the next room. Or you may hear a barking dog outside. And even if you try to get out of the house, your favorite coffee shop may have music blaring and people talking loudly.

Popular meeting apps — including Google Meet, Microsoft Teams, and Zoom — have risen to the challenge by adding noise cancellation features. But those may not be enough, so consider these additional strategies for cutting down on noise:

>> **Buy a good pair of headphones and a microphone.** Then you can block out more outside noise.

>> **Use an internal room, if you can find one.** If you're close to a window, you're close to your neighbor's kid who likes to play basketball for hours on end. But don't have a meeting close to a popular location where people walk. (If you guessed the bathroom, pass Go and collect your $200 in play money.)

>> **Ask your spouse for help.** If your spouse is at home with you, have them do you a solid and take the kids and the pets for a walk. (We suspect that you'll have to return the favor in some way.)

>> **Ask your kids for help.** Talk to them ahead of time about what you'll be doing. Bribes may be necessary.

>> **Keep your pets happy.** Put the pets outside with some of their favorite treats and play toys to keep them occupied.

>> **If all else fails, consider renting a business suite in your area so that you can get out of the house.** Review the suite so that you're satisfied you'll be able to get out of the house with your laptop and "attend" a meeting in a quiet environment.

TIP

You can easily enough search for headphones and microphones for online meetings in a web search, but you can also quite easy become overwhelmed. We found a *What Hi-Fi* article with a list of the best microphones and headphones for 2022, which is the year this book was published, and we think it's a good place to start. You can find the site at www.whathifi.com/us/best-buys/best-headphones-with-a-mic-for-voice-and-video-calls, as shown in Figure 3-1.

Be respectful

It can be hard to remember that you're talking to a real person when you're sending an email or text message. Even in a video meeting, you're seeing only part of a person and it's hard to fully connect.

A running theme of this chapter is that you're talking to real people, and so a core tenet of online etiquette is to treat others respectfully. That's especially true when they make mistakes and violate the rules of your meeting or your classroom, or when they flout online etiquette in the wild.

FIGURE 3-1:
See whether any of the headphones and microphones in the *What Hi-Fi* article strike your fancy.

2

Social Media Etiquette

Chapter 4

Learning the Language of Social Media

Social media allows people to post updates about their lives as well as engage with others via various forms of communication. As a frequent place for all types of people to go for communication, social media is (unfortunately) quite easy to engage in incorrectly — or even maliciously.

In a world that continues to appear more divisive, how can everyone use social media to communicate their ideas and opinions in a way that's effective and appropriate? Making this question even more complex is the large number of social media platforms and the unique rules of etiquette that govern each one. When it comes to etiquette, people should follow the written (as well as unwritten) rules of etiquette for social media in general and for each platform in particular. There's also a fine line between eccentricity and inappropriate behavior. In this chapter, we tackle social media etiquette across social media as well as on specific platforms.

Defining Social Media Etiquette

Social media *etiquette* refers to the guidelines that companies and individuals use online so as not ruin their reputation or stand out too much while using social media platforms. The thing is, social media etiquette includes not only the written rules but also the *unwritten* rules on how you should behave when networking on social platforms, such as Facebook and Twitter, if you want your actions to maintain respect from others who follow these same practices. Complicating matters further is the fact that social media etiquette is a moving target — an evolving set of guidelines that aim (hopefully) to encourage thoughtful engagement with others on topics relevant to the website you're using. Observing these guidelines allows those reading your posts or comments to better appreciate them and to give more thought-provoking responses, thus improving the conversation overall.

REMEMBER

Everyone recognizes that social media is a vital part of many people's lives, but it can also have some negative effects. One way that this happens is when you break the social rules on your favorite platforms!

Though there's no exact rule for what should go where when posting across multiple networks like Facebook vs Twitter (or even Instagram), certain behaviors are generally understood because they've become norms over time, based on user experiences with other users who may share similar interests within specific online communities.

Why you should care about social media etiquette

What would you do if you visited another country and knew little about the customs or language or how to connect with other people? You wouldn't be able to communicate successfully or easily find what you're looking for. Going into social media platforms can be similar. If you try to treat your contacts on LinkedIn like you do on TikTok, it won't go over well.

Social media is an easy way to communicate one-on-one, with your family and friends, or with anyone online — and sometimes, too easy. Social media can help people communicate better when said people choose their words wisely and remember that it's easy to miscommunicate online. For example, kidding around with someone online or saying something in anger can be seen as offensive if the person on the other end is unable to properly interpret your humor or your intentions.

REMEMBER

Besides communication, you want to consider another reason that social media etiquette is important. The reality is that on social media, you're representing yourself in a public forum. No matter how private you think your comments are, they're happening in a public forum. So, if you communicate clearly and in a respectful way, people will appreciate it. And conversely, if you communicate in an offensive or inappropriate manner, it reflects badly on you.

Recognizing bad social etiquette

Here are some signs that someone may have poor social media etiquette:

>> Being overly persistent when trying to engage others online

>> Repeatedly posting negative comments on posts they don't like

>> Making posts that are condescending or sarcastic in tone

>> Name calling

>> Being combative when communicating

>> Using social media platforms in ways they're not meant to be used

This list isn't exhaustive, but it's a start. More important is the fact that, if you're considering posting something on social media, you need to keep in mind that anything can go viral within seconds. (No, were not talking about an infectious disease here; *going viral* in this context means "spreading like wildfire," to use another metaphor.) This often leads to massive amounts of people viewing and sharing the content, regardless of your privacy settings or other users' copies. You might think something is private, or just being shared to a small group, only to wake up the next day to find that your post has been viewed by hundreds of thousands of people.

This makes it even more crucial to understand and follow social media etiquette.

REMEMBER

The Internet has a memory, and everything you put out there is not just viewable but also *archived* for future reference. One small mistake can haunt you forever, so it's important to think before you post.

Being mindful of your audience

You've been practicing the latest dance trend on TikTok and want to share it with your friends. Here's a hint: Don't start by posting it on LinkedIn. Unless your contacts on LinkedIn are part of your dance team, you're probably more interested in demonstrating your social media savvy and awareness — a savviness that recognizes that LinkedIn isn't the place to show off your Nae Nae moves.

It's *crucial* to understand your audience on social media, because you might end up posting something that's inappropriate for anyone in your network, even if they're all adults. Many factors are in play here, including what kind of online community you're browsing or interacting with, the age of individuals in your network, and what other types of posts they're typically exposed to.

Consider what social media platform you're on, how you know the audience, and how they know you. Ask yourself the following questions:

>> Seriously now, are you talking to everyone or to a smaller group?

>> Are you talking to your work colleagues or friends in a direct messenger chat?

>> Are you commenting on someone else's post, or posting and responding on your own?

>> Do they expect you to be merely friendly, steadfastly professional, or "part of the gang"?

It's crucial to keep in mind who your audience is and how your communications will be received. Even if you're already a social media ninja, take a step back and remember that, when you post online, the whole world basically has access to what you post. You just have to be careful about who can see or share your posts.

REMEMBER

Social media is an important part of today's society, and the best way to communicate effectively on it is to be aware of who you intend your message to reach, who your message might reach, and how you would feel if your message reached people outside those circles.

Managing your online presence for different purposes

When you're on social media, you have different ways to manage your presence, and different reasons you might want to. Typically, people use social media for either their personal, day-to-day life (pictures of kids and pets, for example) or professionally (business- or career-related). Consider a third aspect: your personal brand. Your *personal brand* is how others perceive you based on what they know about you — your experiences, words, style, and tone, for example. In this day and age, your personal brand is becoming your online presence and legacy, whether they see you on one social media platform or across every platform you're on.

TIP

Take into account your purpose for using social media in general and specific platforms in particular. Carefully consider how you want to show up and what your online presence should be. What do you want people to think of you, and how do you want them to feel about you?

Social media platforms are designed to keep you on them. They want you to spend all your time on their site rather than hop to something else. As such, they like to show you content that they know you like. Most social media sites use different algorithms to understand what content you like and to show you more of it.

REMEMBER

People often see social media as too political, or too divisive. What they often don't understand is that what folks see on social media is dependent partially on the folks themselves. If you feel that your social media pages are too political, that's because you've been reacting to a lot of political topics. If you feel that your social media feed is filled with news about your industry, or talking dogs, then that's also because of your actions and behavior on social media. If you like, comment, and share pictures of cats playing the piano, you'll likely see more content of talented, piano-playing cats.

Posting publicly versus privately

If you think your posts are private, you might want to think again. Nothing on social media is truly private. Though most people think that private messages or the things they post only to friends aren't visible or accessible by anyone else, that isn't always the case. With the ability to take screen shots with the push of a button, you can easily share someone's information that was posted on a social media site or messenger app and share it with others.

So, how can you start taking control of your online presence when it comes to privacy? First and foremost, you need to understand each social network's different approach to privacy as well as your own language, tone, and mood before getting started using any of the many social media sites.

Secondly, you need to be aware of the fact that social media users also have a responsibility to be mindful of their privacy. If you want your posts or pictures to by seen only by people you want to see it, make sure that your privacy settings are set up on the site. This gives you the opportunity to limit who can see your content. So, if you only want your family to see updates about your kids, that's one way to manage it. Just remember that even if you set your Instagram account to Private or adjusted your settings on Facebook, anything shared online still could potentially be seen by others; all it takes is a screenshot shared by someone who has access to it.

Some social media sites are better suited for particular audiences. Some users will find that they enjoy or gain more value from one site over another based on specific interests and demographics. By understanding each social network's different approach to privacy, users can make sure their posts and pictures are visible to only the right people.

You can take certain measures on some of the social media platforms to increase the level of privacy somewhat — for example:

>> **On Facebook,** you can set your privacy settings to keep your profile, specific posts, and images private as well. You can decide who can see your information (including what data Facebook can share with advertisers).

>> **On Instagram,** you can make your account private so that people have to be accepted by you in order to see your posts.

>> **On YouTube,** you can set specific videos as private and available only to those you share it with.

There's no such thing as truly private on social media. Though it's true that you can set your account settings to Private and allow only certain people to see your posts, you should never post anything online you wouldn't want the world to see. The Internet has a memory, and everything you put out there isn't just viewable but is also archived for the future.

Knowing the Culture of Each Platform Before You Become Involved

People who want to succeed with social media need to understand the different cultures to be found on each platform. Each community has a distinct personality and rules, and if you don't respect those principles, you're likely to be called out for it. Almost all social media platforms have a certain etiquette that users must follow to ensure they get the most out of their experience.

Learning the rules for each platform is simple, and it's worth taking the time to understand them. Each platform has its own community guidelines and terms of use, but let's face it — you're unlikely to read them unless you make posts that violate the guidelines. Instead, spend a little time watching or listening to what's happening on the platform before you dive in.

What might be appropriate on Twitter or Reddit can get you banned on Facebook or Instagram, so it's best to know the rules of etiquette before you make any assumptions. And that goes beyond the rules. The culture and purpose of Twitter are totally different from Facebook or Instagram, so understanding what is appreciated and appropriate on one is also what will get you roasted on another.

TIP

Spend some time on a particular platform watching or listening to what's going on before you dive in (especially if it's a new platform, such as when Clubhouse or TikTok emerged and grew in popularity). Doing so can significantly improve your online interactions and help you avoid making the wrong impression, looking like a novice, being flagged as a spammer, or worse — messing up to such an extent that your account gets terminated.

Many sites, such as Facebook and Twitter, have built-in ways to help users understand how they should engage with one another. Other platforms may be more restrictive or even geared toward a particular audience. (LinkedIn, for example, is designed for professional networking.) It's also helpful to pay attention to the way your friends and the people around you are using social media.

REMEMBER

Each platform has a culture associated with it, and social media etiquette should conform to this culture whenever possible. The flip side is that on social media, you have the freedom to share whatever you like (within reason and within the guidelines), so, ultimately, you should use your common sense to determine what's appropriate.

Understanding the etiquette of each platform

As we've established, each platform has its own set of jargon, customs, and expectations about how users should behave. Beyond their community guidelines and terms of use, they also have customs and behavior norms specific to each. You wouldn't connect with people on Instagram the same as on Reddit, and the other way around. Another example is hashtag use. On Instagram, you can use up to 30 different hashtags to help other users find images based on whatever topics they're looking for, whereas on Twitter, typically only a few hashtags are also used on each post to categorize tweets by topic. On Facebook, hashtags aren't often used beyond organizing content in groups. Each platform is unique and requires unique considerations when using social media etiquette.

TECHNICAL STUFF

Hashtags are the # sign used in front of a word or phrase (#digitaletiquette, for example) and serve as a way to categorize information. Just keep in mind that they're not used on all platforms!

Before you start using any of the many social media sites, you should be aware of the etiquette. (It's no different when you meet new people for the first time in real-life situations; certain rules and boundaries need to be followed to ensure that things run smoothly.) This is all part of knowing how to use the platform and knowing what is acceptable behavior.

Different platforms work best for different situations but knowing the ins and outs of each one allows you to get the most out of them. Whether you're using social media to help with your business or just for fun, it's important to be aware of what each platform is best at before getting started!

If you're not sure where to start, that's okay. We break down specifics about the social media etiquette you need to follow along the way!

WHY YOU NEED TO UNDERSTAND EACH SOCIAL NETWORK'S DIFFERENT APPROACH TO PRIVACY

Protecting yourself online is incredibly important, and you have to pay attention to a few different areas:

- **Your personal information:** This is strictly personal, and everyone needs to decide how much information they're willing to share. Will you let people know what city you're from, whether you have kids (and if so, how much about them you're willing to share), or your favorite places to visit, for example? Drawing those boundaries for yourself helps you stay comfortable online.

- **Interacting with others (particularly strangers):** It comes down to the same tips and tricks you would use in daily life: Be polite, be aware of what you're doing and saying, watch your surroundings, and, if someone seems suspicious or dangerous, avoid interacting with them.

- **Privacy controls:** How much information about you can strangers see? When you're using Facebook, Instagram, Twitter, or another social network, make sure you understand how privacy works on each platform. This helps you stay safe while expanding your network. Though some platforms, like Facebook, have privacy controls, others, like Twitter, do not. Understanding that there's no true privacy online goes a long way toward establishing how you approach social media.

- **Privacy controls, Part II:** How is your data being used for advertising purposes? In addition, there continues to be significant debate about privacy — not just between users but also between the social media platforms like Facebook and users. The amount of data that the social media companies collect on each individual and how it's used is an important aspect to consider as well. Certain privacy settings on Facebook allow you to more or less control how much of your data is shared with advertisers.

Applying etiquette to the specific social media platforms

You've probably heard the saying, "It's not what you say, but rather *how* you say it, that matters." It may seem like common sense, but this adage is especially relevant when using social media. The way you communicate on your social platforms (Facebook, LinkedIn, Twitter) should be different, depending on the platform.

Why? Because you want to send the right message in the right format to your followers in a way that they expect to see on that platform. So, before you go ahead and post something on social media, make sure that you know what's appropriate for the norms and behavior of each network.

If you fail to do this, your posts could be misconstrued as ignorant or offensive because you didn't follow the unspoken rules of that network.

Once you understand these unspoken rules, your social media presence and communication will be more effective than ever.

Here are a few general tips you can apply to all social media platforms:

>> **Resist the urge to overshare your personal information.** As we discuss earlier in this chapter, nothing is truly private on social media. So, you might think it's fine to share your phone number, or opinions about your boss, in a private group, but be aware that more than one person has been fired for this behavior.

>> **If you're unsure about whether you should post something, don't.** If you experience even a twinge of doubt about what you're about to share, the best rule of thumb is not to post it. You can wait awhile to see whether you still feel the same, ask a friend, or just delete the post without sending. But if you're in doubt, don't do it.

>> **Be polite, respectful, and empathetic.** On social media, it's easy to blast out your opinion, tell people they're wrong, and get angry about the responses. Some people enjoy debating, arguing, and even stirring others up. And then, layer on top of everything else the fact that on social media it's easy to take the tone and words out of context of how they were meant. The best way to combat this is to be polite and respectful. Always remember to try to put yourself in the shoes of someone else who might be having a bad day.

>> **Don't say anything on social media that you wouldn't say face-to-face.** The rule of thumb used to be not to say something about someone that you wouldn't say to them personally. (In our increasingly divisive world, that's

a rule worth remembering.) Add to this the fact that we all have an online reputation and, though you might not think it's important, your employers, clients, partners, and potential dating prospects are all keeping an eye on what you say, how you say it, and whom you say it to. Words have an impact, and they combine to create your legacy. How do you want to be thought of and remembered?

>> **Understand how to use hashtags**. A common complaint by people on social media pops up when people overuse hashtags. Be sure that you understand that hashtags have a time, a place, and a key amount, and keep in mind which platforms embrace them and which ones don't.

>> **Tag and post photos of others cautiously.** You might have had a friend who would tag you in all their posts, or another who would dump all their photos from that night out onto their Facebook account without taking the time to edit or curate them. No one wants to see unflattering pictures of themselves, or they might not have even wanted others to know what they had been doing. Though some social media platforms allow you to review photos or note when you've been tagged in a post, most do not. So always check ahead of time if you're adding pictures or you want to tag a friend in your posts. Who knows? They might be looking for a new job and don't want employers to see photos of them partying in Mexico.

>> **Be aware when you're posting.** You might feel great after a few drinks or the edible you just consumed, but that's still probably not the best time to post things online. When you're impaired in any way, it's harder to stay on track with social media etiquette. If drinking alcohol or taking medications makes your mind less clear than usual, wait until later, when you're more effective, before posting anything online so that what comes out doesn't damage your personal reputation. If you wouldn't get behind the wheel of a car under the influence, you might want to step away from social media as well.

>> **Keep your bragging, posting, and attitude to a minimum.** In other words, don't overpost. The idea is to pay attention to others (and not just brag about yourself) and keep your attitude in check. People are often skimming social media quickly to see what catches their attention. Find the good reasons to catch their attention so that they want to see your content and see what you're sharing.

>> **Don't use other people's content without permission or without providing credit**. Don't take a screen shot of a post and share it as your own — respect another people's privacy.

>> **Don't ask for likes, followers, tags, or shares.** Seriously, no one likes to be asked to follow, like, comment, or share your pages or posts. Unless you know without a doubt that your good friend whom you know well will be interested in the content, don't do it.

>> **Be careful about commenting on articles and posts before you've read them, and/or researched them.** This has become a huge issue over the past few years with the sharing of information, research, or even quotes that haven't been validated. Add to that the rise of clickbait articles. If you plan to fire off commentary about a specific article or post, be sure to read it and validate that it's from a valid or reputable source.

>> **Above all, be human!**

Now, the following sections present a few etiquette tips for each of the top social media platforms.

Facebook

>> **Share your own content and ideas, not just other people's.** Sharing only other people's content (and nothing of your own) is a guaranteed way to annoy people.

>> **Facebook isn't a popularity contest.** You don't need to friend every person Facebook suggests.

>> **Don't be that person — you know the one.** That person is the one who is always arguing, name-calling, and shutting down every conversation with hostility.

>> **Keep everything relevant to your friends and contacts.** Don't create direct message groups for a huge number of contacts, and/or take over message groups to promote yourself, your business, or your interests.

>> **None of us wants to be sold to all the time.** Don't be overly promotional of yourself and/or your business.

>> **Along these same lines, don't invite everyone you know to like random Facebook pages/groups.** Be selective and keep interests relevant to your friends and contacts.

>> **Don't tag friends who have nothing to do with your post.** If they're not in the post or directly related to the post, it's considered spam, and your friends or contacts can report it, mute posts from you, unfriend you, or even block you.

>> **Don't comment inappropriately on other people's posts:** Most people have family and coworkers in their Facebook connections. Don't be the inappropriate, cringy guy who responds to a general photo or comment with a crazy, inappropriate comment. Keep in mind that everyone can probably see it, and it generally isn't funny. It's like the groomsman who tells a falling-down-drunk-and-raunchy story at a wedding. Don't be that friend (or family member).

- » **Don't flood everyone's feeds with pictures and updates about you, all day long, every day**. Share your updates and keep going. If you have a ton of updates throughout the day, use Stories to do so instead of the feed. Facebook Stories (and similarly, Instagram Stories) only last for 24 hours and show up above the news feed, not in it.

- » **Hashtags don't matter (much) on Facebook.** They're usually just used in groups to keep content organized and make topics easier to find. In fact, you can mostly refrain from using hashtags on Facebook altogether. (We're looking at you, people who cross-post from Instagram and leave all 30 hashtags on the Facebook post.)

Instagram

- » **Be social!** Like, comment, and respond to other people's photos and videos. Engagement is the key if you want your friends to see your posts and to increase your followers.

TIP

Genuinely like and comment. If you comment, consider leaving more than just a thumbs up emoji on every single post. This is true, especially if you're looking to increase your engagement to help with the algorithm.

- » **Instagram is about visual content.** Post interesting photos or videos that your friends, family, and followers will like.

- » **Don't post too often.** Don't flood your followers, in other words. If you want your followers to see more updates about you, use Instagram Stories or Reels instead of posting on your feed nonstop.

TECHNICAL STUFF

Stories are live on your Instagram (or Facebook) account for only 24-hours from the time you share them. They are outside of the feed and can be used for more personal or behind-the-scenes types of content. *Reels*, on the other hand, are up to 60 seconds in length, and are typically short and entertaining. Reels often include music, effects, and filters. So, mix it up, have fun with reels and stories in addition to your grid of photo posts.

- » **When you post photos or videos, include a description or comment about the photo.** Say why you're posting it and what you want people to know about it. Your friends and followers will read and comment, so take a few extra minutes to include a few words!

- » **Think long and hard about reposting other people's content.** If you're reposting, gain permission first and always, always, always give them credit.

- » **Don't spam.** No one likes it. More specifically, don't slide into DMs or comments to promote your account or business or create multiple accounts to promote your business in case one gets reported and shut down.

>> **There are better ways to attract people's attention than tagging them in a photo or video that has nothing to do with them.** It's spam, and it's a surefire way to get your account reported — even by friends. So don't do it.

>> **We all like free stuff, right?** You like free stuff, we like free stuff, free is great. But just because you like free stuff doesn't mean that your friends might want to be tagged in a promotion or giveaway. Make life easy for yourself and check with them first if or when the opportunity arises.

YouTube

>> **Keep your comments constructive.** If you don't like a video, the person's voice, or even their face, move on. Nothing good comes from your telling the person that you think their voice sounds like Bill or Ted and that you wouldn't follow their advice if they were the last person on earth. Instead, just move on. Billions of videos are on YouTube — just go and find one that you really enjoy instead.

>> **Don't be the troll.** Seriously, life is too short. Don't forget that there's a person on the other side of the camera and that whatever their motivation is for creating videos, they don't need your opinion about it (unless what you have to say is constructive to the conversation).

>> **If you like someone's content, subscribe to it so that you can see more.** This lets the content creator know that their content is appreciated and also makes it easier for you to find them in the future.

TikTok

>> **Similar to YouTube, though TikTok is more casual, there's still a person on the other side of the camera**. Stop and consider what you're planning to say before saying it.

>> **Your comments are public:** If you're posting or commenting, keep in mind that everyone can see it. That means your boss, your next employer, your family, your future children — everyone.

>> TikTok has younger users. Remember that TikTok has all ages on it, so consider what you're saying and how you're saying it.

LinkedIn

>> **Creating connections:** If you want to connect with someone you don't know (or even someone you do know), include a note and add some context to why you want to connect. Don't make them guess or go all Sherlock Holmes to

figure out who you are and whether they can trust you. A few words can go a long way!

>> **Keep what happens on LinkedIn on LinkedIn:** If you want to connect with someone, don't search for their email address and email them. Instead, keep the messages on LinkedIn, unless they ask you to email them, and then (and only then) it's okay.

>> **Add value when you're messaging someone:** No one wants to see five different versions of the same message. If someone hasn't responded to you after the first or second, let it go. Don't overpromote or continue messaging them. There's no place for spam in their messages.

>> **Keep your self-promotion to yourself:** Way too many people join groups or jump on LinkedIn and then all they do is promote themselves, their business, or their employer. Don't do that. It's one thing to introduce yourself — it's another to tell them your name and immediately offer a set of knives and other products for only $19.99 per month.

>> **Respect the nature of LinkedIn:** Keep your comments and messages professional. LinkedIn isn't a dating site, nor is it a place for inappropriate comments or messages. Respect the person you're talking to as well as the very nature and culture of LinkedIn. And though LinkedIn might want to be the "cool uncle" of social media, it's still more professional than the others.

Twitter

You want to use Twitter effectively to communicate, engage, and connect with others. Whether you're a news junkie and want to stay up on current events or you're an industry expert or you want to learn more about a specific topic, industry, or interest, Twitter is the place to go. Just be sure to follow the rules:

>> **Be respectful.** Make sure you don't tweet anything that might seem offensive, especially when it comes from an account owned by a business or company. People take things very seriously, which means that you or someone like you might lose their jobs over a tweet. (And when we say, "Make sure you don't tweet anything that might seem offensive," we also include anything that might be in response to a passive aggressive tweet, insults, and more.)

>> **Hashtag responsibly.** You don't want to turn into that person who never knows what they're talking about because they've read only the first three words of an article before tweeting it as though you agree with them entirely. Instead, spend a few minutes reading the whole thing, and then tweet with a real opinion.

- **Tweet, but don't overtweet.** You don't want to tweet too much, especially if you're the owner of a company. People are always looking for new people to follow them but following someone who has tweeted 500 times in two minutes can be overwhelming. Keep it fresh, keep it fun.

- **Connect and engage (but don't be desperate).** It's really important to put yourself into the community that you're trying to reach, but don't go overboard. You can retweet other people's tweets too much, so be sure to tweet original content once in a while. People get *excited* when they see their own tweet on someone else's timeline, so make sure you use that excitement to your advantage!

- **Add value, insights, or your unique perspective.** You have your own point of view, so don't be afraid to share it. If you're retweeting content, add a comment about why you are doing so. Give it your own spin. It will make it more interesting to your followers and to everyone else who sees it.

TECHNICAL STUFF

Twitter includes a Retweet option as well as a Quote Tweet option. Selecting Retweet will simply share the original tweet from your account. When you choose Quote Tweet, you have the option to add your opinion and thoughts (or even a reason why you're sharing it) along with the original tweet that you're sharing.

- **Make your tweets interesting.** One mistake people make on Twitter is tweeting too much about themselves, tweeting random thoughts without context, and not engaging with other users. Remember that people love to learn and/or be entertained. And the more context you can give them so that they understand what you're trying to say, the better. It's a big world out there, so make it about your audience rather than yourself.

Reddit

As a social media platform, Reddit is different from most of the platforms we cover. Reddit is aimed more for engaging with others and being involved in a community. As such, it also has a specific culture and behaviors that govern it. Here are the do's and don'ts:

- **Follow what the admins say for their particular subreddit.** Similar to Facebook Groups, each subreddit has slightly different rules that govern behavior, so pay close attention because what's allowed depends on who is running the subreddit.

- **Share permanent links.** That means avoiding using temporary links so that access to the content can last longer.

» **Post only links that are relevant to the point you're trying to make**. If your link doesn't contribute to your main topic, please do not post it. This includes memes and other frivolous self-promotion-type posts.

» **Avoid clickbait or misleading subjects.** Clickbait subjects are designed to attract attention and make you click on them but they often don't match the content that's inside ("You won't believe what happened next . . ." is a classic clickbait opener) Instead of using clickbait tactics, make the title of your post descriptive and concise. Redditors vote on how clear your title is when deciding whether they want to click it. Also, be descriptive with your submission; otherwise, you risk having a vague post that no one understands.

» **Don't push yourself on people:** Instead, offer value and engage in conversation.

» **Don't downvote posts just because you disagree with them.** Use your downvotes on posts that sell a product or promote a service or fail to follow the rules.

» **Don't spam subreddits with multiple posts of the same topic:** This advice also applies to content that doesn't belong in their community.

» **Don't troll or post just to post, because you won't last long**. You can't troll on Reddit, because you'll be reported and removed.

» **Using social media as an individual to like, follow, and make connections**

» **Leveraging social media as a business to authentically post and engage**

Chapter **5**

Sharing Your Thoughts in Posts and Comments

eing yourself on social media is at the heart of what it means to connect. When you look at the history of our society, creating connections, conversations, and even debates helps you learn more about yourself as well as others around you. But how does that work on social media? What are the rules or norms you should follow to ensure that your social media conversations don't evolve into online fights that lead you to blocking and unfriending the people around you?

Here's the thing: You have a lot of ideas, opinions, thoughts, and stories you want to share on social media. Everyone has unique perspectives, and something to say. Add in the fact that organizations and businesses are using social media to connect with and engage with new and current customers. When it comes to engaging on social media, there's a definite etiquette and definite norms that are worth following in order to preserve your own personal brand reputation as well as that of your business.

Looking at Followers versus Friends

Social media has introduced many new terms into the lexicon, and new definitions for familiar words. In social media, followers and friends have somewhat different meanings than they do outside of social media.

Let's start with definitions:

>> *Followers* are people who are following your social media account(s). They usually aren't connected to you personally in real life, allowing them to remain somewhat anonymous. People can follow you on all these different mediums if they find your posts interesting enough to follow back. Most often, followers will receive updates and notifications when you post something new.

>> The term *friend* tends to be used mostly among platforms like Facebook. Friends on these sites make up your social network; they're people you're more likely to know in real life than by just following them online.

In some instances, people consider friends to be people they follow and who follow them back.

TIP

Determining whether someone is a follower or a friend depends on two key factors:

>> Platform (are you on Facebook, for example?)

>> Type of profile (are you an Average Joe individual, an organization, or someone with a public persona?)

Most platforms (Instagram, Twitter, and TikTok, for example) are more straightforward and just have followers. It doesn't matter whether you have a business account, a personal account, or a creator account — you still only have followers.

Facebook is different from other platforms because you have both friends and followers, depending on whether you've created a page or a profile.

Your personal profile has friends. If you create a page, it can be of any kind of organization or public person. Pages have likes and followers.

Differentiating between social media as an individual concern and as a business

You're just one person, right? With a personal profile and your own, personal brand, that includes just you. You can show up as yourself and how you would be day-to-day. How you choose to show up on social media affects you only in the sense that you'll be seen by your friends, family, and maybe your work colleagues. Whatever your areas of interest, you might also have followers and friends in those areas. Social media use is often haphazard and based on in-the-moment versus strategic posting.

When you use social media as a business, you represent your company as you talk to your target audience. You're also often held to specific standards for that business or organization. Your posts reflect the larger organization and brand and tend to be strategic and proactively planned, scheduled, and closely monitored based on specific goals.

To friend or not to friend

The issue of who to friend and who not to friend is a hotly debated topic in the social media world. Some people friend anyone who requests it, without worrying whether they know the person. Others have only a small circle of people they trust with the personal side of their lives.

Many people feel that it's difficult enough to keep up with real-life friends, so adding people you don't personally know to your Facebook friends, LinkedIn connections, or even your Instagram private account just makes it worse. Others believe that, after you meet someone in person, you should immediately be able to connect with them on social media, specifically adding them on Facebook or connecting with them on LinkedIn. Such folks approach social media with the mindset of "the more friends and connections, the better!"

TIP

For most people, the decision of whether to friend or connect with others on social media comes down to the answers to these questions:

>> How well do you know them?

>> Do you know them well enough to add to your personal circle?

>> Do you trust them with your more casual/personal side of Facebook (let them in to see your friends and family, in other words)?

>> Do you want to mix your professional life with them?

>> Do you want to be associated with them, either personally (Facebook) or professionally (LinkedIn)?

REMEMBER

Ultimately, it's up to you to determine what norms, etiquette, and expectations you want to establish for your personal social media. If you're going to combine your personal life with your professional life or you want to connect with strangers, you'll want to know where your boundaries are for your specific accounts. And always keep manners in mind when developing your own friending and connections strategy.

Knowing when to unfriend, unfollow, or block

One of the most important guidelines you need to keep in mind is when to unfriend, unfollow, or block someone on a social media platform. People are spending more time than ever on social media and — let's face it — not all of them are taking the time and care that you're putting into knowing how to use it properly. Because of this, it's important to know when certain kinds of online behavior become inappropriate.

People make posts on social media that we may not always like — that's to be expected. But there are also times when we might need to block or unfriend people so that our personal lives can remain private by avoiding any negative interactions. It's vital to know how much discretion we have over our own accounts when it comes to unfollowing, unfriending, or blocking other people, because sometimes it can feel like these social media interactions are happening in real life.

REMEMBER

Facebook gives you a few options to help control what you see on your page. For example, if one of your connections has political or religious views that you don't share (and you simply can't get into yet another discussion with them about it), you have a few different options if you don't want to see their posts:

>> **You can simply mute their posts for a set timeframe.** This means you won't see any posts from them during that period and they won't know that you muted them.

>> **You can unfollow and/or unfriend them.** If you do this, you won't see their posts show up, but if they were to look into it, they could figure out that you're no longer following them.

>> **You can block them.** This means that you'll never see anything from them again, and they can't see anything of yours. It cuts the ties between you quite well.

Instagram offers blocking as well. If, for example, someone keeps commenting on your posts that if you message an account, they'll promote your own post, feel free to block them. Or, if someone "slides into" your direct messages to sell you something, block them as well. Admittedly, it's easy to delete such messages, but if you block the account, they can't message you again.

Posting as an Individual

One of the many advantages of posting as an individual on social media is that it gives you a better chance at creating authentic connections with your friends, family, and followers. You're just posting as yourself — showing up when you want to show up and sharing only what you want to share. It gives you a greater amount of control over your privacy, personal brand, and digital footprint. Your posts will be more authentic and you'll feel less like you're pretending to be somebody else.

Posting as yourself can require some extra effort, depending on which social networks you use and how much privacy customization options they offer. It's helpful to learn how each network works so that you can adapt your behavior accordingly. For example, on LinkedIn, people tend to use their full names, whereas on TikTok, you might see more people using pseudonyms.

Posting as yourself can feel intimidating at first, especially if you're conservative about your privacy settings. However, many people are more willing to connect with you on social networks when they know it's "you" behind the account.

TIP

You never know who might be watching or looking for something new to follow, so you'll want to post interesting content and interact with others thoughtfully. Over time, if you show up online consistently as an individual contributor who has good ideas and knows how to express them well, others will respect that effort and pay attention as well. And that could help bring opportunities into your life that would otherwise pass you by.

Knowing when you're posting versus commenting

People often forget that there's the difference between posting and commenting, from a content perspective, a page perspective, and an audience perspective.

Posting is good for announcing your news, providing helpful information, and sharing tips, experiences, and moments in your life. It isn't as great for passive aggressiveness or clickbait comments, mean-spirited venting, or embarrassing or trolling others.

When you're posting, ask yourself whether what you're saying would be something you'd say to someone's face. If it's not something you'd say in that context, keep it to yourself or take the conversation offline.

REMEMBER

Posting is something you do from your account. It's a new post that shows up on your page or in your feed. It isn't necessarily in response to anything — it just shows up on your account, where it can be seen by your followers. People can address you directly by tagging you in their post, or by posting to your feed.

Commenting is when you respond to someone else's post. Commenting is also where the engagement and conversations happen as people start to reply and can begin a discussion.

Comments made online live forever, so make sure you're taking that into consideration. Even if your name isn't on the post and you're simply availing yourself of Facebook's "anonymous" function, a record will still exist somewhere, so don't think you can get away with saying anything you want without the risk of being found out. If your cover is blown, people will not only hold what you said against you, but they might also view future comments that appear to come from you in a rather dim light as well. More than one person has lost their job, friends, and even family members over saying the wrong thing on social media.

REMEMBER

Once something has left your fingers, it's hard to walk back from it. It might sound like a good post or comment when you're angry, tired, or inebriated, but the reality is that, without any visual or tonal clues, it's easy for your words to be taken out of context, particularly if it has gone beyond the circle of your friends and into the larger, wider world of social media followers.

Determining who can see your posts and your comments

Who can see your posts depends on the platform you're using and your privacy settings. If you're on Facebook and have strict privacy settings in place, your posts will be limited only to your followers. If your posts are on sites like Reddit, they're open to the entire online world. Because of this, before you post, it's critical to remember that your family, your boss, your coworkers, or your future employers might see your post.

Commenting is a different world. When you post, your posts are limited to your audiences. But when you comment on someone else's post, your comments can be seen by their followers as well. So, what you think might be just a fun conversation about your spouse with your friend might turn out to have a much larger audience than you anticipated.

Knowing when to post on social media (and when to keep mum)

As an individual, you can post as yourself on social media whenever the mood strikes you. You don't want to post 20 times in a row, but if you see something that inspires you, you have an update, or you just want to share what's going on in your life, go for it!

You should consider the reason you're using social media in the first place. Posting regularly on social media is important for many reasons. For one, it shows that you're active in the world around you. If employers or interviewers are trying to get an idea of who you are based on what they see in your social media profiles, regular posts will show them that you're generally active in the community and in what's going on around you.

Regular posts also show that you take initiative with things that matter to you, which can highlight your personality and personal goals. Social media postings may seem like small actions, but when taken together become powerful evidence of who we really are as people.

So, social media is a great place for meeting new people and catching up with friends, but it isn't the right tool for every circumstance. When you're trying to decide whether to post on social media, you want to take a look at your frame of mind. Would you be safe driving a car in your current state? Do you have it together? Are you in the proper frame of mind to make good decisions? If you're feeling an extreme emotion such as anger or frustration or you're impaired in some way, you likely want to reconsider posting right in that moment.

TIP

Don't let your current mood make you regret your words later. If you're upset or angry, wait until you're in a calmer state of mind before you post or comment on social media.

REMEMBER

If you're angry about something that has happened or frustrated about a situation that isn't going your way, avoid posting on social media at all costs. In addition to the fact that this could cause an argument between friends who see your post, it can also be detrimental to your professional life. A potential employer may look through your social media profiles before making a hiring decision. Seeing photos or status updates that spell out how drunk you were or demonstrating antisocial behavior won't impress anyone. People should post on social media only when they're in a calm state of mind and have thought things through.

Other times where it might make sense to wait a beat until you're feeling better are when you're feeling down or have suffered a loss. For example, if a friend posts a status update detailing a breakup and everyone comments how sorry they feel for them, it might make that person feel even more alone because they don't want their friends to feel sorry for them. They just want to be able to move on from the breakup. Another example is if someone were to experience a death in the family. Some people need a little time before sharing that news, because the comments, memories, and responses might be too much for them to handle in their initial grief.

Keep these examples in mind when you yourself are posting on social media as well as when you're seeing other people's posts show up. People usually post when they're ready, not necessarily when you're ready or feel like the news should be shared.

And along those lines, be careful of scooping news from a friend or family member. Let them announce their own life events and news publicly first, then you can comment, share, or post it. The last thing you want to do is to be the first to share your BFF's pregnancy before even their family knows, steal a bride's thunder, or be the reason your friend's Aunt Margaret found out about the death of her brother on Facebook.

Commenting on someone else's posts

Before you leave a comment, think about what kind of impression it will make. If you make a sarcastic remark on your friend's page, would someone reading it understand your sense of humor and take it in good faith? Or would they feel that you insulted their friend and feel the need to stand up for them? And how would you feel reading something similar left by someone you don't know on your friend's page? If someone has unwittingly put their foot in their mouth by making an ill-considered post, make allowances for the fact that they were probably posting when they should have been sleeping or they were having a bad day.

TIP

When you're commenting on other people's posts, ask yourself how you would feel if they were saying this stuff about your post? Would you want them chipping in with their two cents' worth? The golden rule is, don't leave a comment unless you have something nice or at least neutral to say!

Imagine that you open up Facebook or Instagram and see your friend Meghan's excited post about her new job. When you go into the comments to tell her how excited you are for her, you see this response from one of Meghan's friends or followers: "What kind of idiot goes to work for XYZ Company? Don't you know they support <insert the name of your least favorite politician>?" You respond, fully intent to stick up for Meghan and her new job. Meghan has been looking for a new job for months, her son has been sick, and what right does this guy have to judge your friend? So you respond, sticking up for Meghan against this guy. You tell him what you think of him, and who does he think he is?

The next thing you know, you're angry and in the middle of an online argument on Meghan's feed, with someone you don't know but who knows Meghan. Is it her friend? Her brother? Her boss? You don't know, and that's one of the things you really should be thinking about — and aren't. You don't know who you're arguing with, who you're calling names, and who they might know. Who else might see it? What happens if someone at your work sees it? Or your own kids?

What impression are you making because someone was incredibly rude to your friend? And how would your own friends and family look at it? Never forget that social media and the Internet are bigger than your comments.

REMEMBER

No matter how much someone might disagree with an opinion expressed by another poster, attacking them personally for it is never a good idea. If a discussion is happening in the comments, offer your opinion and viewpoint, but don't attack other commenters personally and/or call them names. Avoid sliding into the role of a bully in the eyes of their friends and family. If they're saying something you don't like or you think is untrue, save your breath.

If you disagree with a post in your feed or you want to add your own opinion, have the courage of your convictions to speak up. Nobody likes being forced into silence because what they wanted to say was too controversial for others in their circle. Having said that — just remember that when people are passionate about something, even when they're talking about something as seemingly innocuous as which Hogwarts House was the best, it can still come across as sounding mean-spirited and over the top. If what you have to say will be constructive, helpful, or just plain friendly, go ahead and post away. Otherwise, think twice about posting anything that might lead to a heated debate online.

Recognizing the importance of tone

Tone of voice is an essential part of any medium. It makes the difference between a fun post and an angry one or between a serious or nonchalant conversation. When you write on social media, keeping your tone personable and appropriate for the platform prevents you from offending anyone and also conveys the right message to your audience. Tone can be affected by many factors: your relationship with the reader/listener, how much you know about them, and what mood you're in when writing.

Whenever possible, try to stay positive; negativity, more often than not, offends people both online and offline! To keep it simple, tone basically means to carry yourself in a socially appropriate manner, especially over social media platforms. If you want viewers to enjoy your tone of voice, you have to be personable and professional (depending on the platform and your natural demeanor).

Depending on how you feel or what kind of relationship you have with your audience, you should decide what tone to use while writing on social media platforms. If you do say something that is taken the wrong way, consider the situation and, if it's a mistake (like sending the wrong emoji to the wrong person at the wrong time), determine whether you should apologize for what happened and try going back to your usual tone as soon as possible. If you apologize and explain yourself, people will notice that you're a good person without being too much of a pushover.

Creating meaningful discussions

Social media is often seen merely as a way to keep up with friends and family, or as a platform for people to follow celebrities and influencers. You can also use it as a tool to explore ideas, engage in meaningful discussions, and make new connections. More than one online friendship that started out in social media groups and virtual conversations has become a real-life friendship.

The key is to add value, ask questions, and be genuinely interested. Most people genuinely want to talk about their area of interest or expertise and answer questions about themselves. Many meaningful conversations have taken place on social media when we have open, respectful conversation where everyone benefits from seeing different perspectives.

There are several ways you can use social media to create meaningful discussions:

>> **By joining online groups and forums:** Join groups, Twitter chats, subreddits, and more, based on your area(s) of interest. Whether it's politics, RV living, or professional wrestling, you can almost certainly find at least one community on social media where you can participate in conversations about your topic of choice.

Twitter chats are scheduled discussions that you can join by following and using a specific hashtag — for example, every Wednesday is #BCWineChat here with the local community and the third Wednesday of the month is #CanadaChat which is an open tourism Q&A from Destination Canada. Using hashtags keeps the content organized and the Twitter conversations easy to follow.

>> **By sharing inspiring articles and news:** Share links to articles and blogs that have inspired you or that talk about a topic in more depth than the original article. This works best if you share information that's highly relevant to your own life or work and link it back to how the ideas apply to you.

>> **By sharing exciting personal news (keeping up with friends and family, in other words):** If you do something newsworthy, share it on social media — whether it's an appealing photo of an event you attended, your new baby, or some exciting news from your company. This is a useful way to build rapport with people online. For example, if you're celebrating a birthday, wedding, or promotion, sharing the good news on social media can help you connect with friends and family who may not have been able to make it to your special day.

>> **By starting conversations and responding to others:** Comment genuinely on the posts of others! Whether this means liking a friend's post or leaving a comment on their page or photo, this is a sign that you were actually reading what they had written and took time out of your day to engage in the conversation. This is a great way to build rapport with others online.

TIP

In all matters, you have to limit your own posts and comments. Don't post or comment about something unless you can genuinely say that you're interested in the topic — otherwise, people will see through your attempt at being nice! To engage meaningfully with other users online, it helps if they know that you have a genuine interest in what they have to say.

Reserving judgment

Social media platforms such as Facebook and Twitter have given people the chance to express their thoughts about news, current affairs, or any other topic that is interesting them. Though this may be all well and good, there is always the worry about how information can be interpreted before enough background information has been gathered. For instance, a photo may be taken out of context and used as an example of why someone isn't suitable for their job. With this in mind, do not make assumptions about what you see on social media until you have more information on why or how an image was posted.

With this in mind, you should always think twice when reading someone's message before you make any judgement on whether that person is suitable for their job. The truth is, something they do in their own free time doesn't necessarily reflect how capable they are at work. Sometimes a photo out of context may be used without knowing more about why it was posted in the first place.

Avoiding certain topics

Social media is a great way to connect with friends and family across the world, but it also has its downsides. Many people find themselves arguing about topics on social media that they would never get into arguments about in person.

REMEMBER

One of the best rules of thumb for using social media is to avoid certain topics, like politics or religion, because if you start an argument, it will be long-lasting and can cause some serious damage.

Another thing to consider when chatting with your friends on social media sites is how much information you share. Make sure that you're not giving out too much information about yourself or where you live without even realizing that you're doing it.

Do these examples sound familiar? They should, because they are common talking points among social media users.

TIP

If you find yourself coming up against conversations that are turning ugly about politics, religion, or which K-Pop band is the best, consider taking a break from social media and try again when you're feeling less passionate about the subject.

Respecting the person's page you're commenting on

If you're thinking of posting on someone else's page or tagging them in a post, think twice before venturing into the areas of politics or religion. That person may feel disrespected by what you post or may have such strong views about these subjects that they start arguing with you online. Avoiding controversial topics means respecting the other person and their feelings toward this subject. Don't stir up trouble when you have no intention of ending the conversation in a positive way.

REMEMBER

You wouldn't like it if others came to your page or feed and posted something that addresses you directly, knowing that you disagree with the philosophy, political statement, or opinion. If raising it with them in private doesn't resolve matters, block or unfriend them rather than take cyberissues into your own hands. The last thing you want is for a petty squabble to escalate out of control between friends!

Giving credit when credit is due

If you'd like to share someone else's article, a photo, or post, it's important to request permission first. If they agree you can share it, be sure to give credit to the original creator. This is essential to maintaining goodwill online and to ensuring that you don't get sued by the person whose content you're using. More than one publication and other content creators could have avoided potential lawsuits by requesting permission to use the image or content prior to sharing it.

TIP

Depending on the social media platform you use, you may need to provide credit when sharing others' content, in order to avoid being held liable for copyright infringement in the event that someone who created the post takes offense. The simplest way of providing attribution is to include a link back to the original source along with your shared post.

When you're sharing posts on social media sites, remember that someone else created that content. So, if you want to share a post that someone else wrote or created, make sure to give them credit. It's not only social media etiquette but also adhering to copyright law.

Posting as a Business

Posting on social media can be a helpful way to build your brand. It gives you the opportunity to reach and connect with your prospects and customers. It can be used for marketing, customer service, research, and more. The sheer nature of social media means that it also has high visibility, and it can have a negative impact just as easily as a positive one, if you don't understand how to use it or if it's not carefully managed.

Before anything else, it's important to remember what business social media profiles are for: They're used as platforms for brands or people to share information with others. This likely doesn't mean that you'll want to post much about the office party last weekend — unless having an office party is part of your brand or mission statement! Be conscious of who follows you and what work-related posts would be appropriate for them to see. People following your business might be interested in behind-the-scenes information, photos from the office, or press releases and announcements about new projects. In short — anything directly relevant to your business.

Verifying content ownership

Imagine opening your email or mailbox one day to find a notice suing you for thousands of dollars because you used an image that was owned by someone else. Would that make you happy? Probably not. Businesses need to be extremely careful about what they post on social media accounts. Content ownership becomes especially important because social media posts have the ability to spread messages to a large audience. If a company were to upload copyrighted material (photos, videos, written content — you name it) without permission, it could be sued for copyright infringement by the owner of that media. It's possible for businesses to become embroiled in long legal battles because of one wrong move on social media, which would result in not only wasted money but also negative publicity that lasts long after the case has been settled.

REMEMBER

Before you share something on social media, ask yourself whether you or your employees created the content you're about to post on social media. If not, did you get the images, music, or video footage from a reputable royalty-free site? If the content wasn't royalty free, did you pay for the media assets? And if not, do you have written permission to use them? You have enough to worry about without breaking the law and dealing with copyright infringement.

Promoting your business in a spam-free fashion

Social media is a helpful way to interact with your customers, but you can *easily* get carried away. One of the biggest mistakes you can make is over-posting on social media. Make sure that every post is meaningful and adds value for your customers. In other words, never spam your followers by flooding their newsfeed with content that doesn't matter, just because you have a new product or could share a link. You need to strike a balance between making posts that are valuable enough for people to choose to follow your business and not being annoying.

REMEMBER

Add value to your content by taking the time to learn about your audience. Find out what they want to know and what interests them. Then post content about it. The key to engaging your followers is to limit your promotions to 20–25 percent of your content.

> *Hi there! Buy from me! Don't you want to buy from me? How about now? How about in an hour? How about tonight? How about tomorrow? You really should buy from me. I'm just posting on social media and tagging you in the post to make sure you see it so that you'll buy from me.*

Don't be this person or business. No one wants to be sold to nonstop; that's just advertising, not social media. The key to social media is to emphasize the *social* aspect of it. People want you to educate, motivate, or entertain them. They don't want you to sell to them 100 percent of the time. And they definitely don't want to be tagged in posts that don't relate to them or have you show up on their feed or in the direct messages out of the blue without giving you permission.

TIP

Always use an official account for your company rather than a personal account, even if you manage the page yourself, because this keeps everything aligned from a branding perspective.

Refraining from posting if it doesn't align with your company's values

Posting as a business on social media can be beneficial to the company and those following it. By aligning your content with your core values, you create an authentic voice that consumers will notice and appreciate. Authenticity is invaluable when building brand loyalty and trust, which can lead to increased sales and revenue for years to come.

TIP

Your tone should always match your values and vision, allowing people to know who they're messaging with or following on social media at all times. Doing so helps build consistency across platforms, creating uniformity in messages, which customers then learn to recognize as the true message from the company itself.

In addition, if consumers see your posts utilizing hashtags or trending topics without context or relevance, you run the risk of being seen as condescending or self-serving rather than a helpful contributor of valuable information.

If you're a company that sells medically focused cannabis or hemp CBD products, and your values are education, health, and wellness, posting content with scantily clad models or joking about being high doesn't align with your company's values. It isn't right for your audience, or your brand, and it likely doesn't align with your values.

REMEMBER

Checking with your organization's values is a quick way to determine whether you should post content, including whether you should respond to major events or news stories.

Being genuine as a company as well as a person

People don't want to be talked down to. They want to know that there's a person behind the social media account and the business. Customers prefer and respond better to posts that are written human-to-human. That tells them that there's a person behind the business and that person represents the core values and the vision of the business.

Going the extra mile

As a business or an organization, you should take into account additional considerations when dealing with social media platforms, because every post, comment, and response has the potential to impress and connect with your audience or turn them away from you. Here are a few key tips to help ensure that your posts represent your business or organization in the best light (and keep you out of trouble):

>> **Attributing correctly, verifying sources, and banning misinformation:** Social media has had a huge impact on the way people communicate and share information with one another. One of its negative impacts is misinformation spread throughout these channels. The thing is, the sharing of false information doesn't hurt just readers — it can also hurt those who share it without verifying first. Social media can cause problems for everyone — even if you're just trying to share something funny, you should always make sure that what you're sharing isn't fake news, because then other people might believe it too — and that's harmful, no matter what.

REMEMBER

The way to combat the sharing of misinformation is to verify sources and include attribution when you share information.

TIP

One of the most important things when posting and tweeting is to make sure that you always source your information and that you check whether it's reliable and trustworthy. This helps your friends and followers trust your sources and your posts. We recommended that, whenever you post any news or articles on any social media platform, you reference where you got that data.

Also, don't forget to acknowledge comments and responses to your post. If others share an interesting link or background info on your subject of interest, let them know what you think about their contribution. It lets them know that their effort was recognized, which encourages them to keep participating. You can also post questions or ask for more information on the subject if you think it would be beneficial. It's important to give credit where credit is due, so always refer back to your sources and use them whenever necessary.

>> **Verify it before you say it online.** You want your friends, family, and followers to trust you and you want to be seen as someone who is reliable and trustworthy — and knows where to find good information that you're then able to share online. This is even more crucial with the rise of sketchy news outlets that have been using social media as a platform to spread misinformation. In some cases, people think that sharing these articles will encourage others to do their own research into the story at hand or prove wrong those who disagree with them. Though this may sound like a good thing on paper, it creates more problems than it solves.

People are now consuming information with no regard for whether that source is credible, leaving readers susceptible to propaganda masquerading as factually sound news stories. This can be harmful to everyone involved — even if you're just sharing something funny, there's always the chance that it will be based on fake news.

TIP

Here are some tips on how best to verify that your information is accurate before you share it on social media:

- *Use your own common sense.* You're the final judge of information, so use your own common sense when determining the validity of online sources. If something seems outlandish, it most likely isn't true. Use resources to help guide you in making this determination, if needed.

- *Check the author's social media profiles.* When sharing information on social media, always check to see whether an established journalist or news organization is reporting responsibly for updates about an event before sharing any misinformation that may arise from citizen journalists. Professionals at these organizations have their entire reputations at stake and undergo extensive training to ensure that they're being responsible with what they report.

- *Read the entire article before hitting the Share button.* It's easy to get moved by headlines — be smarter than that. Sharing articles that are complete hoaxes only perpetuates the spread of misinformation. Before you share anything, read it to the end to ensure that its information is valid.

- *Share only current news and information.* Always check the date on the article or post. Often, this simple step gets missed, and old information makes the rounds as "new."

>> **Think strategically when posting on social media:** When posting as a business on social media, you want to consider three key factors:

- What type of business you're in
- Who your target audience is
- What your goals for using social media are

The answers to these questions will help you determine what platforms are best for your business to use. They also help you determine what to post on social media.

TIP

One way to determine the type of social media content to post is to audit your own social media posts as well as a few of your competitors. You can learn a lot about what your customers are responding to and what your competitors' customers are responding to.

The formats you can use to share your posts can include posts, links, images, and video. Social media platforms love video.

These are the types of content:

- Educational
- Motivational

- Inspirational

- Entertaining

- Sales/promotional

REMEMBER

If you're trying to decide where to begin, start by sharing the answers to your customers' (and prospective customers') most common questions. Ask yourself and your sales team, "What questions are your customers asking? What questions should they be asking?"

» **Know what not to post on social media:** As a business, you want to avoid topics that are controversial, off-brand, or not quite right for your target audience. Would your customers care about the post? Would they find it valuable? Would they expect to see it from your business? Is the post aligned with your organization's values? If the answer to these questions is "Yes!" then post away.

TIP

A mix of the different types of content can make a big difference. No one wants to be sold to all the time, so don't make all your posts all about promoting and/or selling your product or service!

For a long time, companies were advised to stay away from politics and religion and taking a stand. But that approach has evolved. Increasingly, customers want to buy from companies that have values similar to their own. This means that organizations need to have values and share them with their customers. Use those established values to guide your business's social media posts.

» **Know how to handle major news and socioeconomic events:** There are a few things to pay attention to when a major news event or socioeconomic event occurs. First, businesses should have a written policy and guidelines in place to act as guideposts for how to respond to news and fraught situations. These documents will help them understand and mitigate the risk of losing customers as well as damaging their brand's reputation. They will also help in situations where it has become difficult for businesses to remain quiet when it comes to certain news and social disruptions.

Second, businesses should pay close attention to the posts they have created and scheduled, to make sure they don't come across as insulting or tone deaf. You don't want to be the business that posts about "getting fired up for our big sale!" in the middle of a state with huge wildfires blazing not far away.

Third, if you're not sure what to post during the event, it's best to pause your posts while events are occurring.

TIP

If your business isn't naturally aligned with the event or your values aren't aligned, don't force it. Your audience will know if your words don't come across as authentic. In addition, in some cases, it's better to wait more than one day before you start posting again. Remember that if you and your team are reeling from the news, your audience is likely reeling as well and won't be paying attention to your posts.

» **Respond appropriately to comments:** Social media is a useful tool for businesses to use in order to connect with their customers. This includes responding to questions, comments, and even complaints that are posted about your business. When it comes to social media, you're not just representing yourself anymore — you're also the public face of your business!

REMEMBER

Engage with customers and reply to messages in a timely manner. Don't forget that the public sees your brand on social media just like they would in real life. In this context, being timely when responding to messages means being professional.

Always be positive and open-minded when responding to a customer on social media. Don't get into an argument with them about whatever they said. If they leave a negative comment, you can always apologize for whatever happened and try to work it out with the customer privately (not on social media).

Even when you're frustrated with the questions, comments, and responses to posts, it's best to take deep breaths and respond with a positive tone.

TIP

Your customers and other people interested in your business took the time to reach out and respond to your posts, so you want to give them the same courtesy. People want to know that their post and their comment were important. They want unique responses, even when they're asking the same question. So, make sure that when you start responding publicly, you mix it up and add in some new information.

Chapter **6**

Handling Negative Comments and Reviews

t doesn't matter whether you're just starting out or have been in the public eye for years — sooner or later, someone is going to say something negative about you. It might be an opinion, a criticism of your work, or feedback on your presentation skills, Whatever it is, most people find themselves wanting to respond immediately whenever they see these posts. But before you do anything else, first ask yourself: "Why am I reacting?" Is this really and truly worth my time? What will happen if I don't react? And, finally: "What would make me feel better?"

In this chapter, you get a chance to explore how to handle negative comments and reviews on social media.

Understanding How Comments and Reviews Differ from each other

Before we jump straight into the steps you need to take to respond to negative comments and reviews online, you need to pause for a moment to understand the difference between a comment and a review, because they are often seen as the same.

Defining negative comments and negative reviews

If you're a business owner, chances are, at one point or another, you've dealt with negative reviews and comments from people online. It's easy to take things personally and become defensive when reading these poor reviews and comments, but the truth is that you can learn to deal with them without getting angry, which can often create a win-win situation for everyone involved. Though there's no possible way to please everyone, and at the end of the day it's impossible to avoid receiving negative reviews and comments, we go over some methods you can use to maintain a healthy demeanor when responding or approaching these situations.

Recognizing the difference between comments and reviews

Before you dive into how you should handle negative comments and reviews, you need to fully grasp the differences between the two:

>> A **comment** is a response to a post on social media, a blog, or a forum with thoughts, feedback, or questions that can be made by anyone who has access to your posts, blogs, and forum discussions. Be sure you understand the privacy settings of your personal profiles and the rules of conduct on the given platform before you start posting, to avoid unnecessary negative reactions or unwanted discussion.

>> In contrast, a **review** summarizes an individual's thoughts on a product, service, or event. Reviews are based on the experiences the reviewer has with a product, service or event. Reviews basically reflect what people think of a company, and these can be on your social media posts, website, or review-specific sites like Google, TripAdviser and Yelp. Reviews can heavily dictate the success of a company. Good reviews can help a company thrive and gain tons of new business, and negative reviews can ruin a company if its leaders aren't careful. You *must* understand that a couple of negative reviews are acceptable, but if you start to see a trend in terms of negative reviews, it's time to take note and address the issues presented.

REMEMBER

It can be helpful to understand star reviews as well. Facebook, Google, TripAdvisor, Yelp, and several other review-friendly sites allow reviewers to leave star reviews for a company, as described here:

- » **1 or 2 stars:** Bad
- » **3 stars:** Average
- » **4 stars:** Above average
- » **5 stars:** Excellent

Don't feel bad if you receive a couple of 3- or 4-star reviews. Consumers are savvy enough to see through a couple of mediocre or even negative reviews — plus, some consumers can become suspicious when businesses have only 5-star reviews. Looking at the overall average of your business is better than focusing on each individual star review.

When it comes to negative comments and reviews, tact is everything. You want to ensure that you aren't offending others or their opinions, adding fuel to the flames of disagreement, and that you or your team are open to learning and growing. How you deal with negative comments and reviews depends on many things, including the tone and intention of the original content. While certain comments can be ignored, your goal should be to always have a response to a review, especially on sites like TripAdvisor and Google where it can look reflect poorly on the business when there is no engagement or responses from management. For a deeper dive into what tone and intention are and how they can heavily dictate how you respond to negative comments and reviews online, check out the following sections.

REMEMBER

If the impetus for a bad review is completely out of your control, like the local mask mandates that you're required to uphold or product shortages from supply chain restraints, your best bet is to turn off comments and pin a message to the top pointing people to the local ordinance or guidelines you must abide by. Several media outlets have done so, including CBC Vancouver. They pin one comment at the top of their Facebook post that says: "We have closed comments on this Facebook post to try to reduce harm to the subjects of our content, our staff and the audience. You can visit CBCNews.ca to join the conversation there, where many of our stories are open to comments."

Sometimes, reviewers and commenters are motivated by their own ideology and are just looking for ways to stir the pot.

Reading between the lines: Tone versus intention

One of the tricky aspects of the online world is that it's tough to recognize the tone in which someone is commenting or reviewing and the true motivations behind the content. The *tone* is how something is said — for example, harsh, snarky, friendly. The *intention* is what someone is trying to accomplish: Attract attention, make their voice heard, or get people to agree with them.

TIP

To better remember the difference between tone versus intention, think of it like this: *Tone* is the loudness of your voice, whereas the *intention* is the poster's motivation behind the comment or review. Is the person voicing a genuine concern or just expressing frustration? Regardless of intent, it's important to respond professionally, taking into account the potential impact on your brand, employees, customers, and public image.

Keep in mind that your tone is also important when you respond to negative comments and reviews. Be conscious that your responses can quickly be taken out of context, so be sure that your content matches your intention.

Don't become defensive when responding to criticism

People who are unhappy with a product, service, or point of view commonly seek out the opportunity to voice their disapproval. This can be challenging for business owners because the Internet has made expressing dissatisfaction easier than ever. It can be tempting to take criticism personally or become defensive when responding to negative comments and reviews. However, this does nothing but hurt your reputation and create more drama than the situation is worth. If you are a business owner, it can also drive away potential customers who may have been swayed by a positive review from others. Do *not* let these responses affect you emotionally or cause you stress.

REMEMBER

The way you respond can help your business more than the negative review or comment can hurt.

TIP

If you find that you're getting angry, taking things personally, or responding defensively, you may want to consider hiring a third party to manage your online reputation. If you're a business owner, or if you're an individual, simply stepping away for a while can help you calm down before responding. Often, taking time away from the situation can help you form a fresh perspective — and you might see things differently.

You'll find that taking the high road actually helps you or your business out more than not responding. It's especially important when you're handling business comments and reviews. People usually appreciate honesty and transparency when they're looking to work with a business. So, respond to your fans with an honest answer about what's going on. Letting commenters and reviewers feel heard can help change their minds about an opinion they originally had, so even if you don't remove the review, a more positive reaction can be a significant step forward. This is also true of winning new business from people who read your responses to negative reviews and comments and see how favorably you respond to challenging situations.

Understanding that most people just want to feel heard can help you choose not to overreact to comments and reviews that you find negative. Allowing someone to air out their grievances might help them feel better or validate themselves. When responding to business reviews and comments, keep your comments professional and avoid getting into an argument with your customer.

REMEMBER

Success is all about how you handle negative comments and reviews, so make sure that your responses align with your brand and company culture — and get to the point.

Dealing with negative comments

When dealing with negative comments on your personal pages and profiles, try to see things from the responder's point of view. Consider where they are and see whether you can meet them in the middle or agree to disagree with no further discussion or argument. Good etiquette requires that you never write something on the Internet that you wouldn't say to that person when face-to-face. Everything you write on the Internet stays there forever, so make sure that, whatever response you give, you're okay with it representing you for a very long time.

The Internet has made it much easier to make friends and enemies. For one, the anonymity of the web makes it easy for people to insult (*or compliment*) others without having to suffer any consequences. This is especially true for social media sites like Facebook, where people can post comments relatively anonymously. The nature of these posts allows negative feelings to be expressed without having a face-to-face confrontation, which usually helps facilitate an understanding between two parties.

Unfortunately, on a related note, you may see a lack of empathy on behalf of the poster because they have no personal connection to the person being commented on. To respond appropriately in this situation, you must first consider your thoughts about online etiquette and feel comfortable answering, given your relationship with the commenter.

For a look at some of your options for responding to negative comments, keep reading.

Knowing when to delete comments

If you find a comment especially hurtful, harmful, or derogatory, you may want to consider simply deleting it. This way, you can focus on the positive and constructive comments that people leave on your social media pages rather than dwell on the negative ones. In certain circumstances, it's entirely appropriate to simply delete the comment.

If you do decide to delete, you should follow a few etiquette rules:

» If someone is leaving a ridiculous number of negative comments (for example, ten in 5 minutes), feel free to delete all of them and consider blocking the person from commenting again if it becomes spammy, distracting, or annoying.

» Don't delete every negative comment — only the ones you feel are genuinely hurtful or out of line. It's also okay to delete comments that simply don't make sense.

» It's always okay to delete comments that are spam or from trolls. It's actually recommended that you clear away spam and trolling comments from your online posts to avoid putting off real responders or cluttering the conversational thread. Though spam is easy to recognize, trolling can be a bit more difficult. Trolling is an online tactic that involves leaving provocative messages on the Internet to draw attention, cause trouble, or hurt someone's feelings. As the saying goes, don't feed the trolls; try instead to avoid engaging with people who are only there to get a rise out of you, by stating unnecessary or unrelated info that is out of context.

» Don't delete comments on business posts when a response is needed or will yield a better outcome, especially if the company is at fault. Deleting a customer-service-related comment or a comment that seems to fall in line with comments that other posters are commenting on is terrible form and is likely to backfire on you. If you or your company posted or commented on something controversial or uncalled for, deleting comments only makes matters worse and can cause your posts to go viral in all the wrong ways. Respond to these sorts of situations with transparency and apologies, not denial and deletions.

» Deleting comments that are out of line, that create unneeded or unwarranted aggression or arguments, or that spread misinformation is totally acceptable.

Knowing when to ignore comments

Sometimes, no response is the best response. Some people have valid complaints, but some other people are also desperately seeking unwarranted attention and aren't truly interested in resolving a problem. Sometimes, it's more appropriate to ignore the comment than fuel the fire. Remember that it isn't always easy to interpret tonality on Facebook or other social media types of forums. In addition, your perception of what is meant by the comment can be skewed, and it may not be a negative comment in the first place. If you're unsure about the intention of the comment, simply ignore it for a while. As time passes, you will likely forget about it or realize that no response is needed, after all.

Though a business owner isn't always wise to ignore comments, especially those with a negative tone, if you're a business owner, there are times when you can still ignore a negative comment:

» **If the comment isn't asking or looking for validation or a solution to a problem,** ignore it.

» **If the comment is from a troll who is posting only for the sake of being annoying,** you can permanently delete it. It's not worth your time, nor is there any way for you to resolve the issue if the commenter is simply trolling you.

Letting your audience do the talking

At times, your followers and other commenters take care of the negative comments for you. This is especially true if you have a lot of friends or connections who agree with your point of view, or if you have a lot of loyal customers, in the case of a business. For example, if you're a restaurant owner and a commenter says that your pizza is horrible but then everyone else chimes in and stands up for your restaurant, as long as things don't get out of hand, you can leave and let live.

TIP

Keep an eye on the thread if your friends and other commenters start to respond to each other. One negative comment can turn into a storm of trouble if things get out of hand. If needed, step in and remind everyone that your page, post, or blog isn't the place for ongoing arguments or derogatory language. Hosting healthy discussions and some disagreement is fine, but there's a fine line between agreeing to disagree and outright war on your thread.

Knowing when to respond

When somebody says something negative about you on social media, it can be tempting to defend yourself or get angry. But before you do, answering a few questions might help you decide the best course of action:

>> **What is your objective?** If you have no objective when dealing with negative social media comments, you can easily make mistakes. For example, if your goal is to gain the trust of your online audience and you respond negatively, you might end up doing just the opposite — making people less likely to believe in what you say in future posts. Before engaging with a negative commenter, ask yourself what you want to accomplish.

>> **Who is the person who wrote this?** If somebody leaves a negative comment on one of your blog posts or photos, it's easy to hit the Reply button and tell them how wrong they are. But before you do that, consider their identity. Is it somebody who has written something positive about you in the past, for example? If so, it might be best to let it go.

However, if the commenter has a negative online or offline history, your response may actually help bring them back into line. Perhaps they were hurt when you canceled an appointment at the last minute and are now taking it out on your business page. In this case, a response may be appropriate. If you're not sure who they are, ask them!

>> **Do you have the time to do this?** If somebody has written a negative social media comment about you and you want to reply, make sure you have the time to dedicate to it. If you're in the middle of a busy day when the comment is written, it might be best to leave it for later. After all, if you get into an argument with them, they will just go online and complain about how unprofessional you are!

REMEMBER

Even if you do have time to respond, consider whether your reply will benefit anybody. If it won't help you or the person who left the negative comment, don't bother — there's no point in doing something that brings no value to your business!

>> **Have you given what they've said serious consideration?** Before you respond to somebody who has been negative online, take a step back and consider what they've actually said. If somebody leaves a comment that expresses their disappointment or anger, try not to dismiss it or tell them they're wrong. Instead, perhaps ask for more information about why they feel this way — if people think you don't care about them, they're less likely to support you.

REMEMBER

Social media is a two-way street. It might feel like all your customers or friends are behind you, but keep in mind that what goes around comes around. If somebody leaves a negative comment on your Facebook page, don't retaliate immediately — instead, consider what they're saying, think about how it can help you, and then maybe send them a private message to find out more.

If you feel the need to respond with a positive or constructive comment, do so. For example, if someone says, "My dog had fleas after visiting your clinic," rather than reply by saying, "Well, that was the first we've ever heard of it!" you say, "We totally understand how frustrating that can be. We take cleanliness very seriously and will look into this issue right away. In the meantime, we have a helpful blog post about how to deal with flea issues here:" and direct to the blog.

Good etiquette mandates that you be polite to your connections and business customers, so it's essential to consider how you reply to negative comments. If someone leaves a negative comment on social media about your company or on your personal social media posts, remain calm and resist the urge to respond immediately. Responding in haste can result in your saying something you will later regret, so instead, consider what the person said and whether your reply will benefit anybody.

Responding to Negative Reviews

Few things are as harmful to a business than a bad online review. But the way you respond to a negative review can not only solve the issues presented in the original review but also help you gain future business from people who read reviews and your responses. In the next few sections, you get a chance to explore how you can respond to a negative review so that you always paint your business in a good light.

Developing a response strategy

Though it's easy to get mad at a reviewer who has left you an unfavorable review, there are many ways to respond that will help you maintain your dignity and save face.

REMEMBER

Do *not* let the negative review get under your skin. The reviewer had enough interest in your work that they felt compelled to share their thoughts on it with the world, which is something of an honor. It may also be helpful for you to take note of the constructive criticism they offered so as not to repeat those mistakes in future endeavors. By responding graciously, you open yourself up for more positive reviews from other readers who appreciate how professional and polite you were about the situation.

A negative review isn't always as big of a deal as many businesses perceive them to be. Often, people just want to be heard or simply share their individual experiences, and they mean no real harm to you or your business. Depending on what industry your business is in, there are quite a few ways you can adequately respond. Universally, there are some specific strategies you can use that will help all parties involved.

Depending on the situation, apologizing for how a reviewer feels and being empathetic to their concerns can help set the tone and show you care about your customers. You do not have to always apologize for the specific transgression or issue the reviewer is complaining about, but empathy is always a good way to start. Just make sure you do not come off as condescending when attempting this. The last thing you want is to make a negative reviewer or anyone reading perceive you as uncaring.

REMEMBER

Never make excuses for your actions. It may be easy to develop reasons and logic for why something went wrong, but reviewers don't care about any of that. They care about how you respond and what steps you will take to fix the situation and prevent it from happening again in the future.

Offer solutions, not excuses. Not taking responsibility for customer service or product quality issues is a recipe for failure. We understand that it can be a difficult pill to swallow, especially if you're a business owner. It's easy to take things personally, but remember that this is business. Though the customer isn't always right, they do pay the bills. So, if a resolution can be found, that's what you want to do. Therefore, rather than make excuses for a poor experience or a defective product, create solutions that help make the reviewer feel better. This can be a simple solution, such as a coupon for 50 percent off their next purchase or offering to send a new replacement product for one that may have broken in shipping.

For example, if you're a restaurant owner, you can apologize for lousy service and let the reviewer know that you and your staff always strive to make the customer experience stellar. Explain to the reviewer that this experience isn't standard fare and ask whether they would be willing to give you a second try. Sweeten the deal by offering to get them dessert on their next visit. Often, if you can get a restaurant reviewer back into the restaurant and show them a great experience, they will come back and update their review.

If your company offers products or services, again, apologize and empathize about their frustration. You can ask them to send you a private message on the business page or profile with their customer-service ticket number to follow up and get to the bottom of what is going on in order to find a solution for them. If they say they have no support ticket, tell them to send you a private message anyway, and then you can address their concerns and give them your proper channels for customer support to resolve their issues.

TIP

Do not simply send a customer a canned response telling them to call or email customer service. This response can come across as impersonal and may leave a bad taste in their mouth. It also sends the message that you aren't taking them seriously enough to respond. If there's no way for you to contact them, try your best to work with Google or Facebook to help give the reviewer an alternative route, because sending a canned response doesn't show you care about the customer or their concerns. And they will most likely know it's canned and therefore feel even more frustrated with your business.

Additionally, do not engage in back-and-forth comments on a public thread. Be friendly and courteous but move the reviewer into a private discussion to help them resolve the issue. Often, a bad review takes place after at least one or two attempts to work with customer service departments with little help or fix. You do not want to get into a war of words with them if you can help it. Do your best to try privately to resolve the situation instead of publicly arguing with them on a thread.

TIP

If a reviewer continues to complain on public channels and threads, even though you know you're trying to help and customer service is working with them, it's acceptable to kindly remind the commenter publicly that you have been helping them by email or that the ticket is waiting for their action. You don't want to be combative but having a clear understanding to anyone following along that the company is doing everything they can is the key.

Do what you say you will do. If you take on the task of tracking down the reviewer's customer support ticket, then do so. Make the handoff to customer support transparent and as frictionless as possible. We have seen many instances when a bad review turned into a stellar review because someone took it upon themselves to be helpful and treat the customer with compassion. Sometimes, the small things that the social media or customer support teams can do make all the difference.

Avoid offering customers any kind of compensation, refund, or returns publicly. The last thing you want to do is train your audience to complain to get something for free. If you do need to offer a refund or gift card, do so in a private message or by way of the proper customer service channels.

If the reviewer is attacking your company with profanity or derogatory comments, it may be best to just ignore them. They are an outlier and don't represent most customers who purchased your products or services. If you feel that the person may be getting personal or that their words are inciting others to join in on the conversation, we recommend having your legal or customer service team politely ask them to stop. If the commenter continues, let them know that you will be blocking them from your page because of their language and derogatory comments.

REMEMBER

Customers are human beings, too. The best thing you can do is remember that statement when responding to reviews. They have a right to feel frustrated and honestly express themselves, and you have a right to choose how you will react and deal with their situations. First and foremost, consumers aren't just numbers on a spreadsheet — they are people, too.

Do your best to do what's right by those who comment, even if it means swallowing some pride or taking some lumps along the way. Your fans will respect you for it. Stay constructive, stay calm, and always do your best to respond positively, showing that you're genuinely interested in helping out the commenter.

We hope this advice helps give you some ideas on how to better deal with negative reviews, both personally and professionally. It isn't easy, but if you can find a way to help them without it being too much work, showing compassion can sometimes go a long way.

Avoiding a bad review in the first place

It's pretty standard for businesses to experience bad reviews. Even if you take every precaution, some things can still remain outside of your control. Although it's impossible to avoid *all* the bad reviews, it's possible to avoid getting a lot of them. Here are some ways that will help you manage this issue and keep your business afloat, despite any mistakes or misunderstandings on your part:

» **Do your best to keep your promises.** Even if you can't accomplish something right away, let the customer know when you'll have it — rather than keep them in the dark. Letting your customers know what to expect makes unpleasant surprises less likely to affect their opinions of your business. Showing that you pay attention to detail also prevents misunderstandings, because you're able to understand what exactly they asked for.

» **Giving customers options can provide a big boost.** Customers are more satisfied when they receive the product or service they actually need instead of having to settle for something else. Be clear about your services and provide suggestions if one of them is better suited to the person's needs. Clear up any confusion about the services you offer, with a professional-looking website and customer support, so that no one has to feel like they're being tricked.

» **Customers who have their issues resolved by your business before they ask are much less likely to leave a negative review.** Listening to your customers, following up with them to determine how their experience was, and anticipating their needs can help you turn around bad situations before they even start. If issues do arise, try to find out what is causing them distress, and either fix it or offer a suitable replacement — without waiting for them to complain online. Be sure to send out regular newsletters about updates and new product lines because your customers will appreciate your continued attention and support.

» **Be consistent and reliable.** If you consistently take care of your customers and stay consistent in the quality of service you provide, you earn their trust and loyalty and they are more likely to come back. Of course, keeping up this level of work is easier said than done, especially if you have a lot of customers, which is why you need to provide reliable customer support as well as check in with them regularly.

The bottom line is to do your best to provide what customers want when they want it. When you do this, negative reviews are less likely to be a problem for your business because your customers will appreciate the effort you've made on their behalf and will trust you with their loyalty.

Handling Positive Reviews

How a business responds to a positive review is just as important as how it reacts to a negative review. But the good news is that responding to positive reviews is a lot easier. Responding to positive reviews shows the reviewer and anyone who reads your reviews that your company cares, and that its leaders are active and participate when needed. People love to see companies whose employees care about their customers in good times and bad.

Here are some tips for responding to positive reviews:

» **Thank the reviewer.** A simple thank-you goes a long way. Sometimes, that's all people want from you. You might think that saying more will make them happy or expect more from your company, but most of the time, all they really want is a response from you.

» **Make it personal.** Don't use a stock response; rather, provide a unique message to each reviewer that acknowledges their review and lets them know how much they matter to your company.

» **Respond quickly.** When you read reviews, use the tools available to reply quickly. Sites like Google and Yelp notify you whenever someone posts a review on your company's page. Take advantage of that notification system to let the person know that you're happy they took the time to write about their experience with your business.

» **Be professional.** People often get so excited about a positive review that they let their emotions run wild. Resist the urge to be overly excited or elated; instead, just acknowledge your gratitude toward them in a professional manner.

Your customers are thanking you for your product or service, so take a moment to thank them back. Personalize it by mentioning what they said about the good experience with your company and respond quickly so that they know you care. Remember to stay professional at all times — even if it's a negative review. You can't please everyone, but showing appreciation is never a bad idea!

Another great way to capitalize on a positive review is to ask a good reviewer if you can share their quote on social media and tag them. Reviewers typically love it when businesses share their content, reviews, and photos, so this can create a win–win for you and your customer. This personalized touch can also help solidify the positive experience that the customer had and lead to higher customer loyalty. You can use design tools like Canva or Easil to create social media graphics to really enhance the look of the quotes and increase overall engagement on your social media channels.

Chapter **7**

Going Viral: The Good, the Bad, and the Unintended

S ocial media has become such a powerful platform that it can transform lives, create careers, and even start political movements. It can also lead to some unintended consequences. In this chapter, we help you explore some of the upsides and downsides of being an Internet sensation, from your online reputation to your real-life relationships. What are the consequences of going viral?

The Consequences of Going Viral

It's hard to know what to do when you find yourself in the spotlight. It may be a dream come true; for others, it can be overwhelming or upsetting. Whether your moment of fame was well-deserved or not, there are always consequences. In this section, you can look at some of the positive, negative, and unintended consequences that may come with going viral.

Enjoying the good consequences

For some people, being famous for 15 seconds is exactly what they want. For their entire life, maybe they've dreamed of being recognized by friends, family, or strangers for doing something special. Fame can be both validating and rewarding in unexpected ways. It seems like nowadays every child wants to grow up to be Internet famous, so the trend to go viral will only continue to grow over time.

Of course, being famous doesn't always have to be about self-validation. You might pick up thousands of new Twitter followers who are interested in the same topics as you are, and they might support your Patreon account with regular donations for being so clever. The more visible your online presence is, the more opportunities come your way. (If you are one of the millions of people who do not know what Patreon is, don't sweat it. Patreon is a membership platform that makes it easier for creators to get paid on the things they are already creating like videos, songs, and so on.)

If you go viral on a business account, the benefits to your business can be huge. You can appear on local news, be featured on industry publications, or draw shout-outs from popular influencers. This level of exposure is a dream for some businesses. The more people who see your social media posts, the better chance you have of turning some of them into customers. Going viral will help you drive more website traffic and create more opportunities in the marketplace.

TIP

The best way to go viral as a business is to create content that people can identify with. People love to see your company's personality shine through in the content, and it should be something that gets people excited about what you do. You have a good shot at going viral if you can get people to laugh, feel inspired, or be surprised by your content without turning them off.

Tolerating the bad consequences of going viral

Many people want to be Internet famous, and businesses are always looking for ways to go viral, yet few people think about the bad aspects. The Internet is an unforgiving place, and people will attack anything they dislike with the power of their thumbs. The Internet has created an environment where anyone can be harassed, insulted, or even threatened.

When everyone has a high-definition camera in their pocket, anyone can go viral at any time, and there's little to prepare you for what happens next. You're no longer safe from being ridiculed or bullied online. This list describes some of the more common problems that come along with going viral:

>> **Cyberbullying**: Preparing for cyberbullying is challenging. One of the worst consequences of going viral, it takes a thick skin to handle. Going viral opens you up to all kinds of unwarranted criticism. You have to have a thick skin to avoid falling into depression after having so many opinions thrown at you about how you look, sound, and act.

>> **Lack of privacy.** Even if you go viral by accident, your privacy — both online and offline — can become nearly impossible to keep. You will have to grow accustomed to living your life in the public eye.

>> **Job loss**: When you go viral, there's a good chance you'll have to endure a backlash at work. Your boss might find it necessary to let you go or put you on leave. Perhaps you go viral for an opinion you have, or the company might also receive backlash. Either way, when you go viral, your job can be at risk.

REMEMBER

Before going viral, you probably had an online presence, but it was limited. Going viral changes that situation completely. After going viral, you give up privacy and welcome all kinds of unsolicited attention, not to mention the potential for people who do any digging into your credit history and find things that could come back to haunt you. There's no way to prepare yourself for the downsides of going viral, but at least now you know what can happen.

Managing the unintended consequences

When going viral, you can expect many things to happen. But what about the unintended consequences? Whether the results are good or bad, they can be overwhelming for anyone who isn't ready to be famous at any scale. Growing anxiety and experiencing depression are the most significant unintended consequences of quickly gaining Internet fame. Any reality star can tell you that the public is brutal. Between cyberbullying and the constant pressure to produce more content, plus the loss of privacy, your mental health can take a hit.

Another unintended consequence of going viral is the overwhelming amount of media inquiry and management you need to take on. Media outlets are commonly on the lookout for the next viral social media star, and your inbox can quickly become overrun. Not to mention that managing the ongoing abuses of usage rights can be a full-time job. Many media sites don't wait to gain approval to share your content, nor do they do their due diligence to ensure that it's even the property of the source they're citing. It can be a tedious and mentally exhausting experience to continually field inquiries and keep your reputation intact.

As a business, going viral also has unintended consequences. You may find that you have many more followers, but they may not turn out to be the ideal customer you were hoping to convert into sales. The noise from people who will never buy from you can drown out the people who are your customer base, and you can lose out on creating more business and meeting the needs of existing customers.

In the end, going viral has positive *and* negative consequences, which is why it can be challenging to prepare for and handle — it's a double-edged sword. Dedicating yourself to being happy and healthy is one of the best ways to deal with the challenges of Internet fame. The next section describes ways you can handle the viral consequences that come your way.

Staying Sane When The Situation Goes Off the Rails

Loss of control and virality go hand in hand. One of the biggest fears associated with going viral is having no control over what will happen. Comments and incoming messages can quickly become overwhelming. Whether you're trying to go viral or never intend to, you should know how to handle things before they career out of control if you're online creating and sharing content.

Knowing your options

Knowing your options can mean the difference between a positive experience and one that leads down a painful path when the situation escalates and going viral is on the horizon. If you have an established audience, this means building trust through consistent communication and engagement. It also means being transparent so that followers feel like they understand where you stand and why. When you build credibility as a creator, others are more likely to listen to what you say. This is especially true for influencers who already enjoy a large following, and you need to earn their respect first.

You have many options when you start to go viral and feel like you may be losing control:

>> **Be authentic:** People love authenticity, and they appreciate honesty and transparency. So don't try to fake anything — just be real!

>> **Don't panic:** Many content creators freak out when their work starts to go viral, and they assume it's terrible and immediately look for a way to stop it. Panicking is the worst thing you can do, because there's no way to control something that takes on a life of its own after others share your work.

- » **Set aside sufficient time to focus on the situation:** Social media platforms are all about sharing and engaging. However, if you're trying to go viral, your schedule can become pretty crazy. You need to carve out time for this kind of social media interaction.

- » **Establish boundaries:** One of the main ways you can maintain control is by establishing boundaries online. For example, if people request a phone call or start bombarding you with requests, send them to your voicemail and write back that you will get back to them within a specific time frame. Sometimes, avoiding an interaction altogether is the best way to maintain control of things.

- » **Know when to let go:** For some businesses and content creators, going viral isn't about generating sales or gaining customers — it's about creating awareness. If gaining customers from your virality isn't your primary concern, you may need to assess what you want from it. Having a goal in mind can help you better prepare for success and failure so that there's no way you can be blindsided.

- » **Get help:** You can easily become overwhelmed by the demands of going viral. And it can influence your mental health and personal relationships if you aren't careful. Finding help before the situation gets out of control is essential for positive outcomes. There are many ways to do this, including hiring virtual assistants or finding new creative partners that you can work with, either full-time or on an as-needed basis.

- » **Consult a lawyer:** Between dealing with usage rights issues and handling the legalities of sharing content, your options can quickly become limited as you go viral. To avoid tedious legalities, you may need to hire a lawyer specializing in copyright matters and social media contracts.

- » **Prepare for the worst:** Although going viral should be fun and rewarding, you have no guarantee that things will always turn out positive. For this reason, you must prepare for the worst and know what you will do if things turn ugly or spiral out of control.

- » **Maintain a positive mindset:** There's no way to predict how going viral will impact your life but maintaining a positive mindset can help you better deal with the challenges and unexpected turns of events that come with going viral. For some people, it's easy to maintain a positive mindset all the time, but for others, it can be difficult.

You will also want to consider how going viral will impact your relationships and mental well-being. This is something that many content creators often overlook when they start their journey!

Planning your actions

One main reason for a viral post getting out of control is that there's no way to control the exposure after it gets started. Once you press the Publish button on your post, it's available all over the Internet for anyone to see and take screen shots. An innocent post or content piece can start to get out of control when going viral, so what steps can you take when things start to snowball?

You have the opportunity to get ahead of your viral post before it goes too far off its original track. If you start seeing a large influx of traffic coming from a social network or website, put up an official blog post with all the information related to your situation. The blog allows you to take control of the content and put up official updates to concerned people.

Explaining what happened, how it happened, and why it happened helps your audience understand the situation. Without much explanation, your audience can quickly jump to conclusions. A blog post also gives people exclusive information that isn't being shared elsewhere online. Taking control of the chaos of going viral enables you to better influence the narrative and provides a single location to send media and inquiries regarding your viral content.

One of the most critical steps you should take before things escalate too far is updating your privacy settings on various social networks. Every social media platform has some form of privacy settings. You should take steps to protect your personal information and the information and images of your loved ones by using privacy settings.

If you're a business owner, work with your marketing and PR teams to construct messages that will appropriately address common inquiries and comments that start to pile up. Bringing in a lawyer is also a smart idea, if legal implications exist in your social media post.

TIP

Consider creating alerts for your brand or name to monitor how your content is shared across the Internet. You can easily do this in Google Alerts. Media outlets commonly pick up your content without permission and fail to do the due diligence to get the source or context right. Be prepared to reach out to these media outlets to request corrections or complete removal of your content.

REMEMBER

The content you create on the Internet falls under DMCA protection. (DMCA, short for the Digital Millennium Copyright Act, was passed by the US Congress in 1998 to protect the owners of digital content from theft.) If your content is being used without permission, you can send a DMCA takedown notice to the infringing party or request that they update the original content source.

When you need to do some damage control, bringing in a crisis communications specialist can help you get ahead of your social media crisis. This person will assess the current situation, send out official statements and company updates, identify which information has been posted that is false or incorrect, and monitor new content on social networks. They can also call news outlets and reporters directly to ensure that they have the correct information and help schedule interviews.

There are many ways to gain control in the chaos of going viral, but hindsight being 20/20, a plan you have before you go viral is probably your best bet. Read on to learn how to construct a plan so that when you do go viral, you know precisely what steps to take.

Having a Plan in Place

You never know what turns are down the bend on the path to viral fame. Internet users are fickle and can quickly turn on you.

Having a foolproof plan for handling sticky social media situations and viral activities is especially important for businesses. Not only can a company benefit from going viral, but it can also be extremely costly if you don't prepare yourself.

How to react to viral situations should be a part of any business's social media policy. Even if you are not a business but instead a personal brand or content creator, you should try to be prepared.

Having a plan to not only handle the bad results from going viral but also how you will capitalize on the good is only helpful if the plan is done ahead of time. So, before you go much further, consider writing up a plan of attack.

REMEMBER

People will remember how you handle yourself, so it's important to think about what your end goal is before you start going viral. The steps you take after you start to go viral can easily make or break the situation.

TIP

A good social media viral plan answers the following questions:

>> What is your main goal when it comes to going viral?

>> How will you handle comments, both positive and negative?

>> How will you handle media inquiries and the influx of incoming messages?

>> In what ways will you address negative backlash?

>> What next steps will you take if you want to keep the momentum?

>> What is your exit strategy?

Responding to positive feedback

There is an etiquette to going viral. People will remember how you handle yourself, so it's important to think first about what your end goal is. The steps you take after you start to go viral can easily make or break the situation. You should respond to the positive and negative comments with sincerity and gratitude. Responding with humility and authenticity can be a successful response for going viral in a positive way. If you can respond to the positive comments with gratitude, you will keep the momentum going.

When going viral is a good thing for you, you will want to keep it that way. Keep up the positive and don't allow any of it to go to your head. The best thing you can do when going viral in a positive way is to continue to do what got you there. Don't try to be something you're not or take on the attitude that you're unwilling to accept negative and positive feedback.

Make sure, when responding to comments and commentary on your viral post, that you're genuine and authentic. If you handle your social media with grace and stay true to yourself, you will manage your social media beneficially and memorably. If you're confident in the message you want to convey, make sure that it comes across that way when responding online. Authenticity is the key when going viral in a positive way.

REMEMBER

It's always better to be yourself when going viral than trying to be someone you aren't. Your personality is what got people interested in the first place, so make sure it carries through to your online response to the viral situation.

When given opportunities like these, if you want to keep the momentum going, you need to know precisely what you're doing and why. This is where having that preplanned social media policy and content strategy comes into play. A well-thought-out plan helps you understand all aspects of your campaign, from beginning to end. Having a clear understanding of who you are and what makes you unique allows you to create content that resonates with others.

Avoiding plagiarism

With the Internet being the giant place it is, it's hard to know where content comes from sometimes. You want to share something interesting with your friends or social media followers because you find it entertaining or relatable.

Perhaps you share a screen shot that someone else took, thinking that it was fair use, or you innocently share an image you found online in a Google search. No matter how innocent your actions are, sharing content that you lack the right to is not only illegal but can also have some severe repercussions, especially if the content goes viral.

If you're the one who has shared content that doesn't belong to you and it starts to go viral, you should apologize for your mistake. You can then link back to the original content creator and give them credit for their hard work — unless, of course, the original content creator has requested that you take down the content. In that case, you must do so promptly.

Most of the time, people who share content without permission do so because they think it's a victimless crime or that no harm will come from it. In reality, the person whose content you have shared may experience a loss in revenue, damage to their brand, or loss of opportunity that you get instead of them.

REMEMBER

Asking companies, influencers, or other creators for permission to use their content or concept ideas might feel like a hassle, but it's always better than taking an idea and running with it. You never know whether sharing this content piece will come back to haunt you.

It can get even trickier on platforms like TikTok or Instagram Reels, where creators commonly replicate the video ideas of other creators. In this case, it's always good etiquette to credit the source of the content idea, even when you're putting your spin on it.

TIP

Most social networks allow you to tag or mention other accounts in your posted content or description. Make sure any mention of the originator's account is clickable. If you list only their name but not a way to link to the creator, it doesn't count and isn't helpful to the source.

If you have already shared a photo that doesn't belong to you, the best action is to take it down and apologize. In your apology, make sure you provide a link to the original creator of the post so that people can find them more easily.

REMEMBER

The Internet is a big place, and sometimes it can be challenging to find the original content source. Make sure you always do your due diligence to properly research who created the post or clip or idea — before sharing it with your followers.

Managing a crisis

The first step in managing a crisis is to identify what went wrong and why and then determine how much of an impact it had on your reputation or business. Next, it's time to address any public relations issues that need addressing as soon as possible with accurate information. This includes being proactive about answering questions from followers, media outlets, and other individuals impacted by your actions.

Knowing that you're wrong and then apologizing

Knowing that you're wrong and apologizing is a step you should not skip if you want to win back public trust. When apologizing, you need to be sure that you admit what went wrong and take full responsibility without excuses. Though it might not be your fault, the actions of those associated with your brand need to be acknowledged as well. You can state how you will prevent similar incidents from happening in the future, but this doesn't mean you should make any promises you can't keep.

Always avoid the "non-apology apology," where you say something like "I'm sorry if you somehow felt offended by my actions" — this sort of apology does not take personal responsibility and history has not been kind to people or brands who take this approach.

Taking responsibility and not blaming others is the key to coming out of a viral crisis relatively unscathed. Even if it's not your fault, you need to take responsibility and apologize.

REMEMBER

The Internet never forgets, so deleting a post without an apology doesn't do you any good and may even encourage more public outrage. Before you issue your apology:

>> Take a quick step back.

>> Consult your team or a trusted advisor.

>> React calmly and not from a place of high emotion.

Often, your first reactions to high-stress situations aren't the ones you should be sharing online.

It's important to be sincere and genuine when apologizing because people can tell when you're not. One way to make sure your apology is sincere is by keeping it short and straightforward. Keeping things simple helps avoid any defensive language that shows up in written apologies. It also helps you avoid making mistakes that can make things worse than they already are. You want your message to be understood, so ensure that the words you choose are understandable. As you apologize, acknowledge that what you did was wrong, and spell out what you will do to prevent it from ever happening again.

After making your apology, share it to all the appropriate sites, including your website, Facebook page, Twitter account, YouTube account, and any other social media accounts that are applicable. After you have your apology out there, continue to monitor your social media accounts and respond to anyone who has a question or concern.

Crisis management is the process of working to mitigate and prevent adverse effects when something negative happens. You need to know that even if your reputation has taken a hit, it doesn't mean there isn't hope for recovery. It would be best if you were honest with yourself about what happened so that you can move forward. The best thing you can do for your reputation or your company is to be proactive and let the public know what's going on as soon as possible. Be transparent about why these things are happening and why it was a mistake, and make sure that those impacted by your actions are taken care of first before worrying about yourself.

WARNING

Do not simply try to sweep the situation under the rug. If you do, there's a bigger chance that public outrage will continue and that your business will suffer long-term, permanently damaging your brand and reputation.

Knowing when to cut your losses

When going viral for the wrong reasons, you will find that things can quickly get out of hand, and the damage starts to add up. If you have taken all the necessary steps to help de-escalate your situation to no avail, it may be time to cut your losses. But you cannot simply delete the post and move on. When you're deciding whether to cut your losses, you have a lot to consider.

>> Is it better for your reputation and your bottom line to walk away? If you find that your sales are slumping and the damage to your brand is continuing to grow, the best thing you can do is delete your account.

>> Can you rebuild and if so when and how? It may have taken you a long time to build your social media following to what it is. When considering cutting your losses, you should plan for how you will rebuild and what you will do better.

>> If you cut your losses and delete your accounts, will it escalate things further? If you have yet to address the issues head on and have not apologized when necessary, deleting an account can look like a cop out and can end up costing you more in the end. Do not leave a social media channel until you properly address the issue.

>> How will you move forward conducting your business and your marketing after you close accounts? You need to put a plan together for how you will move forward and ensure you have the tools and resources it will take to recover with as little collateral damage as possible.

DELETING YOUR POST

If you have posted something online and things go wrong, one of the worst things you can do is ignore the situation and fail to address the controversy. As we state earlier, issuing an apology is important, but can you take down the post in question? The answer is yes, but when you give your apology, you need to address the fact that you have removed the posting in question. The last thing you want to do is remove a post without making an apology or addressing the issue head-on.

REMEMBER

Your content has likely been screen-shot by many people, so removing a post without addressing the issues that the viral crisis presented is a recipe for further backlash.

It's hard to know what to do when these moments arise, but if you do all the right things and work quickly, you should be able to salvage a social media crisis. If it ends up seeming like a no-win situation, however, understand that there's nothing wrong with cutting your losses and deleting your post from the social network. Make another post to address the problem, apologize, and explain why you deleted the original viral post.

With time, things will blow over. Don't let a viral moment define who you are as a person or business. You can recover from it, although it may take time and effort on your part.

LEAVING THE PLATFORM

Knowing when to cut your losses after going viral for the wrong reasons is different for everyone. If an issue becomes too much, you may need to delete your post, shut down your accounts, and leave the platform. But this should be done only as a last resort after consulting with an attorney specializing in crisis management. There is no one-size-fits-all strategy when you go viral for the wrong reasons. Knowing when you should cut your losses, therefore, requires a lot of consideration and self-reflection.

One simple way to cut your losses is to delete all your social media accounts. Although this step will undoubtedly stop the noise, it may not be the best strategy to take if you're trying to recover from a viral crisis. If you delete all your posts and accounts, you're basically saying that whatever you posted was so egregious that no one should ever read anything else you have written or watch anything else you have created.

WARNING

For a business, deleting all your social accounts can be a death sentence. Be sure you have weighed all your options and consulted with others before making such a big step. Even if you decide to shut down an account on only one of the social networks, you need to understand that the issues from one platform will follow you to other platforms where you're active.

Knowing whom to trust to help out

When things become too much for you to manage on your own, you will want to bring in other people to help you with moderation. But whom do you trust? What kind of person makes a good moderator, and what kind of additional skills should they have? Here is a list of traits that will help you determine a good fit for a moderator position:

>> **A good moderator takes initiative:** If they have a problem with a user, they should report it and take action. They must have the ability to know when to step in and help with moderation and when to let you handle it yourself. Initiative is an important trait to have because they should be able to intervene before things escalate and go viral.

>> **A good moderator is tolerant:** You should know that your moderator(s) will have people calling them out as well as name-calling. They need to handle people who are angry and upset without getting involved in a Twitter war. They should be able to hold back from responding even when they feel the urge to say something. Tolerance is essential because they need to stay strong in bad situations and not get too caught up in the noise.

>> **A good moderator practices empathy and has a high EQ level:** You must choose moderators with high levels of emotional intelligence (otherwise known as emotional quotient, or EQ). Comprehending, utilizing, and healthily managing your feelings is crucial in a moderation capacity. Empathy allows a moderator to see the problem (rather than become defensive) and helps them understand why people are upset. Having this level of emotional maturity is crucial in a viral environment, where things move fast and emotions are high.

REMEMBER

Have a section about moderation as part of your overall social media policy to help moderators stay on track and manage your online reputation accordingly. A guide like this helps your moderators to keep responses consistent and helps you avoid any misunderstandings.

Community management and moderation can intersect, so be sure you're clear in assigning roles and responsibilities when hiring a moderator. It's best to go with moderators who are familiar with social media and understand the platform's environment they will be moderating. Assign moderation tasks with clear goals and guidelines in mind, and make sure your social management, PR, and the moderation team are on the same page.

Chapter **8**

Group Decorum

A social media group can be an incredible way to connect with people worldwide and learn from them on topics that interest you most. But some etiquette is involved, to ensure that these connections don't sour into arguments or hurt feelings. In this chapter, we cover how to behave appropriately in your social media groups so that they remain fun and productive places where everyone gets along well together. Additionally, you'll see what it takes to be a good group moderator so that your group thrives in the online space.

What Exactly Is a Social Media Group?

Social media groups or communities are, at their most basic level, spaces where members can share information, stories, and photos. The most popular groups are those centered around hobbies, interests, sports teams, politics, and religions.

Social media groups are all over the World Wide Web. You can find groups on Facebook, LinkedIn, Reddit, and Discord, to name a few of the most popular social media platforms. These groups allow people who share similar interests or locations to connect over shared topics. Some of these groups have memberships in the hundreds of thousands; others, only a few dozen. The size of these communities has no bearing on their value or importance to other community members, though — it's simply a reflection of the group's overall popularity.

Recognizing the importance of online groups

The Internet has given a voice to groups and communities of people who, before its existence, would never have reached such a broad audience. They allow people to connect with others who share similar interests, interact with new cultures, and find like-minded individuals.

These online spaces are an incredible tool of empowerment for people of every age and economic status. Like the town halls and gathering places of the past, online groups help people foster community and feel connected to others in a sometimes isolating online environment. These online groups give people a space to feel connected to others in a way that may never have been possible. Like the mom with a premature baby looking for encouragement and not feeling so alone or the new entrepreneur looking for support and unsure where to start, you can find a group to help meet that need.

Whether it's large communities on Facebook or the unending list of niche Reddit categories (known as subreddits), online groups are incredibly important for today's society because they connect us by interest and can help our lives tremendously, either by helping us find the answers we seek or simply helping us feel more connected to like-minded people or those who are going through similar experiences. Online communities are becoming more powerful every day as they continue to expand and evolve. You can find thousands of different types of online groups and communities, ranging from large platforms that have hundreds of thousands or even millions of monthly visitors to small forums with a few thousand regular users.

Groups can also help businesses of all sizes. A robust online following on a popular social media platform can be an incredible resource for a business looking to market its products or services. The large communities of Twitter, Instagram, and Facebook can significantly boost exposure to companies of any size. However, if your company is more interested in looking to build a loyal fan base who will regularly buy your product and recommend it to friends, you may want to look into building a smaller community inside a group.

A business looking to build a community should start looking at its ideal clients and build on those platforms where the desired audience already hangs out. For instance, if your company already has a huge following on Facebook, building up a group within Facebook is an excellent place to start. These brand-managed groups are useful for building customer loyalty and for growing a customer base of like-minded individuals.

REMEMBER

Groups vary in purpose and size, but they all have one thing in common: bringing people together. Whether it's a music enthusiast looking for friends with similar tastes or a new mom who just moved across the country and is looking for recommendations on baby stuff, a group is out there waiting to be joined. The Internet has opened up opportunities that were never before available for people. Online groups and communities are invaluable to today's society.

Categorizing online groups and communities

Groups are by nature exclusive. A common thread connects members intimately with each other while at the same time giving them the opportunity to set themselves apart from everyone else.

These are the most popular types of groups online today, with a few examples for each one:

>> Hobby groups (baseball, cycling, golf)

>> Interest groups (travel, party planning, cooking, political movements)

>> Social communities (moms, dads, towns, neighborhoods)

>> Fan clubs and fandoms (superfans of a TV show, movie, singer, or singing group)

>> Support groups

Some groups exist online to serve a broader community, such as

>> Nonprofit groups fighting for environmental or social causes

>> Business networking and industry groups where members can connect with other professionals in their field and gain valuable insights by way of discussions and sharing information

>> Groups sponsored and run by businesses to highlight their latest product updates, resources, and how to's, and to foster a community built around their products

Regarding the most popular types of social media groups, it seems that groups exist in all corners of the web. Facebook has groups, LinkedIn has groups, Discord (which is now one of the world's most popular community hosts for gamers — among other topics of interest) has groups. Unlike all the other social networks, Reddit's groups are referred to as *subreddits.* These various platforms can fall into different categories; for example, you can find communities dedicated to specific interests and groups devoted to more general topics that may span multiple interests.

REMEMBER

You can also find countless forums on the web to join, subscribe to, and participate in. These online discussion boards differ from social media communities because they require more of an investment by members (time). The nature of these forums is usually to discuss an organized series of topics on a set schedule, with one moderator or sometimes a group of moderators (admins) who take shifts to manage the discussions.

There are many different ways for companies and marketers to make use of social media groups and communities. Many successful businesses have hosted communities on their web pages or via private networks like Mighty Networks or Circle.io and multiple social media platforms (such as Discord and Reddit). If you make a point to engage with members by asking questions, providing helpful information and content, and replying and updating regularly, your company will likely inspire a warmer reception than if you're there just to advertise or spam links.

Secondly, you can create your own social media groups or fan clubs to benefit your business. By creating a group for customers to connect and share information, they're more likely to stay interested in what you have to say and much more willing to spread the word about your brand if given a chance. There are many ways that you can leverage these groups to increase your visibility online, such as providing discounts or exclusive offers for members, offering valuable prizes or giveaways, and encouraging customer feedback on products.

TIP

Building communities/groups can be an excellent way to improve your reputation among customers and build loyalty and trust, both of which lead to increased sales.

Being Respectful (and Respected)

Being a member of an online group is an easy way to connect with people worldwide. Whether you're looking for new friends or inspiration or you want to chat with like-minded individuals, joining these online communities can be beneficial. However, if you're going to participate in online groups and forums, you need to follow a number of written (and unwritten) rules. The last thing you want is to be an uninformed community member.

Group posting etiquette

When you're looking to contribute to the group, be sure that you take the time to read up on the group rules. Though most groups post their specific guidelines on what is acceptable content within that group, many groups follow some general guidelines.

When deciding what content should be posted to a group, ask yourself, "Is this relevant to the purpose of the group?" or "Does this bring value to the other people in the group?" If your answer is no, it might be best not to post.

Before posting to the group, do a quick search of the group's posts to see whether your content has already been covered. If you find a similar post and yours contains more information, feel free to post, but if it offers little value beyond the original post, maybe just comment on the original post instead.

REMEMBER

By posting only relevant content, you will not only be a better community member but also save yourself from being reported or removed by a group admin. (*Being reported* sounds like something the secret police would do, but all it means is that another group member has signaled to a moderator or administrator that your content is either not relevant or goes against that group's rules.)

Avoid overposting or taking over the group with too much of your content. Generally, it's best to give more than you take, so although most group owners and moderators encourage sharing within a group, neither do you want to take it over. Give your contribution, and then let the other members have a turn. On this same note, be sure that you aren't a direct competitor of the group owner. It's not good etiquette to post as an expert in a group where you're in direct competition with the owner, unless they have given you permission to do so.

Also, avoid sharing spam or overly promotional content that is not relevant in a group or promoting your own business or services, especially as a new member. Most groups prefer that members not promote themselves unless it's on a dedicated thread. When in doubt, ask a moderator or an administrator. When it comes to group interaction, it's better to be safe than sorry.

Though you should always be mindful of the rules, it's equally important to remember that not all groups are alike. Though some are quite strict about who is allowed in and what members can post, others might allow more freedom when sharing content or posting comments. The best thing you can do is take the time to familiarize yourself with the group's vibe before you start sharing your content or asking questions.

Commenting etiquette

In addition to being a good group member when it comes to posting content, think about your interactions with other members. This includes how you respond to comments and what kind of content you put on the feed.

There are many different kinds of comments you can post in groups, so it's important to be mindful of how your words may come across. Though some members might want to start heated debates over controversial topics, it's generally best to stay out of such conversations.

If you find yourself in a heated exchange, you should also avoid personal attacks against other members. It's okay to voice your opinion, but do so thoughtfully and respectfully. Calling another member names or even responding to a rude comment with one of your own can lead to removal from the group or being banned from posting in it.

The rules of the group

The most important thing you can do in a group is respect the group rules. Taking the time to read the rules and making sure you follow them sets an excellent example for other members — and makes it easier for the administrator to run the group.

If you have a question about what's allowed, it's okay to reach out to the administrator or other members. Taking the time to read the group rules and familiarizing yourself with how the group runs can save you from being blocked in the future. One thing you should avoid doing is starting a post with the instruction "Please remove if not allowed." If you're unsure if your post is allowed and want to avoid breaking the group's rules, it's better to reach out to a moderator or an administrator. This will ensure not only that you're not posting inappropriate content but also that you're not creating additional work for the group moderators.

REMEMBER

When you're in a private community, you should never take screen shots of the group to share outside of that group. It's a violation of many platform policies and shows a complete disregard for the etiquette of private communities. In the same category, you must remember that other members may violate this unspoken rule and take screen shots of your posts and comments inside a private group. Never post anything you would not want the world to see.

Avoiding Common Mistakes in Social Media Groups

Because it is so easy to be active in social media groups, millions of people do so. Unfortunately, many people don't realize that they're making common mistakes until it's too late. If you want to avoid these mistakes and learn how to use a group effectively, read on!

Posting at the wrong times or to the wrong groups

Being timely when posting and responding to other members is vital. It's not helpful for group members who have questions if you don't answer them until weeks later. Additionally, if you're making a post, make sure it's relevant to the group. If it's not, the only thing your contribution does is lead to unwanted noise, making it difficult for other members to find what they need. It's also good to use the group Search feature, if one is available, before you ask a question. Often, members end up asking the same question that has already been asked many times.

REMEMBER

Before you ask a question, post a complaint, or share information in a group, you should first assess whether this channel is the best one for the job. For example, if you have a tech support question for a company, navigating the proper support channels is often better than visiting a community-driven group and asking a question that most members would be unable to help answer.

Most groups are useful for finding answers to your questions; be sure to ask the kind of questions the community can help you with and do your due diligence to ensure you aren't being repetitive.

Making false claims about yourself or others

Don't make any false claims about yourself or others inside of a group. For instance, it's not okay to say that you have experience in an area you don't have or that someone else has done something they have not done. These false claims will only lead to trouble for yourself and other group members. If you want to grow your reputation as a community member, stick with the truth about who you are and what you know. Give value when you can, but don't try to be something for everyone.

REMEMBER

What you share online never really goes away. So, if you lie or misrepresent yourself, it may come back to haunt you.

Trolling and harassing in social media groups

A *troll* is someone who goes out of their way to harass someone online with little reason besides upsetting or humiliating someone. To avoid being a troll yourself, never make fun of, insult, harass, or troll other members. Though it's okay to disagree with people, purposely trying to upset them isn't okay. If someone deliberately harasses or trolls you, report them to the group administrator. If it's a personal account that starts the problems, you can certainly take it a step further and block them along with reporting them to the hosted platform, like Facebook or LinkedIn.

REMEMBER

The people in online groups are real-life humans, they have real feelings, and yes, they have bad days now and then. So, try to be empathetic to others, and don't go out of your way to make other members feel bad or attacked.

Spamming

There are many forms of spamming — some more blatant than others. For example, if you make the same post in multiple groups in a short period, the post is considered spam. It's also spamming when you're soliciting or pitching your products or services to other group members in their private messages without explicit permission. Avoid any form of cold outreach — those unsolicited messages sent to people you don't know in hopes of landing a sale. Also avoid posting content lacking context into any group, let alone multiple groups.

Additionally, you should avoid joining a group and immediately posting content that is self-promotional or irrelevant. By that same token, avoid posts that have a call to action to solicit other members — for example, making a post about the secret to selling more online courses and asking people to comment below or send you a private message for the details on how they can learn more. It's best to give more than you take when it comes to online communities.

Trying to be sneaky and create a post that at first glance doesn't seem promotional or spammy but is designed to drive people to your material or website — neither of which has anything to do with the group's content — will also likely get you in trouble with the group administrator.

Sharing without context should also be avoided. If you plan to share a video, an article, or a link, it's best to give context in the description that connects the dots between the group's intention and yours. Successful posts can be both relevant to the conversation and used as a launchpad to other discussions.

REMEMBER

When in doubt about the rules for a given group, be sure to check first with the administrator before sharing.

Being a Good Moderator

The moderation of a social media group can make or break the group's success. As moderator of a group, it's up to you what goes on in there — deciding which posts are allowed or not allowed in the group, deciding how much sharing is appropriate, and keeping members safe by reporting any inappropriate content. It might seem like a lot of responsibility at first glance, and it can be, but don't worry — you're not alone! This section presents some tips to help you make the most of your new position.

Assuming the role of the moderator

First and foremost, a group moderator is a manager, which means that they're responsible for organizing and overseeing all aspects of the group. As a group moderator, you're also responsible for ensuring that members follow all the platform's terms and conditions as well as the group rules. These guidelines include not sharing anything pornographic or offensive, not sharing personal information (such as addresses and phone numbers) without consent, and removing any bullying, scamming, trolling, or other inappropriate content that may be shared within your group.

You're the host, facilitator, and perceived expert all rolled into one! As a moderator of an online group, you're responsible for how your members interact with each other.

Whether your goal is to generate a lively conversation or to weed out trolls and spammers, you can do it by following a few simple tips:

>> **Be responsive:** When a problem arises in your group, address it promptly. If someone has been posting inappropriate content or hurting others' feelings, make sure they know what they've done wrong and ask them to stop.

>> **Be welcoming:** Make your group open to everyone, but don't allow it to become chaotic. Make sure you're setting clear expectations for what is and isn't allowed in the group so that people know exactly what they can expect when joining. Create welcome posts and encourage new members to introduce themselves.

Think of a moderator as a community evangelist. This person not only ensures that members are following the rules but also encourages engagement and timely discussion. As a moderator, you're responsible for the success of the group. Let members know that you appreciate them — if you're friendly and active in the group, the group members are sure to follow suit. (Well, most of them, at least.)

Growing your group

As a moderator, one of the important jobs you may have is helping to grow your group. There are right and wrong ways to grow a group. Some ways to grow your group include sharing it with friends, promoting it on other social media platforms, and inviting people interested in joining via email. You might also offer training, resources, specials, or a service or product of value inside your group.

Engaging with members and being active in your group will naturally make people want to do the same. And the more active a group is, the more likely it will grow. One of the most important ways you can engage with members is via conversation. This means that you, as moderator, should watch for opportunities that arise during discussions and chime in when appropriate. The more active the dialogue, the better! If you see a topic that no one has responded to yet, but it looks like people would be interested in commenting, comment yourself so that others are encouraged to join the discussion.

You might also want to see whether there are any other ways, besides conversations, to engage members. For example, creating polls or surveys can help generate new discussions and get people talking again. Encouraging members to share content they find interesting can do the same thing.

When you invite nonmembers to join your group, be sure you're inviting only people who genuinely have an interest in the group's topic. Ending up with a ton of members who don't interact or share content won't make the community stronger.

REMEMBER

The numbers don't matter if the people don't care. Having people added to your group to show you have more members and not because they're interested can hurt the group in the long run. The engagement will be lower, and those who care about the topic will likely get lost in the crowd.

Avoid adding people to your group without their permission. Adding to a group without permission or without making a request is a pet peeve of many online users and can immediately leave a bad taste in the invitee's mouth. Instead, politely invite people to join while giving them reasons the group would bring them value.

Setting expectations and rules

Group members must know exactly how they should be engaging in your group — which posts are appropriate, what kind of links can or cannot be shared, what type of content is allowed, and what isn't.

The first step to setting expectations for group members is to create a clear mission statement for your group. A *mission statement* helps you stay focused on providing value around that topic or subject area. Next, come up with a name for the group — a descriptive group name allows visitors to know whether they're in the right place.

It's essential to set guidelines for discussion and share them widely because you want to ensure that everyone is on the same page to avoid confusion about what content is appropriate. The last thing a group moderator wants is a heated argument over whether a topic should be allowed in the group, so being upfront about the guidelines is helpful for group members, too.

Handling issues in your group

It's inevitable, when participating and managing a group, that issues will arise. The anonymity of the Internet has changed how people interact and treat each other. You need to take steps that you may not be used to when you first start managing your group.

Sometimes, the issues that arise are in direct violation of group rules or are blatant attempts to spam or harass other members. At other times, it can be a misunderstanding that spirals out of control. Tonality and intention are sometimes difficult to read in an online group setting, and comments can quickly be taken out of context.

You have several options for dealing with various problems in your group.

Problem: Spam and misinformation

Social media groups generally have stringent guidelines when it comes to spam. They have been known to shut down entire pages and even close groups that foster spam and misinformation. To prevent this, you as a group manager *must* take quick action as soon as spam is noticed. Preventing these issues can be as simple as deleting the post or editing or removing comments. The action you need to take depends on how much spam has been posted. As for misinformation, it is your job as a moderator or administrator to be familiar with the given platform's stance on how they handle misinformation. It does not matter if you agree with the stance or not; when you are using a specific platform, you must abide by their rules.

If a great deal of misinformation is being spread, it's usually best to delete all comments and start a new thread with correct information or point to official documentation on the topic. This prevents the further spread of misinformation while allowing people to raise the points and questions that need to be addressed. It's better that you end up deleting a few legitimate comments than allowing misinformation and people's fears or anger to escalate. If you don't want to start a new post, simply remove the post and direct the poster to your group rules on sharing spam or misinformation in your group.

Problem: Blatant trolling or harassment

Trolls will do whatever they can to elicit a reaction from your group, including starting fights, provoking anger, or going out of their way to hurt feelings. They want to cause disruptions and then disappear into the shadows — only to come back later when you're less prepared to deal with them. They're the kind of troublemakers you' need to address immediately if they become an issue in your group. Your best action is to have a rule disallowing trolling or harassment and immediately remove the offender from your group.

TIP

Be prepared. Trolls have been known to address the original post from a new account. This can be frustrating because their profile is often private, so you cannot see all their posts and comments on other groups. If they continue to be a problem, you need to block them and report them as spam, if necessary.

Problem: Simple rules violations

In most cases, a simple rule violation doesn't warrant the removal of a member from your group. Simple violations could be a first time offense of a promotion of a blog post or breaking an implied rule. In these situations, it's best to remind the offender of the group rules and take down their post or comment with a warning. If the individual doesn't understand and continues to violate group guidelines, you need to remove them from your group.

Problem: Dealing with a disagreement or a heated debate

Despite our best efforts and intentions, group members can sometimes disagree, and arguments can ensue. Remember that everyone deserves a voice and to be heard. That said, there are ways to deal with a disagreement without letting it spiral out of control.

If the argument is growing out of control or commenters are making personal insults, closing the thread's comment section may be best. If members are fueling the flames, send them a private message with a warning or, in extreme cases, remove them from the group. You can also simply reference your rules on bullying or harassment. It isn't necessary to delete comments from people who are being respectful and thoughtful when sharing their opinions just because there's a disagreement.

In most cases, simply closing the commenting section after members have been reminded of the group rules will be enough to calm angry feelings.

REMEMBER

Disagreements as such are fine; what you should be on the lookout for is when people take matters too far. Creating an environment of respect and empathy is best for growing the kind of group people want to participate in.

Having those clear rules and community guidelines makes your job easier when handling issues, because you'll be able to point back to the written rules. It's best to treat all members the same and not play favorites. If the rule is No Promotions, do not allow some people to introduce promotions and not others. Consistency is the key when upholding the community guidelines.

To keep the peace, here are some issues to consider when it comes to moderating:

>> **When closing comments on a post, be sure to add a final comment yourself.** You need to explain why you're closing the comment thread.

>> **Be clear about why you're removing a post from the group.** Send a private message to the original poster explaining why and, for clarification, pointing to the rule they violated.

>> **Be transparent with your community about what can get them banned.** Having a zero tolerance policy for behavior like spamming or trolling is a good start.

>> **If you need to remove someone from the group, do it privately.** Removing someone in the open can cause unnecessary drama, especially if they didn't realize that their actions violated your rules.

>> **Be consistent when it comes to whom you allow to stay in the group.** If there's a specific rule that one person has broken but another is allowed to stay for doing the same thing, you'll cause further confusion. It's crucial that those who join the group know what they can expect from being a part of it.

REMEMBER

When handling issues and interacting with group members, your tonality is essential. Tonality is incredibly hard to read online, so take extra steps when you can to come across as friendly as possible and not overly stern.

Creating a positive environment and being active yourself helps others do the same. As a reminder, here are some tried-and-true methods you can use as a moderator to foster a valuable group experience for all members:

>> **Encourage engagement.** Use polls, share your own posts and content, utilize video content, and ask members to engage thoughtfully.

>> **Provide ways that members can promote themselves or share more about their own interests without overpowering the feed.** One way to do this is to create dedicated posts in your group for these purposes, where members can share that post's comments.

>> **Encourage members to tag their posts with relevant hashtags.** This action, which helps others find their posts within your group when searching, is especially helpful if you manage a large and active group.

>> **Encourage contributions from members that go beyond just posting links to their own content.** Though sharing your own content is a great way to utilize the power of having your own group, try to keep it to a minimum to prevent burying the rest of the feed with your posts. If the group is all about promoting your own stuff, people will be less likely to stay in your group and engage.

It's also helpful if you, as moderator, ask for feedback or opinions on improving your own posts. Your group members are the experts on what they want to see, and you can learn a lot by asking for their feedback.

REMEMBER

Moderating with a heavy hand can actually hurt a group. You want members to feel comfortable sharing and asking questions. Make yourself available if someone needs you, but don't be a dictator.

IN THIS CHAPTER

» Knowing what live video is and why you should care

» Being a gracious host

» Being a wonderful guest

» Avoiding embarrassing mistakes

» Engaging in the etiquette of watching and engaging in a livestream

Chapter **9**

Being Likeable During Livestreaming

A s the world of social media continues to expand, so does our human need for effective communication. In recent years, one medium that has undergone a revolution is livestreaming. This type of video broadcasting is becoming more and more popular among users on social media platforms. In the beginning, live broadcasting was made popular via platforms like Meerkat and Periscope. But as it became more popular, livestreaming has been rolled out to most major social networks as well as shopping platforms like Amazon.

Though this new form of communication may seem daunting at first glance, there are a few simple ways to be likable during livestreaming that can make all the difference in your personal or professional life. Being likable while livestreaming makes you an enjoyable person to watch and engage with and provides viewers with a better experience overall when watching your broadcast.

What's a Livestream, Anyway?

Live video is a type of streaming media where the content is broadcast in real-time to an audience. Live video can be anything from a live sporting event to a news bulletin or even just your own personal thoughts and feelings. The Internet has transformed how people share information with one another, and live video is no different. Gone are the days of waiting for newscasters to read headlines on TV at 6 P.M. — now, you have access to all sorts of breaking stories as they happen, thanks to social media providers like Facebook Live and YouTube Livestreams.

Many people use live videos for their businesses because it gives them an outlet to create relationships with potential customers by providing valuable content related to their industry or niche market. Livestreaming is an excellent opportunity to attract attention that will hopefully turn into a business for those looking to gain a foothold in the competitive online world.

Livestreaming has taken off like wildfire, thanks to how accessible it is now. Anyone with Internet access can post live videos on many social networks, and tools like Ecamm (www.ecamm.com) and Streamyard (https://streamyard.com) make it accessible for anyone.

Livestreaming natively to networks like Facebook, Instagram, YouTube, and even Amazon is free and easy for desktop and mobile devices. It allows you to reach a broad audience that is already using the platform every day. It also provides an opportunity for businesses to interact directly with customers, by way of trading comments and engaging in conversations. Niche networks like Twitch, which is dominated mostly by gamers but has loads of opportunity for other interests, allow you to tap into an audience that has similar interests. Even TikTok has gotten into the live streaming game by offering the feature to users with over 1000 followers.

One of the most exciting and profitable uses for livestreaming is interacting with your audience via an online course or workshop. By holding a live training session, you create a sense of community and engagement with your customers while providing them valuable content they can use to build their business.

REMEMBER

There are many different ways to use livestreaming, all of which can help you grow your business, launch your personal brand, or share your interests. Whether you're a lawyer, web designer, yoga instructor, or anything in between, there's a way to use live video that will work with your industry and allow you to reach new customers in real-time.

Going Live

With the advancements of the Internet and the adoption of streaming tools and technologies, it has never been easier for individuals to go live. Whether livestreaming on platforms like Facebook, Instagram, YouTube, or another social network altogether, they all provide tools to help you create content and share it with people who will be interested in your niche.

So many people are starting to use this communication method because it opens up avenues for new relationships, personal branding, and business opportunities.

What you need to know before going live

Before you go live for the first time, there are a few questions you need to have solid answers for. First, where will you be going live? The best option is a site dedicated to live video, such as Facebook. You have access to not only a broad audience right from the beginning but also analytics about *who* is watching and *how long* they're watching. This can help you tailor your content better so that it serves your customers' needs more efficiently.

You next need to determine what kind of equipment you need in order to go live. Luckily for you, the list isn't long. All you need these days is a web camera, a mic, and a strong Internet connection. A laptop or desktop computer works best, but your mobile device may suffice if it has a strong enough connection. One of the benefits of using a mobile device is you have more flexibility when it comes to when and where you do your live broadcast, so long as you have a good data connection or fast Wi-Fi speeds.

The other important consideration is to make sure you have quality sound. Outside of your content, sound is the most important component to your livestream. Sound can make or break the success of your broadcast because no one will stick around if your sound is poor. An easy fix is to use headphones with a built-in mic. Even the mic and headphones that came with your phone will suffice.

TIP

To ensure the best-quality video and audio, you need an upload speed of at least 10 Mbps. Sometimes you can get away with less, but you risk having a spotty connection. To use Facebook Live or YouTube Live, for example, you need a minimum 3–4 Mbps upload speed. For Twitch you'll need 6Mbps — but again, that is the bare minimum. Even though you meet the minimum requirement, the quality of your feed may be spotty.

TECHNICAL STUFF

Broadband speeds are measured in *megabits per second* (Mbps). This is a unit of measurement for how fast data goes through your Internet. The higher the number of Mbps, the faster your Internet will be.

The next thing you need to figure out is what exactly you'll say. Although the live video does give you some leniency to go off script and break from tradition, it's still essential to have an idea of what you're going to say before you go live. This helps ensure that your video is engaging and interesting, which helps attract more customers in the long run. Viewers don't want to watch a live broadcast starring someone who really has nothing of substance to say. Having an idea of what you want to talk about and even having a couple of bullet points with key concepts written down will go a long way in keeping you on topic and your audience tuned in.

Finally, what do you want to get out of the experience? This question may be hard to answer right away, but it's something that will definitely affect how you convey yourself during your first few tries at going live. What is the purpose of this first video, and what do you want it to lead to? It may help to take a few steps back and ask yourself what your overall goal is in using live videos. Knowing these answers helps you refine your content to be more effective in meeting your goals.

TIP

Make sure, before you go live, that you have an enticing title for your video. The title is crucial for attracting viewers' attention during livestreaming. Although you may not be able to do much about search engine results and how you appear in them before your livestream, the title is one that will immediately pique interest and get people tuning in to watch your livestream.

What you need to know while you're live

Once you hit the Go Live button, the real fun begins. Though you're livestreaming, it's important to be engaging. You're now in direct contact with your audience, so you want to make sure they enjoy themselves and take away value from the experience.

Most of your viewers will be those watching the replay later, so don't make them skip ahead or wait for you to start because you're waiting for live viewers to show up. After you're live, welcome viewers and jump right into your topic. Delaying will only frustrate future viewers of the replay and may discourage them entirely from watching.

TIP

While it is okay to ask your initial viewers if they can hear you alright once you start, do not dwell on this too long. An example of a great start would be "Welcome replay viewers and live viewers! Please let me know if you can see and hear me. I am excited to discuss [*topic of the broadcast*] today! Before we start, let me know where you are viewing from . . ."

Think about what you want to get out of this live video. Will you use it as part of a paid webinar? If so, try hooking early viewers with a giveaway or free offer. Will you be using it as a demonstration of your services? Then make sure to engage directly with viewers and answer any questions they may have for you. Taking time to structure your live broadcast and create an outline of your show will help you reach your livestreaming goals.

REMEMBER

You may encounter some technical difficulties during your first few livestreams. That's okay, because it's an opportunity to learn how to improve and it shows off how you handle adversity. Viewers are generally quite forgiving, so don't beat yourself up if things go wrong. This is also the best time to learn how people respond to what you're saying during your live video. Start with your most engaged viewers and ask them simple questions about their experience to better understand what you could be doing better.

When you are going live, it is a best practice to engage with viewers in real time. Viewers of live shows appreciate responses to their questions while you are still broadcasting, as it makes them feel more connected and involved. You can choose to respond to questions as they come or at specific points in your show. However you decide to handle questions, be sure you do not get too far off track from your original message. It is also best practice to go back and review and respond further to comments after you have wrapped up your live stream.

As the video is coming to an end, remember to thank your viewers for tuning in and engaging with your content. If they enjoyed the experience, ask them to spread the word about your live videos! Ending with a clear call to action helps you reach your goals and gets your viewers more involved.

What you need to know after you've been live

When it comes to displaying your video online afterward, make sure to link back to your website so that you can gain more traffic and viewers who missed out on the live experience. (Don't forget to put a link in your live video description as well.) If people who view the replay leave comments and ask questions, be sure to go back and answer them and connect with those viewers you missed in the first go-around.

TIP

Take note of what worked and what didn't during your livestream. Write down anything you need to change in future broadcasts and take some time to check your analytics. Remember that even if something doesn't work out exactly as you planned, it doesn't mean that you shouldn't try it again in the future — but there's also always room for improvement.

Give viewers a reason to come back and watch your video, such as exclusive content or discounts on your products and services (assuming that these are the things they're interested in, of course). Your live videos should be like a TV show: Show new content every time and keep viewers coming back for more.

Don't forget to promote your replay by sharing it widely when you're done. When it comes to promoting your videos, get *creative* and don't just rely on social media and email blasts (although they do work). You have many other channels available to you, such as the ones described in this list:

>> **Your blog:** Create a post about your livestream with a recap of the topics you discussed, plus links to any mentioned resources.

>> **Video snippets:** Take small clips from the replay to share across all your promotional channels. These clips should be engaging, thought-provoking, or enticing to inspire people to watch your whole video. Don't forget to link back to the main replay video.

>> **Social media:** Include links in all your social posts that drive people back to your replay video.

>> **Email marketing campaigns:** Send out a reminder message via email about the replay and give subscribers another opportunity to engage with you and your brand. This is also an excellent time to remind them about the other ways they can connect with you, such as livestreaming, blog posts, or messaging.

>> **Promotional images:** Create images that promote the replay and post them on social media sites where users will see them.

>> **Email signatures:** Put a link to the replay directly into your email signature.

Now that all your promotion is done, it's time to monitor the results and plan for your next live broadcast. Pay attention to which channels are driving people back to your video; this way, you can focus your efforts in the future.

Being a Gracious Host During a Livestream Interview

One of the most potent ways to create engaging live content is to host guest interviews and panels. Having a guest join your livestream takes the pressure off you and allows you to interact with someone else and keep the conversation flowing. It also brings highly valuable content to your audience that you alone wouldn't normally be able to provide.

Live shows that feature guests also tend to be more engaging; audiences are more likely to tune in for a lively discussion between two or more people. As a bonus, your guest can help you promote the content and attract more people to tune in, introducing you both to new audiences.

Set up your guests for success

Before you go live with a guest, you should do a couple of things to ensure a smooth broadcast experience for both of you. First, give your guest(s) a brief overview of what to expect during the interview — what kind of discussion you'll have, how formal or casual it will be, and what, if anything, the guest should prepare in advance. Be sure that they know how long the broadcast will last and any special segments that may be included. If you are using a third-party broadcasting tool, it is helpful to have your guest show up five or ten minutes before starting your livestream so that you can test their connection, camera, and sound.

TIP

Let the guest know if you want them to answer specific questions or touch on any particular topics. Also, let them know if they *cannot* share a topic — sensitive industry information, for example. A prepared guest is a good guest.

You might consider giving guests a couple of pointers in advance to help make the quality of the broadcast better. Many top live broadcasters provide guests with a list of tips for going live — info such as lighting tips and camera angles and reminders to wear headphones to eliminate sound feedback. Also, remind guests that live broadcasting takes a lot of bandwidth, so a strong Internet connection is a must.

Respect your guest's time

Nothing is more critical when hosting a guest on your live show than respecting their time. Most times, your guest is doing this broadcast as a favor to you and is likely taking time away from their busy life to join you live. Be respectful of their time. Do not request that guests show up more than 15 minutes before a live broadcast if the time isn't necessary. If you're planning to have other guest segments or long promotions as part of your live show, schedule your guest to come in only for the time they're needed.

Show up on time yourself. If you tell your guest to be there 10 minutes early, you should be there 15 minutes early. You need to be fully prepared to complete the preshow checklist with your guest and handle anything else that arises before you go live.

One factor that separates a good host from a great host is knowing when to call it quits. Your responsibility is to keep your guest engaged, have them return for future broadcasts, and provide value during their time with you.

REMEMBER

Do not keep your guest longer than necessary. Having a disregard for your guest's time will earn you a bad reputation in the industry, making it harder for you to book guests in the future.

Make the visit worthwhile for your guest

If you want to be a good host and continue to offer your audience interesting and valuable content, you need to help your guest succeed. If your guest is there only for the promotion and not because they care about the conversation, their contribution will lack authenticity, leading to their disengaging from the broadcast. Give the person an interesting topic to talk about that is valuable to their brand *and* to the audience.

It's your responsibility as a host to know what your guest brings to the table so that you can ask about it during the broadcast. The best hosts have done extensive research on their guests, especially if they're reaching out cold (without an introduction).

REMEMBER

Recognize that it's your responsibility as a host to keep things moving and to make your guest's time with you worthwhile. Come prepared with the right questions and interesting conversation starters.

Providing value to your guest is just as important as delivering it to your audience. Here are some reasons that someone may want to be a guest:

>> Promoting themselves or their business

>> Getting in front of a new audience

>> Creating content

>> Furthering their reach

With these reasons in mind, here are some things you can do to make their time worthwhile. Ensure that you've done the necessary promotion in advance to attract live viewers watching the show. Allow your guest to share their expertise and connect with your audience. Share links to their website and social media in the episode description, and make it easy for people to learn more about them. If you want to truly impress a guest, consider creating a blog post recap or a series of short video clips that they can use on their own social media and blog site as a thank-you gift.

And, of course, the easiest way to show your appreciation is to send a thank-you note.

Following the Guidelines for Being a Great Guest

There are considerable benefits to being a guest on other people's live shows. It can not only give you greater reach and exposure to a new audience but also allow you to be a part of video content without having to do much work. But before you agree to be on someone's show, do your due diligence. Make sure that the show's audience aligns with your own. Check out a past episode or two to decide whether the branding and messaging would be beneficial or perhaps detrimental to your own branding.

Once you decide to be a guest on someone's live show, make sure it has value for both you and your host. If you don't see it as a good fit, there's nothing wrong with politely declining the invitation.

TIP

Make the most of your time by getting familiar with the audience and their interests. You want to ensure that you bring unique value to the broadcast and that you leave them wanting more.

It's also good etiquette to help promote the live broadcast ahead of time. This is especially true if your host has provided you with graphics and other marketing materials to make it easy for you to do. Doing so creates a win-win for everyone involved and shows that you're excited to participate in the live broadcast.

REMEMBER

Being a guest is a two-way street. You should be sharing links to your host's social media and website in the description after you appear on their show. If the host has helped make it a bit easier for you, make sure you do your part by promoting them. In addition, if someone has been particularly nice or the show was particularly easy to participate in, a short thank-you note goes a long way.

In the end, being a great guest is all about being both helpful and authentic. Help your host create engaging content that will drive more traffic back to their site and provide value to your own personal brand.

Show up on time

Being a good guest means showing up on time. Nothing is more frustrating for a host or an audience than watching a guest arrive late. Most hosts will give you a couple minutes of grace period after the scheduled time before they start the live broadcast, but if you're more than five minutes late, it can be pretty disrespectful to your host and what they're trying to accomplish with their show.

Being fashionably on time is about being early, so you have enough time to set up your equipment as well as test out lighting and sound levels. If something comes up during the day to unavoidably cause you to be late, give your host a call or send them a text to let them know beforehand. And, if nothing changes on the horizon, just go ahead and show up on time.

TIP

Find out well in advance when your host wants to have you arrive and be sure to block off time on your calendar to accommodate that window.

Be prepared

People don't respond well to an unprepared guest. Nothing throws off your host more than having to stop the show and figure out what you need from them when you should already have at hand everything you need.

REMEMBER

Have all your equipment, lighting, sound, and other resources ready before you arrive on set. Test everything beforehand so that you have no surprises when you go live.

Be professional in your appearance and in your messaging. If you show up in sloppy clothes or use vulgar language, it reflects poorly on you and the host who invited you to be there. The way you present yourself publicly says a lot about what people think of you, so make sure you always look your best when going live. This advice goes back to taking the time to research the show's messaging and audience. This way, you know how to present yourself as well as what will be allowed or what should be avoided.

REMEMBER

Know the topic in advance. It's good to be a person who takes the initiative and prepares for situations that will improve the quality of the livestream. Knowing what you will talk about in advance is a great way to ensure that both parties have a positive experience during the broadcast.

If you know what topics and questions will be asked beforehand, you can prepare your responses ahead of time. This ensures that the broadcast runs as smoothly as possible and that the topics discussed are as current as they can be.

It also shows the host that you take them seriously and respect them enough to put the time into researching before you arrive. This goes a long way in the eyes of your host and can potentially lead to additional opportunities down the road.

Avoid the takeover

Being a good guest means being willing to relinquish control. If your host has asked you to come on and help with the show, this doesn't mean you're the host.

If everyone tries to be the star of the show, there won't be a show at all. Be sure that you don't try to hijack the broadcast to accommodate your own needs. If you have an opinion or a discussion topic, that's great, but let the host lead their show. This is especially important when you're part of a panel of several guests. You want to make sure that you give other guests a turn to talk and avoid talking over anyone.

REMEMBER

Give your host space to do their job. If you try to *be* the show, it just comes off as rude, and everyone will have a less enjoyable time.

This is not to say that you should not speak up if you have value to give. As a guest, you're expected to have a unique point of view and to share your thoughts — just make sure you're not the only person doing the talking. Also, be sure to not take the conversation too far off course. The host will probably have a run of a show or at least a primary goal for the broadcast, so you don't want to go too far down rabbit holes if you can help it. Stay on topic and bring as much value as you can without hijacking the conversation.

Avoiding Embarrassment

Just like in life, things can go wrong or unplanned things can happen in a live broadcast, leading to embarrassing moments. Whether it's your child running into the room while you're livestreaming in front of the world or your roommate walks by in their underwear in the background, you can count on unexpected events happening. When you're live, there are no takebacks. So, it's helpful to prepare yourself and prepare the other people in your office or household before you go live. Let everyone know that you will be live, and be aware that they will be seen and heard if they come into your broadcast space.

Try to choose a location for your live broadcast where it's less likely for things to go awry. Scout out areas where people and pets cannot walk behind you and distract you or your viewers. (If you can be in a room with a door that locks, that's even better.) If you cannot find a quiet place to broadcast live, it may be best to reschedule until you can. Noise and distractions can be cumbersome for you and a turnoff to your audience, if not handled correctly. Some minor distractions are acceptable, but constant noise or interruptions are to be avoided.

If you're livestreaming and something goes wrong, don't dwell on it. Quickly fix whatever needs fixing and move on. Don't cry over spilled milk, because it will only make things more awkward. Most people will be totally fine with your scooping up a wandering child and continuing with your livestream or needing to step away for a second to attend to an issue off camera. Just be transparent and then move on.

These kinds of seemingly embarrassing moments make everyone more human and thus help you build rapport with viewers. They're following you because they want to know you better by seeing what makes you laugh and seeing how you handle challenging situations — and seeing that you're just like them. This makes you more relatable. So be yourself, even if it's not perfect! Take these situations in stride and carry on.

REMEMBER

You should avoid drinking alcohol while live broadcasting. A single beverage is fine, but staying in control of yourself is essential. The last thing you want to do is get tipsy and start oversharing or tossing your inhibitions out the window. There are countless examples of broadcasters who drank too much while live and learned to regret it.

Adhering to the Etiquette of Watching a Livestream

Being a good audience member is an important element of any live broadcast, and broadcasters rely on engaged audiences to keep things fun and interactive. So, if you're going to tune in, try to be a good audience member by following some simple etiquette.

Respect the broadcaster

A lot of work goes into creating a live broadcast that is full of value for audiences like you. You must still be respectful even if you disagree with the broadcaster or the guest on the show. Don't troll the host in the comments or try to dominate the feed with unrelated chatter. Also, refrain from spamming your links in the chat.

The chat is not a place for people to advertise their services or products; it should be a place for conversation and friendly banter.

By design, livestreaming is an interactive experience. So, interact in the comments, answer the host's questions, and give them a thumbs-up or click the Like button if you enjoy what they're sharing. Your participation goes a long way in encouraging a live broadcaster to continue showing up again and again.

If you show up late to the broadcast, avoid asking the host to repeat themselves because you missed what they have already discussed. It isn't fair to the other audience members, and it can downright derail a broadcast if the host feels that they have to go back and revisit earlier material. Instead, after the broadcast ends, go back later and watch the parts you missed.

Respect the other audience members

Live broadcasts can be subject to trolling, spamming, and other disruptive behavior — this isn't okay and should be moderated when it happens. If you see troublemaking in the comments, report it to the host so that they can take care of it when the broadcast is over.

If you see other viewers trolling or being disruptive, avoid feeding into their bad behavior. It can be quite distracting for a live broadcaster to see the heated exchange of audience members in the chat. Being respectful of the other viewers by practicing good chat etiquette is essential.

Good chat etiquette is simple:

>> No name-calling or harassing other viewers.

>> Avoid side conversations that don't pertain to the live broadcast.

>> Do not answer questions in the chat with your own business promotions.

>> Being a good audience remember means respecting the host and respecting the other people engaging in the chat. It's easy to lose control of the chat if everyone tries to hijack it.

REMEMBER

While you may be watching the live videos at home and thinking you don't necessarily need to be engaged, being active in the chat does have its benefits. Sharing your thoughts and actively participating are just some of the benefits of coming together to enjoy a live broadcast by engaging. That is the wonderful thing about watching live videos. It is an engaging experience where you get to not only participate in discussion with other viewers, but you can get real time responses from the presenter.

Benefiting from actively participating

Showing up and watching livestreams can have many benefits. Livestreams are not only entertaining but also quite educational. When you watch livestreams from industry experts, you can learn from top leaders in your field. Such livestreams allow you to gain new insights into your private and professional lives as well as putting you on the cutting edge of what's happening in your industry or in the areas you're interested in.

TIP

Explore new topics and join live broadcasts from creators who you have never seen before. Doing so can expose you to new topics that inspire you to develop new ideas and grow in your specialties.

There's also the added benefit of socializing with other like-minded people from around the world. Engaging with other people in a chat around a common interest can be an excellent opener for networking and making connections. Being active and interactive in the chat during a livestream can be the first step toward building new friendships and relationships.

3

Email Courtesies

IN THIS PART . . .

Familiarize yourself with email best practices

Learn how to stay professional in your email use

Navigate the legal twists and turns of email communication

Chapter **10**

Email Best Practices That Won't Let You Down

E mail is email is email, right? You open up your email app, start a new message, write a note, and then send it off. Easy!

Then, if that's the case, why are we constantly overwhelmed and frustrated by email?

Email has become a key source of communication, both professionally and personally, so how can we make our email as effective as possible? In this chapter, we review the fundamentals of what makes email email. You'll find out how you can be more effective in your email communication as well as how to make those around you thank you for your email — instead of deleting it before opening it.

Emailing for Personal Use versus Emailing for Business Purposes

Email has become a key source of communication personally and professionally, but there are some differences in how you should use it, depending on whom you're communicating with. So, how can you make your email as effective as possible?

Let's start by looking at the difference between emailing for personal use versus for business use.

Personal email comes from someone using their private account to contact their friends, their family members, their dentist, their financial advisor, or anyone else related to their private life rather than their professional life. *Professional email* refers to email in those situations when you use a work address or one associated with a business. In these emails, you're presenting your professional self, not just you as a person. Professional emails can be linked to businesses, non-profit organizations, government entities, associations, and more.

The etiquette for personal email is much different from the etiquette for business email. The main difference between the two is that with personal email, you want to *maintain* a relationship with the person you're communicating with, though with business email you're trying to *build* a relationship with the person you're communicating with. Another difference is that when sending a message via personal email, it's okay to be more informal and use abbreviations, whereas when sending a message by way of business email, you have more things to pay attention to because the stakes are often higher.

When you're emailing someone with whom you have no personal relationship, it's important to take a more professional approach — including using proper grammar and punctuation and being mindful of your tone. you should remember that the recipient may not be familiar with you, so including context about why you're reaching out can be helpful.

One of the most common mistakes people make when using email is mixing up their personal and business email accounts and sending out messages from the wrong one. This is obviously a big mistake because you want to maintain professional relationships with your clients and company partners. Using the proper email account — and proper email etiquette — is important in maintaining those relationships. If this isn't done correctly, it can have negative consequences, such as losing trust from the person on the receiving end of the message or even being blocked by them altogether.

TIP

When communicating via email with people who are outside your company or organization, mixing up personal and business emails is the last thing you want do, because it will definitely damage your professional image. It can reflect poorly on how well you communicate, and it also allows for the chance that confidential information might be sent outside the organization. Using a personal email address that's separate from your professional email address is an easy way to avoid this problem.

Keeping things personal

Personal emails are the type you would send to a friend or a family member or to people with whom you already have an existing relationship. These emails are primarily to people you already know. As a result, they're usually more casual in tone and content and don't have to follow any specific format. You can write them based on your personality and your own style — and however you're most comfortable.

When emailing for personal reasons, you're generally more relaxed in your tone and more comfortable using less formal language. This might include using contractions (*I'm*, for example) or slang words (*awesome* or *bussin'*). The emails themselves tend to be about whatever topics you feel like sharing with your friends and family. You can also be more creative with the formatting, such as adding images or colorful text to your messages.

REMEMBER

Though personal emails are often less formal than business email, there are still a few rules you should follow: Be respectful and professional (of course), keep your message short (no one wants to read an essay in their inbox!), and avoid sensitive or confidential information that might break confidentiality agreements.

Personal emails are a handy way to communicate with friends and family members. It's easy, fast, and convenient. However, it's important that you remain respectful when sending personal messages.

Here are some more guidelines to follow when using personal email:

>> **Write how you speak!** Avoid using formal language — unless your friends and family are formal, be as formal as you feel like being.

>> **Resist the urge to use all CAPITAL letters in your emails:** It's considered shouting.

>> **No one likes a spammer:** That's the honest truth, so don't send the same email to everyone on your contacts list (especially not at the same time).

>> **Respect your friend's information and privacy:** That means you should always use the BCC feature of your email program for their email addresses when emailing a group of people who don't know each other.

>> **Be respectful of people's time and space:** Don't send long emails if they're not interested in reading them.

>> **Try not to email when you're angry.** Wait until you've calmed down before sending your messages so that you don't get emotional and say something unkind or offensive.

>> **Many of your friends and family likely think that spelling mistakes are annoying.** That's reason enough to proofread everything carefully before hitting Send!

>> **Avoid pressing Reply All to emails from friends and family unless everyone on the list needs to know what you have to say and unless what you say is adding value to the conversation.** If you're responding just to respond, reply directly to the sender — no need to fill up everyone else's email boxes.

>> **Keep your personal emails personal and separate from your work emails.** There are several legal reasons for giving this advice, and many company policies explicitly forbid it. But the bottom line is that personal emails shouldn't include any information about work so that they don't get confused with business emails by mistake.

>> **Think twice before you forward emails:** This one applies even if you think it's funny and everyone you know should read it.

TIP

Watch out for spam and phishing emails that can spread malware and gain access to your other accounts. Do not open emails from people you don't know or from accounts you didn't sign up for! Don't click on links that seem suspicious.

Emailing for business

Business email is a more formal way to communicate with coworkers, clients, and other business associates. The etiquette of business email is important because it can often be the first impression you make on someone you're trying to do business with.

Business communication is all about clarity; whether you're trying to build a relationship with a client, launch a new project, or deliver bad news, you need to make sure your message is clear. Miscommunication can lead to all sorts of problems, from missed opportunities to lost revenue.

One mistake people often make when communicating via email is failing to understand the difference between personal and business etiquette. Another mistake people make is using their work account for personal messages, which can lead to mixed up messages and damaged professional relationships. The best way to avoid these mistakes is by having separate accounts for each type of communication, using your personal email address for friends and family members and using your work email address only for official company communications. You should also be aware of how to write formal and informal emails correctly so that you can better tailor your message depending on whom you're sending it to.

A CAUTIONARY TALE

Bryan received an email to his Gmail account from someone he didn't know. Other people were listed on the email, but it was addressed to him.

"Hey, Bryan — what did you think of the auditions? Should we cast Person #1 or Person #2 for the new TV show?"

Because Bryan is a computer programmer and not a casting director, he couldn't resist responding with this vague reply: "Who did you think was better?"

The email exchange went back-and-forth for a while until the other people made a decision and cast Person #2 for the now-failed TV show.

This situation could have been avoided if the real Bryan — the casting director Bryan — had used a business email instead of a generic Gmail account.

This was inspired by a true story. Don't let this happen to your business. Don't let your business decisions be left in the hands of people who aren't involved in your business because your decision makers (or anyone else) are using personal emails instead of business ones.

TIP

Know your company's email policy, and follow it when sending out any form of business communication. If you're unsure what the policy is, ask someone in the human resources department or see whether you can find a section about it on your company's website.

Writing with a Clear Purpose

Email is one of the most common forms of modern business communication, but, unfortunately, it's also one of the easiest to misinterpret. As easy as it is to shoot off an email, you need to be aware of the impact your words can have.

Picking the right communication tool

There are a number of different ways to communicate with someone, and not every communication needs to be an email. Sometimes it's better to communicate in person, over the phone, via text, or even with the help of a messenger app.

In some cases, email is simply better than other types of communication. If you need to ask a quick question or check the status of an order, email is usually helpful for getting a fast response. In other cases, however, you should pick up the phone or schedule a face-to-face meeting instead. This not only protects your reputation and relationships with colleagues and clients but also saves you from the possibility of making a costly mistake.

Choosing a call, text, message, or email

The main thing to remember when deciding which technology to use to communicate your message is what you're trying to achieve; this list describes the four types:

» **Instant messaging** is used for sending messages quickly and clearly.

» **Emailing** has the benefit of being able to send complex messages and attachments, for example.

» **Text messages** are used for communicating specific information that needs to be sent in a short amount of time and in a reliable manner.

» **Calls** are used when you need to have an actual conversation about something or to discuss a sensitive topic.

Email is also useful if you want something that can be tracked and you're not in a time crunch. And, of course, you should always use the communication method that's most appropriate for the situation.

If you're not sure which method to use, try asking the other person how they would prefer to communicate. You can also check with your company. Many companies have policies about how to best have conversations, store files, and track information about projects in a centralized place. Companies have realized that project management apps — whether it's Slack, Asana, or pr Basecamp — are their best bet when it comes storing files and information centrally. Relying on email or messaging apps to have the "latest version" is so 20th century.

These are the most common reasons for sending an email:

» You need to connect with a person located in a different office or time zone.

» The information you want to share isn't time-sensitive. The act of sending an email is instantaneous, but that doesn't mean the person receiving it will see it — or respond right away. Unless its urgent, email is on their schedule, not yours.

» You need to distribute information or files with one or more people.

>> You need a written record of the communication. Saving important emails can be helpful if you need to refer back to what someone said in an earlier message, provide some kind of proof (for example, proof that you have paid for a service or product), or review the content of an important meeting or memo

Knowing why you're sending an email

The importance of knowing why you're sending an email cannot be overstated. Knowing *why* you're sending an email is the most important part of sending one. If you can't think of a reason, don't send it. It's that simple. Emails should be reserved for important matters, not trivial matters that can be easily handled with a phone call or in a messenger app. Before you hit Send, ask yourself whether the email is truly necessary. If it's not, don't send it. You'll save yourself and the recipient a lot of trouble.

REMEMBER

If you have no strong rationale for sending an email, chances are that all the time and effort you spent composing it will be wasted! That's because it stands to reason that, if you can't think of a good reason to email someone, they probably won't think there's a good reason to read it. So, before you hit the Send button, ask yourself: "What am I trying to accomplish with this email?" and "What is the best way to achieve that goal?" If you can answer these questions, your message will be a lot more effective.

Knowing what you want to happen

If you don't expect your email to prompt an action of some kind, why are you sending it? Most of the time we're sending an email to make something happen. Whether your goal is to gather an opinion, educate in order to move a project forward, keep people updated, or make a decision, you want to make sure that the action you want someone to take is clear and easy for them to understand.

TIP

Make your email as easy to read and follow as possible! Include a clear Subject line, bullets, bolded section titles (if necessary), and a clear call to action with a timeframe that you need it by. Another suggestion is to keep your emails limited to one topic or project. It makes them easier to search, find, and get a response when your email is about one specific topic or project versus making one *long* email that remain unopened and unread for weeks.

Context is everything

When you write an email, it's important to remember that you don't know how the recipient will read it or what their mindset will be when they do. (For example, if they just spilled coffee all over their desk, they might not be in the happiest state of mind when they open up your email, so they might read more into it than you intended.) Therefore, you should be careful with the tone, word choice, and context of your email, and make sure to include all relevant information. This helps avoid any confusion or misinterpretation on the part of the recipient. Additionally, taking these extra steps helps save time and frustration in the long run.

REMEMBER

When you add context to your emails, you're proactively improving your communication. You want the reader to have the key information they need in order to understand the content in your email. Adding context doesn't require long, detailed descriptions; instead, you just need to include enough that reminds them or tells them the basic context of what you included in the email.

Tone is important

The tone of your email can greatly impact how readers perceive it. When you send an email, the tone is one way to show your emotional state toward that person or the people receiving it. Many types of tones are available for writing emails and understanding which ones help convey meaning while also maintaining professional relationships can be complicated. Learning how best to use them in communication can make life easier on yourself when dealing with coworkers or clients alike.

How many times have you received an email that made you frustrated because you inferred something less-than-complimentary from the tone of it? The thing is that the sender likely didn't intend it to come across that way. Instead, because of the day you're having, the meeting you just got out of, your feelings about the project . . . whatever the reason, you're reading the email in a certain light, through your frame of reference, though the email was written by the sender in their communication style, through their frame of reference.

They might not realize they're being abrupt, overly descriptive, condescending, or even rude. Instead, they might be working through their task list and quickly replying and sending emails to everyone they need to reach out to.

Instead, pay attention to the tone you're using to compose emails and be aware of how you're feeling when you read them sent from others. You'll quickly see the important role that tone plays in email communication.

Because tone is so important in face-to-face communication, it's even more critical in email communication. You need to be crystal-clear about the emotional tone you're trying to convey in your emails.

Here are a few tips on how to handle tone in your emails:

>> **Use the Subject line to set the tone.** If you start with a question on the Subject line, it can change the tone in your email. For example, a Subject line reading "Email from John Doe" sounds formal and professional whereas a Subject line starting with "Quick question!" has a more casual tone.

>> **Keep your goal in mind when writing each email so that you stay on track.** If you're writing an email to request that a meeting time be changed, don't get sidetracked by other topics while composing your message. Your goal isn't to discuss how you feel about the current schedule but rather to let the person know what time works best for you and why.

>> **Don't make assumptions about how your recipient interprets your message.** Rather than write, "Apparently, last week's event was on Thursday, not Wednesday, so, obviously, I missed it." it's better to say, "I'm sorry I missed the Accounting meeting. I thought it was on Thursday. Was that incorrect?"

It may take more effort to write an email with the right tone than just sending out a message, but it will prevent any damage that can be done by conveying the wrong impression to your recipient.

Use the right words

The words you choose in your emails can mean the difference between clarity and confusion, between action and procrastination (or email deletion). When communicating over email, it's important to use language that's concise and easy to understand. Using too many words can clutter your message and make it difficult to get your point across. On the other hand, using too few words can make your message seem abrupt or unprofessional.

REMEMBER

Email isn't about you as the sender — it's about the recipient. When you're sending your emails, you need to keep in mind the person you're sending it to. Do you know them well, or is it someone you haven't met? What do you know about them? As with any form of communication, you want to try to meet the person where they are. If the person prefers succinct and brief communication that goes straight to the bottom line, then communicate in that style.

The words you choose are just as important as the tone and context — and they all work together.

TIP

Remember who you're emailing. If the person you're emailing is older than you, try to avoid using slang words or text language. You should have perfect grammar no matter who you're writing to, but if the person is older or senior to you in the company, you should consider using more formal language when emailing them to show respect.

The clues are in the context

Tone, word choice, and context all work together to create clear communication and help you achieve the goal or desired action of your email.

When you send an email, it's important to provide context for the reader. Without context, the recipient will likely be confused about the purpose of your email, or why you're sending it, which can lead to frustration and a lack of response. Providing context in your emails makes them easier to understand and more likely to be acted on.

The context in email communication typically includes information about the purpose of the email, the sender's relationship to the recipient, and any background information that's relevant to the topic of the email. Including this information allows the reader to understand why you're sending the email and how it relates to them.

TIP

Help the reader understand why you've sent it to them, why it should be important enough to take up some of their time, and what you want them to do with the information.

Including context in your emails makes them more likely to be read and acted on. Providing this information upfront allows the reader to understand why you're sending them an email, which helps keep misunderstandings at bay. It also shows professionalism and saves time for both parties.

One way to provide context is to include a clear Subject line that succinctly summarizes the email's contents. This helps the reader quickly determine whether they need to read the email now or let it wait. In addition, be sure to introduce yourself and your purpose for emailing in the body of the message. This helps the reader understand where you're coming from and why they should listen to you.

Use the Subject line as the first step. Then include enough information to help the receiver read your email in the way you intend it. Ask yourself what the recipient needs to know about what you're about to tell them as well as how you can keep it straightforward enough so that they don't misinterpret anything about what you're telling them. Remember that the person you're emailing isn't inside your brain, so you don't want them to feel like they have to play Sherlock Holmes to figure out the who, what, why, where, when, and how of your email.

Chapter **11**

Spam, the Law, and You

We provide you with a good introduction to *spam*, the computing term, in Chapter 2. But we don't blame you for seeing the word *spam* in the title of this chapter and checking it out first thing. We agree with you that spam is a vital topic.

If you're in the United States like we are, and you're in business like we are, you need to know about the CAN-SPAM Act and how to comply with it. Then you need to work on employing terms of service and other policies to make sure everyone in your business understands not only what spam is but also what to do when it's "in case of emergency, break glass" time.

When you're in a specific industry, like health, you need to be aware of HIPAA, which you probably have heard about but don't know the details of just yet. And, if you're in another country, we talk about similar antispam and data privacy laws in other countries and regions.

We know that you want to avoid all the bafflegab and get "just the facts, ma'am." (Look up *Dragnet* on YouTube if that phrase doesn't ring a bell.) Let's start with what the CAN-SPAM Act is all about — and it's much more than spam.

Reckoning with CAN-SPAM

The CAN–SPAM Act, enacted in 2003, applies to all email, not just email sent to a large group of people. According to the Federal Trade Commission (FTC), the agency that administers and enforces CAN–SPAM, the law applies to "any electronic mail message the primary purpose of which is the commercial advertisement or promotion of a commercial product or service."

This definition includes all email that promotes content on not only commercial websites but also business–to–business (B2B). For example, when you announce your shiny new widget to businesses in the area, you have to be sure your message follows the law.

WARNING

The FTC isn't kidding: Each email sent by you to each recipient in violation of the CAN–SPAM Act can cost you up to $46,517. If you want to send out 500 messages to people, is it no wonder your eyes are watering? (Go clean up so that you can read about following the law with nice, dry pages.)

With this information in mind, the FTC has seven requirements, which we summarize here and which you can memorize as often as you like:

>> **Use accurate information in the From, To, and Reply-To fields in your email message.** You also need to ensure that the originating domain name and email address (also known as your *routing information*) identifies the person or business that sent the message.

>> **The Subject line must accurately reflect the message content.**

>> **Be clear and up front in your message that the mail is an advertisement.**

>> **Tell recipients your physical postal address.** It can be a street address, post office box, or private mailbox — as long as the address is current and valid.

>> **Let recipients know how to opt out of receiving all future email messages from you.** The message needs to be up front and clearly explain how the recipient can opt out easily. For example, you can include an email address link in the message so that a recipient can click it and then tell you of their wish to opt out.

>> **Process opt-out requests promptly.** The law says you need to process a recipient's opt-out request within 10 business days, and after you send your email, you have to be able to process opt-out requests for at least 30 days.

WARNING

As with many laws, CAN-SPAM has gray areas. What happens if you don't tell people in your email message that you won't be honoring opt-out requests after 30 days, then someone asks to opt out after 35 days and you don't honor it? You may have already figured out our point: Be clear in your email when a lack of a response after a set number of days (no less than 30) means the user has given their approval to opt in. But remember that anyone can also opt out of your communication at any time by contacting you and asking for it, and you should honor that request as quickly as possible.

» **Here's the main rule: If you've hired an outside marketing firm to handle your email marketing efforts, keep a close eye on what that company is doing.** The law says both the company that sends the email and the company whose product or service is promoted in the email may be held legally responsible for breaches of the law.

The FTC website goes into more detail about what you need to know. There you'll find a Frequently Asked Questions section (better known as a FAQ) with examples of what to do and what not to do. Just visit the CAN-SPAM Act: A Compliance Guide for Businesses website at `www.ftc.gov/tips-advice/business-center/guidance/can-spam-act-compliance-guide-business`. (See Figure 11-1.)

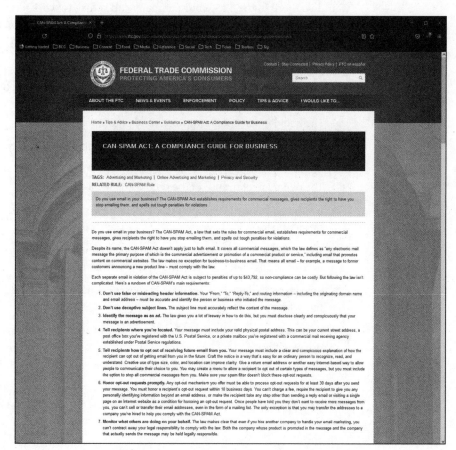

FIGURE 11-1:
Dig into the details about the CAN-SPAM Act on the FTC website.

Looking at Platform-Specific Terms of Service (ToS)

You may have seen the terms of service on a website or on a printed sheet with small text, and we think the chances are quite good that you haven't bothered to read them. If you have a business, though, the terms of service can help protect your business.

The terms of service are usually abbreviated as ToS, but you can also find terms of understanding (TOU) or terms and conditions (T&C) on company websites and product documentation. For companies that provide online services, you've likely seen them on not only company websites but also software and social media.

A terms of service document, which we call by its acronym ToS, for easier reading, protects both companies and customers. If a customer or potential partner doesn't want to adhere to the ToS, your company can refuse to work with the customer or partner. On the flip side, a customer can also take legal action against you if they think they were damaged by your company's breach of those terms.

If you want to create a ToS or (more likely) have a lawyer create one, there are some standard features of a ToS that *must* be in there, including, but not limited to

>> The definition of important words and phrases

>> The customer's (or user's) rights and responsibilities, including the proper or expected use of the service or product

>> The definition of misuse of the product or service

>> Limits regarding the use of personal data, which can be covered in a separate privacy policy

>> A Limitation of Liability clause that limits the company's exposure in case a lawsuit or another claim is made by another party

>> Any payment details such as yearly subscription fees to be paid at a certain time, such as once a year

>> A conduct accountability section, in the case of an online website or social media service

>> An optional dispute resolution clause

>> An optional ability for users to contact a company when the company modifies the ToS

TIP

You can find tools online for drawing up a ToS agreement automatically. Eric uses Termageddon (`https://termageddon.com`), which not only walks you, step by step, through the process of creating terms of service agreements and privacy policies but also updates those policies to reflect changes to national and state laws. These tools are also cheaper than lawyers, but there's nothing stopping you from having a lawyer review the ToS created by one of these tools.

Establishing Business Policies

Because most companies are online with at least one social media profile and a website (or both), we strongly suggest that you add other policies to the mix to help keep your business safe.

That's especially true if you have employees, because a lot of them post not only on social media to communicate on behalf of the company but also on their *personal* social media profiles — and those posts can affect you.

Drawing up an acceptable-use policy

You may have seen an *acceptable-use policy,* also known by its acronym, *AUP,* on some websites. The idea behind an AUP is to inform people about the rules governing how a website or piece of software must be used. Companies use such policies to protect themselves against customers who feel they've been wronged by using the website or software. If you've ever been a new employee (and we suspect you have), you may have been required to sign your employer's acceptable-use policy (or policies) to use the company's network and other IT assets like printers.

If your small or growing company needs to create an AUP for your website and/or your new employees, the good news is that plenty of sample acceptable-use policy templates and examples are available by way of a Google search.

REMEMBER

Even if you create an AUP using a template with clues from sample policies, be sure to invest in a lawyer to look it over and approve it. Chances are good that you're already working with a business attorney to create and/or approve other policies (right?), so be sure to talk with said attorney about the AUP before you begin. Your attorney may create one or recommend good templates.

Creating effective social media policies

When you're building your business, you'll find that social media policies are vital because, even if an employee doesn't use social media personally, they may use it as part of their job to promote the company and/or interact with customers.

2022, we ran a quick Google search of social media users here in the United States and found that every site we visited estimated American use of social media at more than 70 percent. What's more, with more people working from home during the COVID-19 pandemic, it's much easier for people to blur personal and professional social media use.

That's where you and your social media policy come in. You need to create a comprehensive policy that places guardrails on what employees can and can't do on social media wherever and whenever they're working.

TIP

Where do you start? Well, the PostBeyond website just happens to have a blog article with five examples of company social media policies. The article also has guidelines for how to make one. You can view the article at `www.postbeyond.com/blog/5-terrific-examples-of-company-social-media-policies-for-employees`.

To get you started, here are some recommendations we have for creating an effective social media policy for your company:

>> **Assemble a team.** This team should include senior leaders and should also include legal, marketing, IT, and human resources (better known as HR). Work from HR and legal are especially important because you want your social media policy to dovetail with other workplace policies dealing with employee conduct.

>> **Encourage your employees to participate.** Your employees will have valuable insight about not just the guardrails but also their participation to support and promote your company.

WARNING

If you don't involve your employees in creating your social media policy and you try to impose it from the top down, you've created a recipe for legal problems that will waste your time, create a sour work culture, and spur valuable employees to celebrate their departure from the company.

>> **Clearly tell people what they can and can't do.** Your policy needs to explain what kinds of information they can post as well as any regulations they should know. You also need to explain what is offensive and disrespectful, in addition to stressing more obvious things to do, like protecting sensitive company information.

>> **Prepare for problems.** You need to tell your employees what constitutes a problem and when to talk to someone for guidance. (We talk some more about managing public relations crises later in this chapter.)

>> **Train new hires.** Once you have the policy set, you need to put the policy in the employee handbook (and/or on the company intranet) and dedicate time to train new employees about how the policy works.

REMEMBER

Just putting the social media policy in place is not enough. You also need to set up a monitoring system so that you can check your employees' social media posts every so often. (It's not a good idea to do it constantly so that you don't have to field accusations of micromanagement.) You may want to hire a social media manager with monitoring as part of the job description.

Managing Your Public Relations

If your business is serious about leveraging the potential of social media, it likely has a social media team dedicated to that task. Make sure they keep listening to what's going on not just on your social media profiles but also on other profiles and websites (like influential blogs) where your company may be mentioned.

Listening tells you not only whether you're doing well but also, possibly, whether there's a significant negative change in how others perceive you.

People who write bad comments about your company occasionally are a fact of life, but if a lot of people online are saying bad things at the same time, you may have a crisis brewing — or it's already here.

REMEMBER

You may want to put together some criteria for finding out whether there's a lot of positive or negative feedback. For example, if you see enough of the same type of message from a specific number of sites, you can take action.

Any crisis has the potential to do long-term damage to your brand online, and soon enough you'll start to see damage to the business itself. When your social media manager brings you news of a crisis, you need to have a plan.

Devising a crisis plan

As with any plan, you need to create your social media crisis plan in advance of a real problem. You need to respond to any crisis as quickly as possible because, as Charles Dickens said in his book *Life and Adventures of Martin Chuzzlewit*, "[T]here's a true saying that nothing travels so fast as ill news." And Dickens wrote that long before social media.

Any good crisis plan includes some things that seem obvious as well as some that are a bit trickier. Here's what you should consider:

>> **The members of your crisis team:** It should include senior leadership, department managers, the marketing team, the public relations team or

company (if you have one), and the social media team (if there is one). If you have a worldwide organization, you need to have criteria for bringing in leaders of global offices.

>> **The person who will act as backup in case a person on your crisis team is unavailable:** What's more, if someone is unavailable, consider the criteria that warrant your calling that important person during their off time.

>> **Your crisis criteria:** The conditions for deciding whether a crisis really exists and that it's not just a few haters who are trying to damage your company for no justifiable reason.

>> **The communication process for communicating a crisis to the other members of the team:** You should spell out when you need to meet in person and when you can meet virtually.

>> **The method for posting on social media:** This is the approval process for what the company posts on its social media profiles during the crisis.

>> **What the company communicates to the public:** These are the messages you post to the public after you break the emergency glass.

>> **A plan for how exactly you'll tell people about the crisis:** For example, consider whether managers discuss the issues with their individual teams or the messaging comes from senior leadership.

>> **The method for communicating to your employees:** What you'll tell everyone else in the company internally about the crisis, what you're doing to fix it, and what people in the company should and should not do until the crisis passes.

TIP

In all crisis communications, it's a good idea to send a link to the copy of your social media policy that's on your company intranet or on your company's file server. This reminder not only helps employees understand in what way the policy has been violated but also serves as a way for managers and their teams to talk about the policy and have employees' questions answered.

Owning up

You've likely heard of the saying that it's not the crime that gets you into the most trouble — it's the cover-up. (Ask Martha Stewart.) If you at any time look like you're covering up your problem, the bad news will only grow exponentially.

Your best option is not to defend yourself but rather to own up to what's happening. If you don't want to send out an official statement yet, write a quick post telling people you're working on the problem and you will have an official response soon.

REMEMBER

Keep your answers as short as possible. It's *easy* to get into an argument with people, and you'll be amazed at how many of those people have large groups to share the "real story" you gave them.

What happens if people, such as customers and journalists, badger you about getting answers? Then you should ask people to send you private messages (via email, for example) or even to talk on the phone. Keep any private conversations outside of social media — even private messages, like Facebook Messenger — because you'll have less control over who's listening.

Watching your communication

You've probably read about — if not directly experienced — companies not having a plan when you see scheduled posts talking about something completely different and lighthearted during a crisis. (The oft-shared graphic meme comes to mind of a dog sitting at a table inside a burning kitchen and saying, "This is fine.")

So, it should be self-evident that one critical element of your crisis plan is to identify who's responsible for putting all scheduled posts on Pause. If you have just one social media guy in charge rather than a social media marketing team, this may be easier to do, because you can just tell the person responsible to stop.

Debrief

We're all human, and making mistakes is part of the human experience. (Your company's HR policy in general should keep that statement in mind.) As with any mistakes your company makes, you should have one or more debriefing sessions with your social media crisis team after the crisis passes.

You may need to ask yourself several questions:

>> How did this crisis start?

>> How can we prevent this crisis from happening again?

>> Did our crisis plan work well?

>> Where did our crisis plan not work well, and how should we change it?

>> How did our employees react?

>> What can we do to communicate better, both inside and outside the company?

REMEMBER

You may not be able to answer these questions internally, because of political and/ or legal issues within the company. For example, several leaders in your company might lose their jobs if they're found to be derelict of duty during the crisis. In that case, you need to look at hiring a legal service that reviews the situation and provides recommendations for you.

Following Industry Regulations

Depending on the industry you're in, you might have to follow specific industry regulations when it comes to online communication. The three industries most commonly cited are the financial sector, government, and health services.

If you work in the financial industry in the US, you've probably heard of the Financial Industry Regulatory Authority, or FINRA. FINRA provides financial institutions with social media compliance guidelines, but you may also receive guidance from other financial institutions, like the Securities and Exchange Commission (SEC) or the Federal Trade Commission (FTC).

Government bodies have to adhere to laws that manage access to and accessibility of information. For example, government agencies must follow the laws in the Freedom of Information Act (FOIA). European Union countries have to obey laws codified in the General Data Protection Regulation (GDPR).

But the health industry is one that touches everyone, so we focus on health regulations and how you need to respect others' privacy. Here in the US, the best-known law dictating online communication of health information is the Health Insurance Portability and Accountability Act, or HIPAA.

HIPAA and privacy

HIPAA, passed into law by the US government in 1996, created national standards to protect the sensitive health information of patients. HIPAA dictates that organizations cannot disclose patients' information without the patient's knowledge and consent.

The specific section of HIPAA that defines and executes patient privacy rules is, logically enough, the Privacy Rule. The goal of this rule not only explains what the law defines as *covered entities* but also tells those entities how health information should flow so that patients can (hopefully) get the care they need.

As you can probably guess, there's usually a catch, and HIPAA is no different. The law has specific criteria spelling out when an organization can release information in the interests of *national priority*, including

>> Health oversight activities

>> Information about public health activities

>> Information about victims of abuse, neglect, or domestic violence

>> Judicial proceedings

>> Law enforcement activities

>> Stopping or reducing a serious threat to the health and safety of others

>> Identification of deceased people

>> Organ donation

>> Research (under certain conditions)

>> Workers' compensation

Before we talk about how you can find more information about these exemptions, we need to talk about HIPAA and your business because you need to know about some other potential exemptions.

HIPAA and your employees

HIPAA doesn't apply to every business. If your company meets these three criteria, your business isn't what the law refers to as a *covered entity*:

>> You offer a group health plan with fewer than 50 participants.

>> The employer established and maintains the plan.

>> The group health plan is administered solely by the employer.

If you use another company to manage your health plan no matter what size your company, that is what HIPAA describes as a *business associate* and so you and the outside company are covered entities.

You can see more information about HIPAA compliance for businesses and individuals by visiting the HIPAA page (shown in Figure 11-2) on the US government's Health and Human Services (HHS) department website (www.hhs.gov/hipaa/index.html).

FIGURE 11-2:
The HIPAA website page has plenty of useful links, including one to frequently asked questions.

REMEMBER

The HHS Office for Civil Rights enforces HIPAA rules, and all complaints should be reported to that office. HIPAA violations may bring civil monetary judgments against you or even criminal penalties.

More Social Media Regulations to Know

Depending on what part of the world you live in, you've probably heard of laws regulating the use of social media. In Europe, the General Data Protection Regulation (GDPR) governs privacy and behavior on social media. The state of California used the GDPR as a template to create its own state law, the California Consumer Privacy Act. And the CAN-SPAM Act in the United States has also informed other countries' efforts.

We list the prominent laws you should know about and tell you what you need to know without wading into the legal weeds.

California's Consumer Privacy Act

We're talking about the California Consumer Privacy Act (CCPA) not only because we live in California but also because California is the biggest state, in terms of population in the Union. So, if you do business in the state, you need to inform yourself about what California requires.

The intentions of the CCPA are to provide all California residents with these rights:

>> Know the personal data that companies are collecting about them

>> Access any of their personal data that companies may have collected

>> Request that a business delete all consumer information collected from that consumer

>> Know whether their personal data has been sold or disclosed and which businesses have purchased that data

>> Refuse the sale of their personal data

>> Not have a business discriminate against consumers who request privacy under the CCPA

Seeing whether CCPA applies to you

CCPA applies to any for-profit business that collects consumers' personal data — non-profit businesses and government agencies are exempt. If you're a for-profit business, then your business needs to meet at least one of the following three criteria:

>> The company has annual gross revenues of at least $25 million.

>> The company buys, receives, or sells the personal information of at least 50,000 consumers.

>> The company earns more than half its annual revenue from selling consumer information.

Oh, yes, CCPA applies if you live in California; it also applies if you live in a different state or country but you sell to California residents.

REMEMBER

Even if your business doesn't meet CCPA standards, you may still want to adhere to the law's requirements to show people that you care about their privacy. For example, Eric runs his website development business that meets none of the three criteria, but he follows CCPA requirements on his business website. Adhering to the CCPA also shows potential customers that Eric knows about CCPA requirements and can help others implement CCPA in their businesses.

Knowing your responsibilities

The CCPA requires organizations to implement security processes and maintain them regularly, including these:

>> **Add a link labeled Do Not Sell My Personal Information on your business home page.** The link opens a web page so that people can opt out of the sale of their information.

>> **Your organization cannot make another opt-in consent request to a person for 12 months after that person opted out.**

>> **Update your company's privacy policy to reflect the data privacy rights of California citizens.**

>> **Include contact information for people to submit data access requests.** The CCPA requires that you provide, at the very least, a toll-free telephone number to call.

>> **Implement a process to obtain consent if you sell to kids and/or teenagers and want to share their data.** You must secure a parent's or guardian's consent for children under 13 years and secure the consent of teenagers between 13 and 16 years old.

If your brain is badgering you for more, the California Department of Justice website, shown in Figure 11-3, has a page with plenty of frequently asked questions and answers, as well as links to related sites (`https://oag.ca.gov/privacy/ccpa`).

GDPR: Data protection and privacy in Europe

The language in the CCPA was based on the language created by the European Union (EU) in the General Data Protection Regulation, known widely as GDPR. The GDPR is required for all companies that attract visitors to the EU. That includes companies established outside of the EU that offers goods or services (paid or free) and/or monitors the behavior of EU residents.

GDPR in the EU

When it comes to data sharing, the GDPR makes it clear that if you have an urge to share data, you should immediately stifle that urge before it has a chance to grow — that is, unless you can meet one of the following criteria:

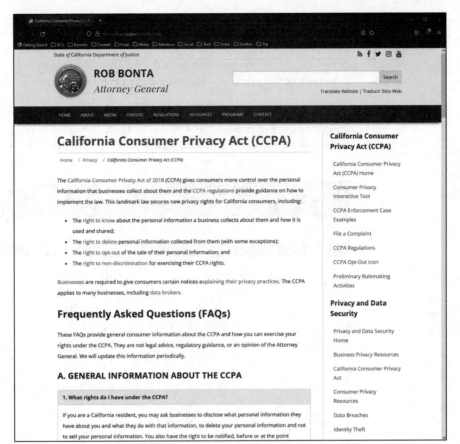

FIGURE 11-3:
The sidebar on the CCPA web page has plenty of links, including how to file a complaint.

>> The person with the data you want to process gave you specific consent, like opting in to your email list.

>> You need the information to do something that's in the public interest, such as perform municipal services.

>> You must comply with a court order.

>> You need to process that data to enter into a contract.

>> The data needs to be shared to save someone's life.

After you read the list and figure out how you qualify, you can't just go ahead and share away. Transparency is the name of the game here, so you need to document the basis for sharing your data and notify the people involved. This can be information included with the signup form for your email newsletter or a private email message if there's a one-on-one agreement.

WARNING

If you receive a complaint, the EU is interested in levying fines that the GDPR website says will be "effective, proportionate, and dissuasive." To drive the point home, the GDPR website also says the maximum fine can be 20 million euros or 4 percent of the previous year's company revenue — whatever is higher.

Article 6 is the section of the GDPR that talks about the criteria for sharing data, and you can read this article, the rest of the GDPR, and find answers to common questions on the GDPR website, shown in Figure 11-4 (`https://gdpr-info.eu`).

FIGURE 11-4:
The GDPR web page also has a list of key issues, such as how to use email marketing in the EU.

GDPR in the UK

Yes, Brexit is a fact of life, but if you already do business in the EU and want to do business in the UK as well, the EU had data privacy on its Brexit to-do list.

The Data Protection Act of 2018 is based on the GDPR, and the Data Protection web page on the UK government website, shown in Figure 11-5, summarizes what's in the act (`www.gov.uk/data-protection`).

FIGURE 11-5:
You can also make a complaint on the Data Protection web page.

Canada's CAN-SPAM laws

After the United States passed the CAN-SPAM Act in 2003, it should come as no surprise that America's northern neighbor Canada created its own law, titled Canada's Anti-Spam Legislation, or CASL. If you're in Canada, here's a quick rundown of what you need to know.

CASL focuses on commercial electronic messages, or CEMs, that are sent to and from Canadian computers or devices within the territory of Canada. The following types of messages fall under the CEM umbrella:

>> Email messages

>> Instant messages

>> SMS text messages

>> Social communications that are a two-way direct messaging system, such as sending a message to someone using Facebook Messenger

As you may have guessed, these messages need to be sent to an electronic address, including email addresses, instant messages, and a phone in the case of SMS communication.

But we haven't answered an important question yet: What kind of messages are under the CASL umbrella? If you've read about spam earlier in this chapter or in Chapter 2, the message is all about commercial activity. The message can ask people to buy something or to promote a company's products or services.

What if your message originates in Canada, is routed only through Canadian servers, and is delivered to a computing device in Canada? Or, what if you communicate by way of fax? (Yes, certain industries — like healthcare — still use faxes). In neither case are you covered under CASL.

You can view the CASL website, at https://crtc.gc.ca/eng/internet/anti.htm.

The website has a lot of information; these six easy-to-remember tips bear repeating:

>> Obtain consent from anyone if you want to send them commercial electronic messages.

>> Keep up-to-date contact lists, such as a database kept by your email marketing software.

>> Process opt-out requests within ten calendar days.

>> Set up an ongoing corporate compliance program to make sure all employees, including senior leaders, are on the same page.

>> Review policies and procedures consistently, especially when the law changes.

>> Maintain accurate records, including who gave you valid consent, training documents for employees, and third-party contracts with separate marketing companies.

WARNING

What happens if you fail to follow the rules? The consequences are, as you would expect from the Great White North, chilling: up to $1 million (Canadian) dollars per violation for individuals and $10 million per violation for companies. As with the CAN–SPAM Act in the US, companies are responsible for messages their subcontracted services send. What's more, individuals at companies have been found personally liable. Need some hot cocoa yet?

4

Virtual Meeting Manners

IN THIS PART . . .

Learn the basics of virtual meetings

Make an appearance at a virtual meeting

Understand the proprieties of webinars and other online events

Chapter **12**

The Basics of Virtual Meetings

t's hard to believe that there was a time when we humans weren't all walking around with laptops and tablets in hand. It seems like the whole world is on the phone these days, so it stands to reason that virtual meetings are the wave of the future. They're a convenient way to meet up with colleagues, clients, or other members of your team. Considering the rise of technology and conference tools, it's easier than ever to snag a seat at the table for a virtual meeting without having to be there in person! All these benefits come with certain challenges, so let's look at the rise of virtual meetings — and at how you can design a meeting for success to get the outcomes you need and avoid virtual meeting burnout.

Charting the Rise of Virtual Meetings

Meeting with people online instead of in person is at an all-time high. Driven by technological advancements (including how cameras are now standard in phones, computers, and laptops), need, and access, virtual meetings have become a popular way to meet up with colleagues, partners, clients, and members of your team. Though videoconferencing was first introduced in 1968, only in the mid-2000s did it became a viable option for businesses. (Individuals had to wait until the rise of smartphones and improvements in cell service and Internet speed for video-conferencing to become practical.)

Even in early 2020, many businesspeople still struggled with the dynamics of turning on and using conference room cameras in rooms filled with people. Teachers and parents struggled with homeschooling via video conference platforms — and let's not forget how much time you might have spent explaining to older relatives how to use videoconferencing to help keep the family connected by way of videoconferencing.

THE LONG ROAD TO VIRTUAL MEETING NIRVANA

The planets didn't necessarily have to align for virtual meetings to become a reality, but a few aspects did have to come together for it all to happen:

- **Technology:** Several technologies were being developed at the same time that began to merge to create videoconferencing and virtual meetings as you know them today, including faster Internet speeds, stronger cell service (5G), one-to-one messaging, group messaging, phone cameras, and webcams. With these advancements came increased ease of use as the technologies started to merge. That's not to say that technology has no challenges, but today they're more limited to the people using the technology. You know — like Mike in Sales who can never remember to unmute himself or Janice in HR who can talk about her dog for hours without pausing to take a breath.

- **Need:** Whether it's the need for businesses to reduce travel to cut costs or a global pandemic that forced everyone to stay inside their homes, there's no denying that the need for virtual meetings has forced the majority of people, young and old alike, to learn how to use virtual meeting technology and attend online meetings. From young students sitting in online classes to older generations wanting to connect with their family members at the same time, the need for virtual meetings played a big part in the rapid adaptation of virtual meetings.

- **Accessibility:** Never before have more people had access to the Internet, computers, phones with cameras, and webcams. Today, more than 80 percent of the global population has smartphones. Virtual meeting tools no longer require applications to download to computers; now they just run directly off the Internet, making them easy enough for nearly everyone to use.

Of course, as with many things, the COVID-19 pandemic changed how many people think of virtual meetings. These meetings — in the blink of an eye — went from a convenience to a requirement. *Everyone* had to quickly get used to being on video calls, after meeting in person was no longer only an option. Teachers had to learn how to teach online; managers, to manage their teams virtually; and employees, to work remotely, which meant that all meetings were online. This sudden shift forced everyone to show up, host, and attend virtual meetings — whether we wanted to or not.

It also meant that you might have found yourself going from maybe one virtual meeting a week to hours of them every day. Like many of us, you probably realized quickly that virtual meetings definitely have their upsides and downsides. They differ from in-person meetings in several ways, and even though you might be tempted to think they're easier to host than an in-person meeting, the nuances and differences are often overlooked. Often, it can seem like all the host needs to do is send out a link for attendees and then everyone hops on at the designated time, but as you'll see, there's more to it than that!

REMEMBER

Virtual meetings require as much planning as in-person meetings do, if not more. There are specific etiquette and norms that should be followed in order to make the most of virtual meetings.

Choosing When to Use Virtual Meetings

In general, virtual meetings work best when people don't have a lot of time to travel or sit in traffic. They need to get down to business rather than take the time to find a meeting time where everyone can get there. Virtual meetings also occur when you need to gather a group of people from different physical locations, especially if travel costs are high, time is short, and the team needs to stay productive while they're together. (The best part of all this is that many virtual meetings often take place over web based services, which means you can join from anywhere — your home, your office, or a local coffee shop.) Of course, it's also possible that a virtual meeting could last longer than an in-person one because no one needs to go home to let the dog out or feed the kids — they have the flexibility to mute themselves for a minute and then come back into the virtual meeting space.

Evaluating the benefits of virtual meetings

Virtual meetings are popular because they can be more cost-effective than traditional face-to-face meetings. Going virtual allows people who don't work near each other to meet, and it increases productivity by allowing employees to work on tasks that relate to the meeting outside of the meeting time. Are you someone who has come to prefer virtual meetings because of the many benefits, which don't even include the popular "business [attire] on top, pajamas on the bottom" look made popular during 2020?

The downsides of virtual meetings often include difficulties with listening and understanding someone remotely who isn't experienced in traditional face-to-face talks.

Virtual meetings definitely have many positive attributes, including these:

» Convenience for people who live in different time zones

» More people who can attend and stay connected and collaborate no matter where they are geographically or what department they're in

» The opportunity to meet people you might not have been able to meet at in-person events

» Reduced business expenses for travel costs

» Employees who have less commuting time and therefore spend less time getting ready (or getting completely dressed in business clothes, in many cases), which makes it easier for them to spend more time productively

Virtual meetings are also helpful in these situations:

» Someone is feeling ill or has a sick child at home and still needs to be connected and kept up-to-date.

» Company growth means that employees are in different offices or working remotely.

» A natural disaster or event causes employees to work remotely.

» Day-to-day occurrences where someone is running late or a car breaks down. Folks caught up I such situations can still call in and be part of the meeting without missing it entirely.

» Individuals who experience difficulties when attending in-person meetings because of disabilities or social anxiety may feel more comfortable in an online setting.

REMEMBER

Virtual meetings provide a way for companies to maintain productivity while still being environmentally conscious. This has been shown to positively affect employee morale as well as company culture overall.

If you take into account virtual events and conferences, there are additional benefits beyond allowing businesses to save on travel costs. For example, it significantly reduces the amount of waste caused by unnecessary products such as paper copies or printed email attachments from traveling back-and-forth between colleagues who don't need them. By going virtual, you're now saving the environment and trees — hooray, you! By going virtual, you're reducing your impact on the environment and on climate change.

And, if you're still not convinced of the benefits of virtual meetings, consider these additional and often unexpected perks:

» **Attendance:** Virtual meetings allow you the flexibility of participating from anywhere with an Internet connection and a computer, smartphone, or tablet.

» **Collaboration:** Online collaboration tools — including shared whiteboards, chat functions, and document sharing — can help you effectively collaborate on projects online.

» **Contribution:** Virtual meetings allow more people to participate in discussions, brainstorms, and decisions. Many attendees find it easier to speak up in virtual, whereas in person they might have remained quiet since you can't "turn your camera off" in person when sitting in front of someone. This also can lead to more conducive contributions and feedback. In addition, the chat function makes it easier for everyone to contribute. Those who may not speak up in the boardroom during an in-person meeting could be more inclined to leave a chat comment in a virtual meeting. Everyone can be heard that way.

» **Efficiencies:** In-person meetings can take time and often have more time spent on small talk than virtual meetings do. Though small talk can give you a chance to get to know each other better, it also can be a meaningless conversation about the weather, for example, which is generally considered a waste of time by all involved. Virtual meetings can be more efficient because they often have fewer distractions, more focus, and less "free" time than found in in-person meetings.

REMEMBER

The benefits of virtual meetings can outweigh any drawbacks, if you know how to keep your audience focused on your goals and specific outcomes. Keep reading, as we'll also be addressing the downside of virtual meetings in an upcoming section.

Determining the true purpose of virtual meetings

Besides the benefits of virtual meetings, sometimes it just makes sense to meet virtually versus in person.

REMEMBER

Virtual meetings can be extremely effective when it comes to solving specific goals.

This list describes a few types of meetings that the virtual environment is perfectly suited for:

>> **Training/teaching:** With the right mix of content and visual and audio cues, online education can be just as effective as the in-person kind.

>> **Decision-making:** Virtual meetings are useful for brainstorming, voting on ideas, or coming to a conclusion together about an issue. All members can contribute even if they're not in the same room and can quickly come to a consensus without the extra time often required by in-person meetings.

>> **Connecting and networking:** Virtual meetings, conferences, and networking have become extremely popular as technology continues to evolve to meet the growing needs of individuals and organizations. For people in sales, business owners, and even people within the same department, meetings scheduled around creating connections — like virtual speed networking events and conferences — allow for businesses and individuals to meet new people, including potential partners and clients.

>> **Crisis management:** If disaster strikes your business, virtual meetings allow you to best use your resources during a time of crisis.

>> **Events:** More and more events are available online, which saves travel costs, travel time, time spent packing, money spent on that conference-chicken lunch you always dread, and more. Online events are often more cost-effective and accessible to a wider audience.

Designing More Productive Virtual Meetings

Before we jump straight into the steps you need to take in order to create the most productive virtual meeting — one that will have your colleagues, partners, clients, and even students vying to attend — it's important to step back and start from the beginning.

TIP

Ask yourself, "Does it need to be a meeting?" Because the last thing you want is to hold a meeting with 15 people, only to hear someone say, as you're wrapping up, "It could have been an email." This is one of the most popular sayings (and memes) about most workplace meetings, and likely you've thought it yourself a time or two. So, before we dive into how to design more productive virtual meetings, it's important to step back and ask yourself whether you need to have a meeting in the first place.

It's a common misconception that meetings are necessary. Though there are many benefits to face-to-face communication, they can be difficult for some people or in certain contexts. A meeting might not be the best option if you need to communicate sensitive information, have busy team members, or are just trying to keep your team up-to-date.

You should answer a few key questions when deciding whether you need to have a virtual meeting:

>> **Is a specific decision or outcome needed?** Having a specific decision or outcome is the key for meeting success. Two uses for meetings are when they're used to get everyone up to speed quickly so that everyone is on the same page and when you're collaborating and discussing a pending decision. Often, repeated meetings such as status updates have vague outcomes, which can cause attendees to become frustrated and disengaged.

>> **Does this decision require real-time input and consideration from others?** If the decision or outcome requires no real-time input or consideration, it could be an email or chat message — which allows everyone to chime in on their own schedule. Real-time discussions can help you reach decisions faster and reduce the back-and-forth that can fill email inboxes with confusion and overlapping messages.

>> **Is the decision time-sensitive?** Similar to the need for real-time input, if the decision is time-sensitive and requires no more than a few people, sometimes a quick call with those who are impacted can help drive to the conclusion you need. But if a meeting isn't time-sensitive, it can be scheduled to help drive to the consensus, assuming that the schedule and due dates allow for it.

>> **Does everyone involved have the information they need in order to contribute?** If a decision needs to be made, or brainstorming needs to happen, ensure that all attendees have the information they need ahead of time. If the goal of the meeting is to share the information, it can potentially be an email rather than a meeting.

>> **Are the people involved located in one place, or are they spread out across the city or country or world?** If spread out, virtual meetings are definitely easier to schedule and more cost-effective than in-person meetings. They also help ensure that the right people can attend versus people being left out because they're not located where the meeting is being held.

>> **How many people are directly involved with the decision?** A Harvard Research Study in 2018 found that the most productive meetings have between five and eight people, and other research suggests that having more than seven people in meetings can limit the effectiveness of the meeting. The key is to not invite everyone, but instead to limit the number of attendees to only those who are involved and have the authority to make sure you reach a clear decision.

>> **Is the meeting worth the amount it will cost the business for all required people to attend, calculated as [meeting length × number of attendees]?** In other words, if you're going to schedule a half-day working session or an hour meeting, is it worth the cost of time for all your attendees to be there instead of doing other work?

If, at the end of all these questions, you find that a virtual meeting is a key to moving forward, let's get started!

Choosing the right format for your virtual meeting

The right format and technology for a virtual meeting depend on a number of factors. The meeting needs to be comfortable for the participants and easy to follow, and it should avoid any distractions so that people can focus on what's being said. It also goes back to the question of whether it needs to be a video meeting or can be a phone call.

The technology you choose depends on the purpose and format of the meeting and the number of attendees. Here are few questions to consider:

>> **How many people need to attend and participate?** Some virtual meeting tools work well with a small group but cannot accommodate 10, 25, or more than 100 people. For example, if you're talking to only one or two other people and don't need to share your screen, it might make sense to use a quick video-chat tool like Facetime or Facebook Messenger video. If, however, you have more than 10 people or you're presenting to your entire department or company, you need to consider tools that allow for more people and collaboration (Zoom, Microsoft Teams, Google Meet, and Webex, for example).

>> **What is the purpose of the meeting?** Is it to share information with just a few colleagues, or will it serve as a framework for a larger discussion where everyone needs to not only be heard but also be able to share their screens?

>> **How will people join the meeting?** Will they all be on laptops from a location with fast Internet access, or will some be traveling and be on their phones or tablets? The devices people use to attend and the Internet speed at the

location where they join are two important factors to consider when deciding on the technology to use.

>> **How familiar with technology are the attendees?** Many funny videos and skits circulate around the Internet after people try to use videoconferencing technology, but the reality is that you don't want to select a tool that's too complicated for your attendees. If your audience is less tech-savvy, you should use a platform that's easier for them to use.

REMEMBER

The purpose of the meeting and the number of attendees are the two biggest factors when deciding what type of meeting format you should use. If your decision or outcome is time-sensitive and you need to discuss it with only one or two other people, picking up the phone for a quick conversation can often be the most efficient way to communicate. And, you have the added benefit of not needing to add yet another meeting to their calendar!

Taking advantage of technology

Choosing which technology you should use can be tricky if you're unsure what works best for your needs. Don't worry! You can avoid many of the problems that cause so many virtual meetings to go off track when technology or participants' use of it fails. Though you can't control how your meeting attendees use the camera or Mute button, in this section we give you some common-sense guidelines to remember when selecting a technology to use.

The most common technology options are described in this list:

>> **Conference call (audio only):** A conference call takes place when two or more people are on a telephone call. It often requires a teleconference number that attendees can use to connect from a landline, mobile phone, or a web app to be on the call at the same time. It's used for quick discussions, putting everyone on the same page, and discussions or collaborations that don't require visuals.

>> **Video call (video and audio only):** Often used for smaller groups, video calls can be Facetime, Facebook Messenger, or Google Hangouts. These are often short, more casual conversations intended for quick questions and conversations where you want to speak face-to-face.

>> **Videoconference (video, audio, and screen sharing capabilities):** This option has been the most popular one for businesses — particularly since 2020. Tools such as Zoom have risen to the forefront when it comes to videoconferencing. The host and attendees can dial in using a telephone number or they can log on through various devices, show up on video, share their screens, chat off to the side, share links, and more.

>> **Web conferencing (for events, webinars, and larger presentations):** When you have a big presentation, like a keynote presentation, shareholder meetings, and so on and you don't want attendees on video or when you want to keep the meeting focused on the materials being shared and the speakers, larger web conference services are available.

No matter what technology you decide to use, whether it's a simple conference call, a videoconference platform that has an element of the ongoing collaboration and chats, or a link you send out that people can click to join from whatever device they're using at the time, it's important to send clear instructions to your attendees.

TIP

If you're the meeting host, be sure to have a backup plan in mind just in case something goes wrong. We've all been in meetings when someone has a pressing issue or the Internet goes down. Whether your backup plan is to send out an email or a message with a phone number to call into or you want people to rejoin your meeting or the meeting needs to be rescheduled, be sure that the plan gets communicated to everyone involved. Just keep a contingency in mind when you kick off the meeting — your attendees will appreciate it!

Looking at the Downside of Virtual Meetings

The reality is that virtual meetings aren't perfect. If the host isn't prepared, or if you're pulled into too many virtual meetings, it can put a strain on your day and negatively impact how you're feeling. It's also more difficult to keep real-time tabs on how everyone is feeling about a subject because you don't have many of the visual clues you would have if you were in-person, which can make it more challenging to manage the flow of the meeting.

Not only that, but many managers also feel like virtual meetings aren't as effective at building camaraderie among team members, whereas some employees struggle with feeling as though their managers don't see them contributing, which can have a negative impact on their next promotion. Others feel like it's harder to establish rapport over the Internet, and virtual meetings can even contribute to feelings of isolation or detachment in some employees.

REMEMBER

Virtual meetings aren't always better than face-to-face meetings — they can lead to disengagement, reduced productivity, and even more conflict when you're trying to manage an argument across screens and speakers. To avoid this, you want to make sure you're properly prepared — whether you're an attendee or the host.

RECOGNIZING SOME COMMON BARRIERS TO PARTICIPATING IN A VIRTUAL MEETING

Some people have real trouble adapting to a virtual meeting environment. Here are some reasons:

- **Not everyone is as tech-savvy as the next person.** For those people who aren't as tech-savvy, it can be a challenge to log in to a virtual meeting and find their way around. They may find buttons they don't know how to use or technology that allows them to participate but isn't intuitive to them.

  If you know there might be people attending the meeting who might have challenges with technology, it can be helpful to let them know that there is a team member on the call who will act as Tech Support for the event. If attendees have any issues, they can message that person and they will help them out. Hosts might also do a quick rundown of the functions available on the platform (using the Raise feature to enter the queue to ask a question or using the Chat function, for example).

- **Some people are shy or hesitant to speak up.** The reason isn't that they have nothing to add to the conversation, but rather because they don't want to talk over others or interrupt. They may also feel that their input isn't wanted and so they stay silent. Though this is also true about many people at in-person meetings, it can go overlooked more easily in virtual meetings. One way to work around this is to encourage participants to use the chat function; they can even send a private message as opposed to a group-wide message if they prefer.

- **There's no face-to-face aspect of a virtual meeting.** When we humans look someone in the eye, we can get a sense of who they are and how they're feeling. If you can't see someone's face or if their personality type isn't easily transmitted via video, it may be difficult to connect with them and trust what they say.

Avoiding Virtual Meeting Burnout

The term *virtual meeting burnout* has been coined to describe the feeling of fatigue that comes from staring at a screen too long. *Virtual meeting fatigue* occurs when you're in front of your computer or tablet for an extended period and it can be damaging, both physically and mentally.

Virtual meeting burnout can be traced back to a few key causes:

>> People aren't used to staring at themselves on computer screens for long. In fact, doing so can even often result in "Zoom Dysmorphia," where individuals obsessively focus on what they perceive to be flaws in their physical appearance. (With digital screens, people often have a distorted idea of what their face and body looks like.)

>> In-person meetings allow people a chance to look around the room, whereas in video meetings, you need to look directly at the screen and maintain ongoing eye contact, if only to show Mikayla in Accounting that you're paying attention to every word she says.

>> Research shows that the majority of communication is nonverbal, so on video calls, you lack many of those cues.

>> In a natural flow of conversation and communication, there's a rhythm that often includes a few seconds of silence. Online, silence can start to cause anxiety around technology working, if people are frozen, on Mute, or more.

REMEMBER

Luckily, you can do a few things to avoid virtual meeting burnout. Keep in mind that some people prefer virtual meetings because there's a perceived convenience, reduced social anxiety and pressure that can arise in-person, and the reduction of natural biases that can be caused by physical appearance (height, for example). The trick is making sure you avoid virtual meeting burnout. Here's what we suggest:

>> Take short breaks from your screen throughout the day.

>> Use the meeting controls to hide your face from view during the meeting. This helps you avoid looking at (and overanalyzing) your own face throughout the meeting.

>> Vary your communication and use the phone, email, or Messenger apps to give your eyes and brain a rest.

>> Include stretch breaks in long meetings.

>> Use ice breakers, quizzes, polls, or some other interactive element that helps refresh people's brains so they can continue the meeting with fresh eyes and a clear mind.

Chapter **13**

Leading a Virtual Meeting

Running successful virtual meetings may sound like a simple task, but there's one thing that most people who have done it agree on: It takes a surprising amount of planning and preparation to lead a productive virtual meeting. A common misconception is that conducting a meeting virtually is as simple as sitting around a table with your colleagues and talking to each other over an Internet connection. But the truth is, whether you're hosting or joining a virtual meeting, there are specific guidelines to follow to make the whole thing go smoothly. Let's break down how to host a successful virtual meeting!

Doing the Prep Work

Let's face it: You don't want to be stuck in an online meeting where the host showed up late, wasn't prepared, and couldn't get their video to work, and then the only person not on Mute was John from Accounting, who rambled on and on about the new expense process until the meeting ran over by 15 minutes, throwing off the rest of your day. Seriously, if you can start by doing the opposite of what that meeting host did, you'll be in great shape!

The reality is that preparation is essential for every meeting. It's even more critical for virtual meetings because so many variables can affect how well a meeting operates. Preparation can mean the difference between a happy, productive team or decisions that never get made and projects that die a slow, painful death.

TIP

One secret to leading a productive online meeting is to design it so that you'd be excited to attend it. You don't have to have the latest K-pop band playing in your home office, but you do want to make sure the time is spent in a meaningful way that leaves your attendees pleasantly surprised. If you can get Maria from IT to put down her phone and turn on her camera, you're basically winning at life and can take the rest of the week off.

Running successful virtual meetings can result in many positive and energizing outcomes, including these:

>> Team and/or client alignment

>> Streamlined project management

>> Increased agility and responsiveness

>> Resiliency under pressure

>> Improved decision-making

>> Increased innovation

>> And more

All these are essential outcomes for busy teams! To get all those fantastic benefits, you need to start with the upfront preparation to ensure that your meetings are a success!

Answering the why, where, and when of leading virtual meetings

When designing the optimal virtual meeting, you can start with the basics: the why, where, when, and how of it. By answering the following simple questions right from the start, you're beginning to create a framework for your meeting to be successful:

>> **Why are you hosting a virtual meeting?** It might seem obvious, but many attendees of virtual meetings won't hesitate to tell you that your meeting could have been converted to an email. So, rather than face the meme-wrath of unhappy people who feel disrespected because you didn't value their time,

start by asking yourself, "Why am I holding this meeting?" or, better, "What is the purpose of this meeting, and what benefit do I want to get from it?"

TIP

Only by defining the key outcomes of your meeting can you ensure that it helps move forward a decision, project, or innovation. To do this, you want to start with the end in mind. Determine what outcomes you want to achieve from the meeting, and then design it for those outcomes.

You can design the meeting specifically for those outcomes by starting with your reason for holding it. For example, if you're scheduling a meeting to onboard a substantial new client, the meeting would look different from a virtual happy hour for your department. And, if you were looking to launch a new project that required weekly project meetings, you would create goals for each meeting that would help accelerate your project and keep the team aligned.

REMEMBER

Being able to define your reasons for the meeting, and what it will do to increase productivity or accelerate decision-making, also helps you improve the focus and engagement of your attendees.

>> **Which platform should you use to host your virtual meeting?** Now that you have defined the intended outcome of your meeting, you should determine where the meeting will take place. Check out the options we discuss in Chapter 12; that should help you decide which virtual meeting platform is right for your meeting.

Something to consider is that if you regularly host video calls, chat sessions, or webinars, it might be helpful to have a tool that your guests can easily access. Specific virtual meeting platforms include Zoom, GoTo Meeting, BlueJeans, Skype, and Webex Meetings, but don't hesitate to go with something similarly suitable for your meeting, like Google Hangouts or Microsoft Teams, if those are more your style.

REMEMBER

You also should consider how technologically savvy you and your attendees are when it comes to encouraging people to attend and actively participate.

>> **What's the best strategy for determining when to hold meetings?** The next important component of leading a successful virtual meeting is when to host the meeting. Two times of day work best for most people: midmorning or early afternoon. These times work well because they're times of the day when people can focus on work without being distracted by other events going on during their day.

Considerations for time zones are essential when you have remote team members or clients who live on opposite ends of the globe. You don't want to be the person who makes people join video calls at 5 A.M. or at 11 P.M.

When time zones come into play, scrutinize where your guests are located. If they're in multiple time zones, you have to pick an appropriate time for everyone to meet within their defined work hours.

TIP

Make use of online calendars — that's a helpful way to find a time where everyone is available to join your meeting. And, if you can't access everyone's calendars, you can still use an online meeting-scheduling tool (Doodle or Calendly, for example) or create a poll. Just add a list of possible times and give people the opportunity to select which options work best for them. Then you choose the time and date that work best for all involved.

Knowing who needs to be there

If you've figured out why you're holding meetings, the result that you want to come out of each one, when you're going to hold them, and on what digital technology, it's time to step back and dial in who should actually attend your virtual meeting. That list depends on what's on the agenda for the meeting.

Begin by identifying the key stakeholders are and which (or all) of them need to be involved in the conversation/discussion. It's not necessary to bring everyone onboard if it creates a distraction for those who do attend rather than boosts productivity.

To keep it simple, you should include only those key decision-makers along with any individuals directly involved in the discussions/project. If you're tempted to include more people, go back and review the purpose of the meeting to help you ensure that only essential people are invited. For example, if people who are in the meeting can relay the information back to their team, not all team members need to attend.

Let's say you're leading a project status update meeting. In this scenario, you'd want to invite either the team leads or the people directly involved in this specific project. But if you're discussing with your colleagues how to handle a difficult client, you might want to invite people outside your team who have insight about this client or have dealt with similar situations.

TIP

If you're unsure who needs to attend, you can begin by making a list and then identify those individuals whose ideas or opinions are critical either to the goals of the meeting itself or to the larger project. Going down the list, you can then determine who would be nice to include but isn't essential, as well as who needs to know the results from the meeting but isn't involved in the decision-making. Then narrow the list to the Required and Optional attendees. This strategy helps keep your attendee list short and your meeting more on track.

Though attendees depend on the project and purpose of the meeting, here are a few roles that are often required, depending on your meeting:

- » Key decision-makers (hands-on and in leadership roles)

- » Internal stakeholders

- » Project team members

- » Others involved in the project, such as subject matter experts

- » External partners

- » Clients or customers

Finally, people who aren't familiar with, or experienced in, virtual meetings may find it helpful for someone to act as their *proxy* (a designated user who participates on their behalf). This doesn't often happen, because the technology has become much more user-friendly and accessible, but it's still something to anticipate if you're not working with a tech-savvy audience or customer base.

Defining meeting expectations so that attendees know what to expect

No one wants to show up at a meeting and not know why they're there or what to expect. Have you been to those meetings? On a scale of 1 to 10, how frustrated did that make you? How excited were you to respond "Yes!" to the next meeting that person invited you to? Having learned from those mistakes, here's how to ensure that your meeting is meaningful and productive and makes the most of every person's time.

Setting clear expectations helps you achieve the outcomes you need from the meeting and ensures that everyone is on the same page. Attendees need to understand why your meeting is valuable and what outcomes they can expect. You've done the preparation, so now it's time to communicate that information to your attendees. That means preparing an agenda and helping participants understand your expectations to ensure that everyone walks away from the virtual meeting with valuable action items and the confidence that you're leading the way.

Many organizations have set expectations or meeting norms that they expect employees to adhere to. These general expectations can be as common-sense-oriented as "Be on time" or more specific: "Mute yourself when you're not speaking." Though most people have become accustomed to people working from home and interruptions from kids, dogs, and even significant others, there are still norms or best practices that you want to ensure your attendees know. On the flip side, there are expectations on you as the meeting facilitator or leader that you need to pay attention to and apply, including these:

>> **Knowing how to use the meeting technology.** Though you can't help it if your computer crashes or your Internet goes down, you do have control over whether the technology works on your computer and whether you know how to use it.

>> **Send out any necessary "homework" so that attendees can review it before the meeting.** If attendees need to know about any information or updates for the conference, help them prepare. If necessary, create a summary document with a brief blurb about each topic so that everyone can review it before jumping into the meeting. You probably want to send out reminders before the meeting starts so that they know to come prepared for the discussion. When people understand what will happen during the conversation, it helps them stay focused and avoid any unnecessary questions or statements made during the meeting. It also saves meeting time when no wrap-up is required.

>> **Schedule your meetings for 25 or 50 minutes.** Often, people are running from one meeting to the next with no time between them for water or bathroom breaks or to stretch and look up from their computers. By scheduling your meetings for less than 30 or 60 minutes, you're giving people the time they need to transition between meetings and projects. Those five or 10 minutes are essential and help ensure that they won't be late for their next meeting.

>> **Start on time.** The best way to create a good impression is to be prepared and a little early. Nothing kills momentum like a 15-minute delay because people need to download software, coax the video or audio to work, or handle other technical hiccups. Meeting presenters should log in five minutes early, to ensure that all the technology is working smoothly.

>> **End on time (or even early!).** It can become extremely stressful for attendees who have meetings back-to-back and the first one doesn't end on time. Don't be the one responsible for that extra level of stress. Keep your meeting to the allotted time, or, even better, end it a little early! No one ever complained because they got "X minutes back in their day."

>> **Discuss project norms and expectations with attendees.** If you have an ongoing project or team meeting, you might want to consider periodically discussing meeting norms with your attendees. They might have ideas on how to improve on what you're doing, to further optimize the results that come out of each meeting. For example, perhaps they think it will be more effective if the input is limited to 90 seconds, or if meetings are longer than an hour, they should include a 5-minute break for stretching. You may be surprised at the ideas that can help your meeting format evolve and productivity take off!

>> **Know your technology capabilities.** With the increased use of video, it can be tricky to always be on video. And the reality is that not every call needs to be a video call. But some meetings will simply be better if the video is involved. And for that reason, you want to make sure that your Internet connection is strong enough to handle videoconferencing when you're leading and hosting meetings.

TIP

Set up your technology before the day of discussion so that you have no problems during the meeting. You should take some time to test how your device works to see whether any issues may come up during the call. Luckily, many virtual meeting platforms have a built-in setup tester for microphone audio and playback. Sometimes, plugging in an external speaker helps you hear how well your voice transmits through the speakers. If possible, have a backup device on hand, in case something goes wrong with the first one. You can also assign someone in the meeting as your backup so that, in case your technology does fail or the Internet does go down in your area, that person can take over and keep things moving forward.

Creating an agenda that works

Your first meeting with someone is your opportunity to make a great first impression, and if you're meeting with people you already know, they'll expect you to be prepared and guide them through the meeting experience. Your agenda is a vital component of having a successful meeting — one that keeps everyone on track and focused on the goals! Creating an agenda and sharing it ahead of time requires you to consider what questions you might want to ask that will take you to the outcomes you want from the meeting.

TIP

When creating your meeting agenda, consider what style will work best with your virtual teams and what you want to accomplish. Remember that you should plan for more concise topics with less detail on each subject due to everyone's busy schedules and demands for their time.

These are a few key points your agenda should include:

>> **Meeting date, time, access information, and topic:** Include the meeting details on your agenda so that people don't have to check their calendars or scroll through millions of emails to find the one from you specifying where they're supposed to be, and when, and how they plan to join the meeting.

>> **Meeting attendees:** You will want include a list of attendees on the agenda so that others know whom to expect. Consider including their names, titles, and departments (if they're part of your company) and include their company if they're outside your organization.

>> **Purpose of the meeting:** Clearly state why everyone is meeting and what outcomes you need from the meeting. This helps keep people focused on the topic at hand and not on what they did over the weekend.

>> **Outline of meeting:** If the meeting has specific topics you need to cover, decisions to be made, or project statuses that need to be updated, list them out. Include the person who is responsible for each item if someone is assigned to it. If you have a longer meeting, it's helpful to set times for each topic to help to keep things moving along.

>> **Build-in breaks:** If your meeting is over an hour long, build in a short break so that people can stand up, stretch, and come right back to the topic at hand. They'll likely thank you for the 5 minutes to move around.

>> **Action items and next steps:** Leave time at the end of the meeting to cover action items and any next steps, to ensure that the meeting outcomes have a more significant impact than the 25-minute-long meeting itself.

TIP

One thing to consider is building your outline using questions rather than topics. For example, "What is required to launch our new product?" is more thought-provoking than simply saying, "Discuss new product launch." Depending on your goals, it can be a more productive way to approach your agenda. Sometimes, this strategy can help you narrow the attendees list after you see the questions you need answered.

If you need to include background information to ensure that everyone is coming into the meeting with the same information, reference it on the agenda, and include it when you send out the meeting invitation and agenda. It's essential that everyone has access to the same information during the meeting, to compare ideas and share their point of view. This also prevents repeating suggestions multiple times, which wastes time and effort.

TIP

Before the day of the virtual meeting, make sure you have an agenda ready for all those participating in the conversation so that everyone knows what they're expected to do.

Conducting the Meeting

How you lead virtual meetings can set the tone for the team, project, ideas, decisions, and more. If you lead a meeting that no one wants to attend, your outcomes will be subpar at best. Virtual meetings can also be energizing and motivating and help teams make giant leaps on projects. We assume that you've defined what you want to come out of the meeting, where online you're going to hold the meeting, and who is attending. We also assume that you've shared the meeting outline and that you've practiced with the technology. You're ready to conduct the meeting!

REMEMBER

Never lead a meeting you wouldn't want to sit through.

As the leader, you're conducting the different aspects of the meeting. Often, you might find yourself facilitating the discussion, taking notes, watching the chat to see what questions or comments come up, and keeping tabs on who has been talking and who hasn't so that you can gather everyone's input. It can be a lot. Some people find that it helps to ask one attendee to help with notes or to watch the chat and bring up questions and comments. Depending on the size of the meeting, you might want to consider who can help you with these crucial details.

By showing up a few minutes early, you're setting yourself up for success. So, log on, and be there to greet attendees by name as they enter the meeting. You're setting the stage for connections, collaboration, and results.

Creating connections

In meetings, not all attendees know each other. They might be from the same team or from around the globe, so creating connections — particularly in virtual meetings — is the key! It can help people know why others are in attendance and help ensure that they're all working together toward the same goals.

Have you ever been in a virtual meeting where you could feel the disconnect between people? Even though everyone is present and accounted for, a lack of connection can stop people from speaking up or sharing their ideas. It can lead to frustration and less effective meetings overall. That's why it's important to create connections before, during, and after virtual meetings to ensure that everyone is on the same page and moving toward their larger goals as a team.

How do you create a connection with others in a virtual meeting while still staying focused on the tasks at hand? It sounds like an impossible question to answer. But it's not.

Often, it can be as easy as starting with introductions and starting the conversation by asking whether everyone knows each other. If not, ask them to tell others briefly what they do. If appropriate, you can also ask people to share one personal note about themselves, like a favorite morning beverage or whether they have any pets. These kinds of questions can help people feel more comfortable and engaged. It also helps to find common ground between attendees — for example, if Mike from HR has a dog he loves to take for long runs and so does Jennifer in Research and Development, it's a small bond, but it's a commonality they share. It really doesn't take much time, and whether or not everyone already knows each other or they're relative strangers working from different locations, there is power in creating connections and bonds over projects. It isn't just meaningless small talk.

These human connections create a more intimate environment during the meeting and allow you to build trust with your colleagues. Here are several additional ways to make connections in virtual meetings:

>> Keeping the video turned on throughout the entire meeting.

>> Maintaining eye contact with the camera as much as possible. If you move the window with attendees' faces on it as close to the camera as possible, you can maintain better eye contact with attendees. Have you ever been in a meeting where the person talking had two computer monitors and spent the entire time speaking to the screen with the attendees on it, instead of where their camera is? It's distracting! Instead, position the window where you can see the attendees faces near the top of your laptop or near your own camera, in order to maintain eye contact.

>> Call on people by name and ask specific questions to encourage participation.

>> Ask attendees a specific question when you're getting started. Rather than ask, "How is everyone doing today?" try something like this: "Did you go outside yet today?" or "What was something from yesterday that you're most proud of?"

>> Encourage and enable chat for questions, feedback, and ideas.

>> Take the lead and maintain an active presence throughout the meeting.

>> Turn off your notifications and phone so that you're actively listening and involved.

>> Make jokes when appropriate.

>> Remember people's names and their reason for attending the meeting/role in the project or decision-making.

>> Ask attendees about what is happening in their lives outside of work.

>> Share funny photos or videos when appropriate but keep them brief. Nothing is worse than being forced to sit through a 20-minute video that only the meeting leader found interesting or funny.

>> If this meeting is a regular meeting with the same team, ask each person to share something short each time. It can be as simple as sharing something meaningful you keep on your desk, showing a picture of the best place you've vacationed, or telling everyone about your favorite hobby outside of work.

It might sound like it's not much, but when people are working remotely and joining in meetings, they want to find that common ground and know that they can trust each other. Finding ways to develop connections can lead to even more significant results over time!

Moderating the meeting

From the moment attendees enter the virtual meeting space, their time is yours. They are yours to impress, lead, and facilitate through the meeting process that leads to your stated outcomes and goals. It's important to remember that you're in charge of their time, so be mindful of how every minute in the meeting is spent, and make each one count!

You definitely want to ensure that the meeting starts well! As a leader, your mood matters — it sets the tone for others to react accordingly and be inspired by what they see happening before them. It's an essential factor in any successful virtual meeting because people will tend to mirror or match the leader's mood.

If you're stressed, anxious, or frustrated, your meeting attendees will likely pick up on those feelings and display them as well. And when you're in a virtual environment, these feelings can amplify even more. You might end up meeting attendees inside chats, ranting about their irritations rather than being invested and actively participating in the meeting. Instead, focus on the positive, the desired outcomes, and the fact that everyone was available to join the discussion to move the project along, brainstorm, or come to critical decisions. A positive outlook and appreciation can go a long way in virtual meetings!

TIP

Start your meeting with energy! In virtual meetings, attendees see only a small part of you and lack the other visual cues they would have in person. By showing up and starting the meeting with more energy, it often translates to your normal energy levels in person. Attendees can see for themselves how invested you are in gaining alignment, ideas, and specific outcomes. Also, show appreciation of your meeting attendees, and express gratitude to those who join and are invested in projects, clients, and work — even when they're coming in from their home, office, coffee shops, airports, or wherever they might be located!

When you're the meeting leader, facilitation is vital. You have to be active throughout the meeting. If people feel unengaged or ignored, their engagement drops off quickly and they tune out. Or, conversely, some people love having an audience. You've likely been in meetings where one person takes over and tells a long rambling story about . . . something. The next thing you know, the meeting is over and nothing was accomplished.

So, it's vital for leaders to actively facilitate by paying attention to who's talking and who's not, and to encourage people to focus their responses on the topic at hand. You can draw others into the conversation by calling on people and asking specific questions. "Sierra, please share your thoughts about this topic," will draw a better response than asking general questions, such as "Does anyone have any feedback?" It helps ensure that everyone contributes. Pay attention to attendees and their interactions. See whether they speak up or try to "hide" in the meeting. The idea is to make sure that every member has an opportunity to speak while also ensuring that no lone person monopolizes the conversation.

TIP

Check the time throughout the meeting. If you have a short session that's either going off track or looks like it might run long, remember to do a time check and remind people how much time is left and what you still need to cover. One way to do this is to have a timer set up so that participants know when the virtual meeting has ended and it's time for them to wrap up what they were talking about and move on to the next topic.

Wrapping up the meeting

When you reach the point where only a few minutes of your meeting remain, a commonly overlooked part of a virtual meeting lies in these last few minutes. How do you wrap up your online meeting successfully and leave attendees excited about the project or other outcomes from the meeting? Here are a few things you can do that your colleagues will thank you for:

>> **Recap:** Give a quick verbal summary of the results that came out of the meeting.

>> **Clarify:** Provide clarity on what will happen next by identifying who's responsible for each action item.

>> **Remind:** Let attendees know that they'll receive the meeting notes and a list of action items by the end of the workday.

The thing you don't want to do is let Daniel or Christina log off your meeting wondering whether anything was accomplished during the time spent together online. Attendees want to feel that you respected their time, that decisions were made, or that projects were moved forward. By reminding them of the outcomes and changes that came out of the meeting, you'll leave them feeling like they did something useful and contributed in a meaningful way.

REMEMBER

One of the best ways to make meetings better is by asking attendees how they think a meeting can be improved. Asking for their opinion allows for improvement and innovation in future strategies, which we hope you'll continue to apply!

Folks also have ideas about what works well or not so well during these gatherings. Use this feedback as another opportunity when possible — after all, it can't hurt you any more than before, right?

Handling the Meeting Follow-Up

So, you've concluded your meeting, and you have a lot of notes from the virtual discussion. Now is the time to get any action items assigned and send out recaps so that everyone has clear notes about the critical points of the discussion. It's also important in case someone couldn't attend the meeting. Having access to the action items, next steps, and key points lets them contribute their thoughts if needed.

If you had no chance to take notes during the actual event, jot down the key points and ask participants to fill in any gaps. You want to send out the action items, next steps, and key points as quickly after the meeting ends as you can. You might be tempted to wait until the end of the day but remember that many of your attendees will sit in several meetings throughout the day. If everyone waits until the end of the day to send out action items and the next steps, your project might lose its place on the priority list. Consider sending out the bare-bones notes and action items closer to the meeting's end.

TIP

If you cannot take the detailed notes you usually take because you're also hosting the meeting, consider opening an email and starting to type out your initial notes, and then add the action items and assign them. Send it out right away.

» Taking an active role in making virtual meetings a success

» Ensuring positive and productive results as an attendee

» Getting the most out of the virtual meetings you're invited to

Chapter **14**

Making an Appearance at a Virtual Meeting

Some folks believe that just showing up for a virtual meeting is half the battle — those folks tend to earn bad yearly evaluations. Here's a word of advice: If you're attending a meeting remotely, just showing up isn't enough. You also need to know what is considered appropriate behavior and etiquette. In this chapter, you find out how to make attending virtual meetings go from painful to successful. You'll see how to prepare before the meeting begins; how best to participate in discussions; and how to follow up afterward.

Attending a Virtual Meeting

The email arrives in your inbox and you open it up to see that you've been invited to attend yet *another* online meeting. Before you start dreading another meeting where the host drones on and on while you and other attendees around the country roll your eyes, making snarky chat comments to colleagues and counting how many times you have to tell Janice in Accounting, "You're on mute," you'll want to continue reading.

There are several ways to approach attending virtual meetings. Attending meetings only because you're required to isn't helpful for anyone. Instead, you can take an active role as an attendee and help the meeting reach its intended outcomes (and then maybe get some time back in your day if the meeting ends early!).

When it comes to virtual meeting etiquette and being an active attendee, there are a few key things you should understand before heading into your next meeting — they can make a big difference! Understanding company culture, who the presenter or host is, the agenda, and the expectations of the meeting, including the desired outcomes/goals of the meeting, can all help transform the typical dreaded meeting into one that is dynamic and keeps projects moving along, teams up-to-date, and teams motivated toward company goals.

Knowing the company culture

Attendees should be prepared with all the information about the type of behavior that's expected during a virtual meeting so that nothing gets lost in translation and everyone remains engaged until completion. Whether attendees are chatting via an audio-only conference call or on a video call and using instant messages, knowing the company culture and preferred communication helps create a more efficient and positive experience for everyone involved.

REMEMBER

A company's *culture* is the combination of your company's values and goals and the personality it gives off. Every company has a unique company culture that influences how virtual meetings are held. Those sets of rules and norms differ from company to company when it comes to being respectful and communicating in business settings — from emails to virtual meetings, web conferences, and more.

TIP

Whether you're an employee of a company in an internal meeting or you're meeting with a partner, client, or prospective client, you should become familiar with the company culture so that your attendance is in line with the company and meets expectations. You do *not* want to be the person who

>> Calls into a formal corporate meeting from their car or a loud coffee shop, unable to find the Mute button and allowing the background sounds to fill the call.

>> Takes their laptop to the bathroom and forgets to turn off the camera or press the Mute button.

>> Shows up overly casual, chatting freely about their day and not understanding why no one else is indulging in small talk on the call.

These actions make it challenging to connect with other employees at the meeting. They might also adversely impact how people work together or cooperate on projects, making life much harder for themselves and others.

After you have a general idea of how things are typically handled at a specific company, consider how these might impact virtual meetings and interactions between employees. Pay attention to details like these:

>> Do they share personal stories about themselves when appropriate?

>> If so, does this mean they prefer informal communication all the time?

>> What kinds of topics should be avoided so as not to come across as offensive?

>> What are the industry or company acronyms they might commonly use that could limit the effectiveness of their (or your own) communication?

TIP

If you're new to the company (or you're meeting with people from a company for the first time), it's always safer to assume that their culture is more formal than your own. You can also learn about the company culture by reviewing the website, following them on social media, and watching videos of past meeting sessions. You can also ask your colleagues who work at the company what the company culture is like and how company meetings are run. And, if you're still unsure of the company culture, take a look at other employees' profiles (on LinkedIn, for example) to see what they have said about themselves or your potential team members in an online social media environment — this will give you a good idea of what's expected!

Being prepared for different types of presenters

Let's face it: Not all presenters and meeting hosts are created equal. Though we'd like them all to show up early, be familiar with the meeting technology, be organized, and know how to manage the details, like bringing everyone in on Mute to limit distractions and create focus, we know that isn't always the case.

Though you can't step in and make someone organized, you can be prepared to take an active role in the meeting. Offering to manage the chat available on many videoconferencing platforms is one way to help alleviate some of the burdens faced by overwhelmed meeting hosts.

In addition, knowing the background of the meeting host helps give you some perspective on what their goals and desired outcomes of the meeting are. It can help you get the most out of the online meeting and, hopefully, from other attendees as well. When everyone understands each other and knows what to expect from coworkers in a particular context, productivity improves when working together online.

REMEMBER

It may seem like common sense to be on familiar terms with your coworkers, but this isn't always easy when working online with colleagues living around the world. If you and other employees, clients, and partners can connect on an emotional level during your sessions together, it can ultimately lead to forming stronger bonds.

Participating in a virtual meeting (via phone, video, and chat)

There are many different ways to communicate and participate in virtual meetings. Whether you're on a phone call, attending a videoconference, or chatting with other attendees, it's essential to know how to be the best attendee possible so that everyone can have a great meeting experience!

Considerations for conference calls

Conference calls are the simplest form of virtual meetings. All you need is your phone and some headphones with an inline microphone (usually included in most headphone sets). Often, you simply dial into an access number, enter a meeting ID/password when prompted, and then just talk! Though there are fewer considerations than with videoconference meetings, there are several vital points you should keep in mind:

>> Announce yourself when you join the call, so that everyone knows who has entered the meeting.

>> Mention your name when you start speaking if on a call with multiple people. Don't leave other attendees stuck guessing who is talking or asking questions.

>> Mute yourself when you're not speaking, but don't forget to unmute yourself when you're ready to talk!

>> Don't be afraid of silence during conference call meeting discussions! Other participants just might need more time to gather their thoughts and formulate what they'd like to say next.

>> Speak clearly and directly into the mic! Often people are tempted to use the speakerphone when on audio-only calls. Not a good idea! Speakers can pick up more ambient noise and make it more challenging to hear you.

>> Turn off notifications on your phone or computer. This is especially important if you're using a cellphone and you have Vibrate mode for messages turned on. (Yes, you can hear the vibration, and it can be disruptive in meetings.)

>> Be sure not to eat or drink anything while speaking on the call. This sounds obvious, but it tends to happen more on audio-only calls because no one can see you. You don't want your crunching chips or slurping smoothie to come through loud and clear for everyone else on the line.

>> Clearly state your name and who you want to speak to when asking questions and on a call with multiple people. For example, "This is Bryan, and I'd like to ask Kayla a few questions now."

TIP

When attending conference call meetings, remember that different platforms have different intuitive ways of doing things. For example, on most conference call services, pressing the star sign (*) on your phone mutes the microphone.

Navigating videoconference calls

When participating in a videoconference meeting, you usually download specific software or use a link to join the discussion. The very nature of videoconference calls/meetings means that other attendees can see you unless you turn off your camera, just like they can hear you unless you mute your audio. It's therefore essential to show up, have any necessary software downloaded, dress appropriately, and be ready for your close-up when you log on to the call.

Here are some additional videoconference-meeting-specific considerations to keep in mind that will make the experience better for yourself and other attendees:

>> If others in the meeting have their cameras on, it's a good idea to turn yours on.

>> Start by making sure your area is well-lit so that you're not sitting in the dark or silhouetted by the bright lights or window behind you.

>> Test out your camera ahead of time so that you know that your face is visible on camera. Let the other attendees see your facial expressions and gestures in the meeting to help increase communication.

>> Keep your camera at eye level or slightly above eye level and on a steady surface. (You don't want it shaking around as if you're experiencing an earthquake and you definitely don't want the camera looking up your nose.)

>> When speaking, be sure to look at the camera instead of focusing on your laptop screen. It might also help if you can see your presenter so that you're aware of when it's time to jump in with a comment or question.

>> Introduce yourself if you come into a virtual meeting room and don't know someone there (of course, this is more appropriate for smaller meetings versus bigger, town hall type meetings).

>> Avoid eating during meetings. Did you know there is a phobia that makes people violently angry just at the sound of someone chewing? It's rare, but it exists. Whether your attendees will become violently upset or if they're just trying to focus, listening to someone chew, crunch, or crinkle food containers can be incredibly distracting. So, though there are times when you're in back-to-back meetings and the only way to eat is in a session, turn off your camera and go on Mute until you're done eating (if this is acceptable in the company's culture). Otherwise, wait until the meeting has ended. Your colleagues will thank you.

TIP

Add your name to the videoconference platform so that everyone knows who you are. If you're using someone else's laptop/computer for the meeting, remember to change the name from theirs to yours, to prevent any confusion. In addition, many platforms also allow you to add your pronouns. This is helpful when you're meeting with people who don't already know you and it also shows you are inclusive and welcome them sharing theirs.

And, for everyone who has access to the Internet, don't do anything on a videoconference call that you wouldn't do in the middle of an in-person meeting, including

>> Bringing your laptop into the bathroom with you

>> Forgetting to wear pants

>> Standing up from your desk if you're not wearing pants

>> Forgetting to wear pants

>> Eating crunchy snacks while people are talking

Videoconferencing with chat

Most videoconference software platforms come with a chat or messenger app. There are also tools like Slack or even cellphones and texting that can be used during a videoconference call. Being a good videoconference and chat attendee is all about being aware of the meeting and using chat to add to it, not detracting from it. Chat allows you to ask the speaker for clarification or to ask them questions about their comments. Many speakers ask people to respond to inquiries in the chat to have a better idea of where people are in terms of the topic.

The chat can also share links and resources and tell someone who might be having audio issues that they're on Mute if making gestures and writing "You're on mute" doesn't work.

A few things to consider when using the chat as part of the platform include:

>> Try to keep your responses short; also refrain from sending too many messages at a time, because it overwhelms other attendees.

>> Stay focused — and help others stay focused — by commenting or asking questions about the topic and not about the person, their background, or their home. So, no matter how much you might want to comment in the chat about the weird-looking statue in Brad's living room, it's better to ignore it.

>> Write about one topic per message; again, it helps avoid overcrowding and clarifies each post.

REMEMBER

If you're convinced that all the side conversations you're having with colleagues on your videoconferencing platform will stay private, we have some news for you: Some platforms allow the host to access all the chat records, even the side conversations. So, be careful out there.

You might not realize it, but other attendees can often tell whether a few members are messaging or texting each other. It can create feelings of exclusion and cliques, even in work meetings. Try to refrain from doing so, and add to the communication challenges that can take place when attending remote meetings.

Being prepared

Being prepared is always important, especially when it comes to attending virtual meetings. Reading the agenda ahead of time and jotting down any questions or notes you want to bring up is helpful for attendees, to help ensure that the meeting ends on time and doesn't run over or require a second meeting to be scheduled.

Here are a few things you can do to be better prepared for your virtual meetings:

>> Be sure to have login information and necessary documents at least an hour before the meeting time.

>> Use a headset for a better voice-over microphone and so that you can hear the voices of others while not disturbing those outside the meeting.

>> Remove distractions from the area where meeting attendance will be, if possible.

>> Turn off email, text, or phone messages that may interfere with focus while attending.

>> Dress as if sitting in the meeting, because the webcam might be on.

>> Put up a sign stating In a Meeting to prevent people from interrupting.

>> Eat before or after the meeting, not during, because accidents happen — or you might have to field a question mid-chew.

>> Log in to the session a few minutes early so that the facilitator knows when everyone is attending.

Being on time

Another vital thing to remember when attending a virtual meeting is to be on time or early. You don't want to miss out on any part of an already scheduled meeting because your technology didn't work correctly! This way, you can make sure that your end of the video call works well and that you give yourself enough time to prepare for the start of the meeting.

If you haven't already used the specific software or tool, you might want to plan to arrive at least ten minutes early — to ensure that you have ample time to test it out and troubleshoot any potential issues.

Punctuality is also essential when attending a virtual meeting, because you want to be on the video call and situated before the host discusses the agenda items. If you join the meeting late, it causes the host to have to stall and wait for you to arrive or repeat everything that has already been said for the benefit of those joining late. Though in some companies this is no big deal, in others it's the equivalent of being the last person who was late to catch a flight. Don't be the person who held up the flight, or in this case, the meeting, because you didn't test out the software ahead of time.

Understanding the purpose

It's essential to understand the purpose of a meeting when you attend one in person, and it's also true for virtual meetings. You can do this by ensuring that you have reviewed any necessary materials such as presentations, documents, or reports before the meeting so that you're prepared and ready to discuss them. If you have any questions, ask the meeting host ahead of time or jot them down beforehand to avoid getting missed in conversation or forgotten about because of time constraints.

Suppose that everyone takes the time to review the schedule and any required materials before joining the meeting. In that case, it makes the virtual meeting experience a positive and productive one, ultimately leading to better results for everyone involved.

Knowing the technology

You'll want to be familiar with the technology you're using when attending a virtual meeting, particularly if it's your first time using this type of software or setup. This way, you'll be able to navigate the tool. Knowing what each button does, how to turn your camera on and off, and how to manage your audio are practical things you'll need to use in the meeting. Practice joining a meeting ahead of time or be sure to enter early so that you know what to expect and that it all works as it should.

You also want to make sure that anything related, such as having access to Internet services like streaming video or audio, are all functioning so that you can be seen and heard without any issues.

TIP

If you think you might need to share your screen, present, or share a project management software, have it ready to go. Other attendees don't want to watch you do Google searches or click through 47 open browser tabs until you find the one with the information you wanted to show them.

Conducting Yourself in a Virtual Meeting

You're in a virtual meeting — now what? Whether it's a big town hall meeting or a small departmental meeting, or even a one-on-one virtual meeting with your doctor, we can suggest a few recommendations that can make the experience more productive and help you get out of it what you need:

>> Mute yourself when you join a meeting and when you're not talking, to prevent background noises from becoming part of the call.

>> Stay focused on the meeting topic and agenda times.

>> Keep comments and questions concise and to the point because meeting time is precious and usually short.

>> Record personal action items and request or suggest a due date before the meeting closes.

- » Join at least 15 minutes before start time so that you can download any necessary apps (and give yourself enough time if your connection isn't as fast as others).

- » Turn off notifications that could be noisy or distract from the purpose of the meeting.

- » If you have concerns, consider bringing them up with the meeting host after the meeting has finished so that they don't affect everyone else trying to participate actively.

- » Keep your comments concise and pointed rather than give lengthy monologues about your weekend, or that one time this happened before, back in 2012, that is irrelevant.

- » Remember to look at the camera and not at your phone or another computer screen. Seeing people not paying attention can be distracting for other attendees and cause them to lose interest.

- » Use earbuds or headphones with a microphone for better sound and to help ensure that others can hear you.

- » If there's a lot of background noise where you are (such as in an open office space), try moving somewhere quieter so that others can hear what you're saying more easily.

- » Interrupting someone else is never a good idea in person, and it's also true in virtual meetings. Even if you think that your voice will carry over the other person's speaking, talking over people isn't recommended. Instead, wait for them to finish speaking and then say what you were going to say.

REMEMBER

It may seem simple, but being proactive and considerate can help everyone have a better virtual meeting experience.

Presenting yourself

When attending a virtual meeting, it's essential to look professional or dressed in acceptable ways for your company culture. If you work for a digital agency and your accepted attire is "rolled out of bed chic," then, by all means, embrace it! But if your company culture is more formal, you want to take care to dress appropriately, even if you're working from your kitchen table.

Studies have found that dressing professionally increases how much we trust someone and makes us think of them as more intelligent. By dressing professionally when presenting information, you help remind everyone else in attendance that the topics under discussion are serious — that it's not just a casual conversation, in other words.

Be aware of your surroundings. Hey! What's that behind you? Dirty laundry? A messy house? Don't give your colleagues, clients, or your team deeper insights into how you clean your home or do laundry. Instead, turn your computer so that your back is to a blank wall or use a virtual background that hides whatever is in your surroundings that you don't want everyone to see.

Also, be careful with mirror placement and what you're wearing. Don't be the person who looks professional for the camera but can be seen in the mirror behind you wearing *Star Wars* pajama bottoms — or worse, nothing!

Knowing when to mute your audio

When you attend virtual meetings, it's essential to be aware of your audio. The safest option is always to mute yourself if you're not talking. If you're not on mute, you may interrupt other people by speaking over them or distract them with the background noises or even the sound of your keyboard. It also helps to quiet unnecessary noise from your location, like if you're eating, or children, dogs, roommates, spouses, or other noise that could be potentially distracting.

Just don't forget to take yourself off Mute when you're ready to talk. If you're unmuted, you won't find yourself talking to yourself until someone lets you know they can't hear you. Taking yourself off of Mute also indicates to others that you're prepared to speak next.

Knowing when to turn off your camera

When to turn off your camera or when not to use it in the first place is a crucial aspect of virtual meetings and often comes down to company culture.

In some cases, cameras can be distracting for other participants and should be used only if necessary. In other cases, it's common practice to have your camera on in meetings unless you need to stand up or step away from the meeting for some reason. But the bottom line is that it does come down to company culture or the nature of the meeting. Some companies are okay with attendees keeping their cameras off during early morning meetings, for example, whereas others expect everyone to keep their cameras on at all times.

Considerations for using filters

The option to use filters on your camera during virtual meetings comes down to the company culture and the nature of the meeting. If you work for a company that doesn't mind creativity or casualness, then play with the filters. However, if this isn't something that makes sense within your industry, it's a best practice to disable all camera effects before starting the meeting! Having unprofessional imagery may call into question whether other employees who have joined via video chat are able or authorized enough to be representing the company.

TIP

Suppose that you have a question about whether to apply filters during virtual meetings. In that case, it's always a best practice to check with your employer or become familiar with the company culture before doing so! Ensuring that everyone is on the same page when it comes to applying any camera effects helps ensure that everyone can participate without worrying about confusion related to what they see on their end.

Virtual backgrounds

A virtual background is a fun way to hide an unsightly room or any laundry you didn't have time to put away before the call started. It's also an option if your home office is in your bedroom and you don't want colleagues to see that you didn't make your bed that morning. Whatever the reason, virtual backgrounds can add consistency and professionalism to your video feed. It's important to remember that they're not perfect, and the background might end up fuzzy around you. Like many other norms and etiquette considerations in virtual meetings, it comes down to your company culture and the space you're using for work. If you don't have a virtual background, consider using a simple "blur" background that many platforms offer. It is always an easy go-to solution.

Handling sidebar conversations

If you're attending virtual meetings, it's essential to understand what makes a good attendee. This means *paying attention* — which means limiting your sidebar conversation*s, whether they're in the chat, messenger, or text. Sidebar conversations often distract those involved and anyone else who might witness them — in both real-time or on video!

Sometimes you can have some constructive discussion by collaborating with others around you, but you should ask yourself whether the meeting is the best place for it — or should happen outside the meeting.

REMEMBER

Many sidebar conversations happen because an attendee is

>> Seeking attention

>> Distracted or bored

>> Confused

>> Frustrated

If you notice yourself having sidebar conversations, chatting, and not paying attention, ask why that is, and then direct your attention back to the meeting.

Though it's the role of the meeting leader to help people avoid becoming bored, confused, or frustrated, it's also the role of attendees to stay focused, ask questions, and arrive prepared. As another attendee, you don't want to give people seeking attention any more attention than necessary.

Sticking to the agenda

If you're in a virtual meeting, it's critical to stay on topic and help the host guide the conversation, to ensure that you end up with the desired outcomes.

People who join a meeting without understanding this may find themselves distracted by other conversations in the chat or taking part in discussions about topics that aren't relevant to achieving business objectives. These can damage employees' relationships and result in additional time spent covering old ground rather than moving forward, frustrating everyone.

For example, if Mike from Operations brings up a project that isn't relevant to the meeting topic, don't get distracted by his conversation. Things like that can lead to nonrelevant tangents, and before you know it, the entire meeting is over and nothing was accomplished. So, listen carefully! If any questions arise during the meeting, bring them up at the appropriate time.

REMEMBER

Sidetracking an entire meeting with irrelevant topics can lead directly to missing deadlines, more meetings, frustration, and lack of motivation.

TIP

Before you speak up, consider whether your question or comment will help move the conversation along. Is your question relevant only to you, or does it impact others on the call or the project? Will your comment or story help the meeting achieve the desired outcomes, or do you just want to tell a story and hear yourself talk? (Our advice? Keep your stories for later and for breaks.)

Respecting the time

Imagine that you have meetings scheduled all day with no time for email and getting your work done. You've probably had more than one of those days. And you know that if one meeting runs late, it can throw off the rest like a chain of dominoes, each affecting the next. It's essential to respect the preset time for the meeting and everyone else's time.

A lot can go into making a meeting run long, from side conversations and tangents to attendees not being prepared and the host not being prepared — and more.

All meeting participants need to respect everyone else's time. Sometimes, this can mean asking questions or making comments in a way where you're sure they will be helpful toward the overall goals of the project, instead of just your gains. Think about whether what you have to say will help others on the call before saying it — if not, maybe hold off until another point during the discussion when your comment might make sense.

Not taking over the conversation/meeting.

As an excellent virtual meeting attendee, it's your role to attend, and not lead, the meeting. This means respecting your meeting host/leader and not hijacking the meeting for your gain. It also means being an active listener who takes notes on topics discussed and asks questions at the end or when appropriate.

You don't want other attendees to think less of you because you couldn't keep quiet and caused the meeting to run late and not accomplish anything. Neither do you want to do all the talking, because you'll come across as self-centered and disinterested in others' ideas, potentially impacting future meetings with your participation.

However, there may be instances when you might just have specific expertise on the topic or believe you can contribute more than anyone else in terms of information. If the meeting host/leader is open to that, you can share your knowledge or thoughts on a particular topic. However, if they're not allowing additional discussion topics beyond what was planned for in the agenda, it's essential to respect their wishes and follow along accordingly.

REMEMBER Your goal is to capture and share knowledge about the topic at hand. In that case, you'll be an influential attendee by respecting everyone's time, being active in discussions where appropriate, and following along with what was planned for in advance of the meeting.

Chapter **15**

Webinar and Online Event Proprieties

ncreasingly, while as a society, we continue to use the Internet for entertainment, learning, and connection, many people are turning to online events, such as virtual conferences or webinars, to stay informed and connected in their professional industries. These types of events have become popular because you can learn from experts in your field while avoiding travel expenses.

The etiquette of webinars and virtual events is unclear to many people, and there seem to be two types: those who love the convenience and freedom of not having to travel and those who prefer in-person interactions. Whether you're hosting or attending an online event, it's important for everyone to know what they should do before, during, and after the event. In this chapter, we discuss the etiquette of hosting and attending these particular virtual events.

Determining the Goals of Your Event

When you host a webinar or an online event, it's important to have a clear goal in mind so that you know what you want to accomplish with the event. A good way of doing this is to start by first asking yourself what your objective is for the webinar or conference. After coming up with an answer to that question, ask yourself how the event will help audiences achieve their goals while living up to your business's mission statement. If possible, try to establish some sort of relationship between the answers to these two questions.

For example, if your webinar is meant to be a lead-generation tactic for your company's marketing campaign, you should clearly communicate:

>> The right message about what your brand stands for

>> Why people need it in their lives

>> How this specific event will help them live up to these values

In addition, think about how it will help audiences achieve their goals on an individual level.

REMEMBER

Many people don't realize the importance of having a goal for hosting webinars and other virtual events. If you have no clear objective in mind, your online event will end up being useless and ineffective.

Having a clear goal for your online events makes it easier to achieve them and helps ensure that everyone knows what they should be doing at each stage of the event.

TIP

Most webinars or virtual events have four common goals: to educate, sell (promote), connect, recruit. (Okay, let's add a fifth goal — a combination of all four.) Keep in mind that if the only goal is education, that needs to come first — no selling or recruiting.

When it comes to setting goals for webinars or online events, your goals should be specific, measurable, attainable, relevant, and time-bound (SMART). A SMART goal can help ensure that you achieve the results you're looking to achieve from hosting an online event. For example: "To increase awareness of my business by 100 percent" is not a SMART goal. "To increase awareness of my business among the target audience in Los Angeles by at least 25 percent" is a SMART goal.

Knowing who your audience is and what's in it for them

Once you know your goals for the event, it's easier to figure out who your audience is. The idea of knowing who your audience is for an online event may seem simple, but it's quite important. You need to know the type of people you're speaking with and their goals in order to communicate effectively and efficiently.

The more information you have about what your audiences want, the easier it is to make them happy — which means that they'll come back later or recommend other peers or colleagues! Asking a few different questions can help you determine who your ideal attendees are: How old are they? What kind of company/industry do they work for? Would any specific interests or hobbies draw them into this event? What is motivating them to sign up? In addition, try putting yourself in the shoes of each attendee when planning out your webinar or virtual event.

REMEMBER

Knowing who they are helps you better align your event with your audience. Only after you have a clear idea of your target audience can you start to define the value you're offering and let them know what's in it for them.

A great way to get people excited about attending your online event is by telling them exactly what's in it for them. For example, if there's someone who can help attendees achieve their goals while also giving back something valuable that everyone can benefit from, be sure to include all these details! It doesn't have to be anything too complicated, either — just give one simple reason that each person should attend with enough detail that others can understand its value as well.

REMEMBER

You should know why your audience would want to attend your event. Try to find out whether they're attending the event because they want to learn more about marketing in regulated industries, for example, or to meet someone that can help their career growth, or because they want to reach potential clients. Whatever the case may be, try to provide value to everyone who attends. The last thing you want is for attendees to feel like they've wasted their time.

Recognizing the difference between webinars and virtual events

Online events have become extremely popular in the past few years. Webinars, master classes, workshops, virtual conferences, and virtual networking events are found everywhere online these days. You probably have one or two on your calendar now!

At its most basic level, an online event is essentially any event held online. Once you start trying to differentiate, though, it starts to become complicated. The difference between webinars and virtual conferences, for example, can be confusing to people who are unfamiliar with them, but once you understand the differences, it's easier to choose which one is right for your goals. To help clarify the differences between the various online events, here are a few definitions:

>> **Webinar:** A presentation that happens over the Internet. Although often presented live, it's also often recorded so that people can watch it later on, even if they were unable to attend the live session.

Webinars tend to be more intimate than other virtual conferences or sessions because they are usually smaller and involve experts focusing on specific outcomes focusing solely on the topic at hand. If you're the one hosting, make sure all participants sign in by registering, and pay up (if it's not a free event) before you make any content available to them.

>> **Masterclass:** An online event that offers an interactive experience for audiences. Attendees can access exclusive content and special offers in exchange for their contact information. It usually includes a lecture or presentation from a professional in their field of expertise and is often accompanied by questions and answers. Unlike a webinar, a masterclass is often recorded (and not offered live). It can usually be found at a particular web address, and participants have to sign up in advance in order to "attend" the event.

>> **Workshop:** In addition to the webinar and the virtual conference, there's another type of online event: workshop. A workshop differs from a traditional event because it's meant for a more specific audience, and the main goal is often to teach something rather than just communicate new information or share knowledge. It can be a useful tool when you want people to learn about a specific topic that's relevant only to them, such as how certain processes work within their company, tips on reaching new clients in an industry with fierce competition, and more.

>> **Online conference:** An online conference refers to a virtual meeting that connects multiple speakers across various locations into one session with attendees who are located in different places at the same time. If you want your audience to feel like they're attending a real-life event, this should be what you go for!

These events need more planning because there will typically be presenters from all over the world, so it's necessary to establish clear guidelines about how each of them should connect during these sessions, which can make things complicated. The events can be prerecorded, live presentations, or a combination of both.

Online conferences are often more like an ongoing conversation between hosts and participants who share their knowledge with each other. The idea is to contribute or trade information in order to solve problems together. Some examples of this include virtual conferences where content creators deliver sessions about various topics while attendees listen and then participate by asking questions during Q&As after each talk. Content creators can set up breakout rooms as part of the event for more meaningful conversations, as well as sharing their own experiences via social media (Twitter hashtags, for example).

It's important to note that every company does these events differently because there are no rules about how you should go about hosting them or what each must entail. This means that it's okay if you occasionally mix things up and try something new!

» **Virtual networking event:** Online networking events have become a lot more popular over the past few years. Virtual networking events give you a chance to meet new people in your industry, associations, or similar positions as yours. Whether you're looking for partners or clients or just to meet and connect with more people in your career/industry, online networking events have the potential to connect you with people around the world.

» **Entertainment:** From yoga studios to musicians to catering companies, restaurants, and bars, there's no shortage of creativity when it comes to entertainment at virtual events. More than one catering company or restaurant has created shopping lists, shipped ingredients, or delivered meals for people to enjoy together. A tiki bar in Los Angeles offers events where they ship the cocktail ingredients, teach you how to make the drinks during the virtual event, and then flip to a band playing theme music while participants enjoy their drinks. Imagine what other businesses could do when they get creative!

Mastering the Do's and Don'ts for Hosting a Successful Webinar or Live Event

The approaches to hosting a webinar and a live event are surprisingly similar, with a few minor differences between the different types. But largely, they're the same — only online events and conferences require more project management because they're bigger. At the most basic level, here's the process you want to follow for a successful webinar or online event:

1. Define your goal for the event.

2. Identify your target audience.

3. Develop the topic of your event and the value your audience will receive from the event (what's in it for them?).

4. Determine the format. (Is it a panel or a presentation? Will there be multiple presenters on the topic or just one?)

5. Select the day and time for your event that would work for your target audience.

6. Develop promotions and promote your event.

7. Identify the technology platform you'll use to host your event as well as the technical resources you need (headphones, Internet connection, microphone, and videoconferencing platform, for example).

8. Create the content for your event (presentations, scripts, questions).

9. Practice and do a dry run with your speakers.

10. Log in early to check all connections, the audio and video, and presentations — your own and that of your speakers.

11. Consider asking someone(s) to help you manage the chat, questions, and other events that might occur during the event.

12. Follow up with attendees — those who made it *and* those who didn't.

REMEMBER

If you promise your attendees something and fail to deliver, they will be disappointed in the content of what was promised but also by how unprofessional it is. Be sure that all information in webinars deliver on the outcomes before advertising them so that people know where expectations should rightfully lie.

In addition to the process and flow of planning and launching a webinar or another online event, here are several key points to remember when hosting:

» **Plan ahead of time.** Have all necessary materials prepared well in advance of the event (registration links and presentation files, for example).

» **Write up an agenda.** Covers the main aspects of the event: what participants can expect to learn and when they can expect the event to start/end, for example.

» **Make sure all your equipment is in good working order.** There's nothing worse than being on the air and having technical difficulties distract everyone who's watching. Our advice? Test everything before the big day!

» **Keep the discussion on topic at all times, no matter how many times people try to derail it or talk over each other.** It's not rude if the presenters have something important to say, and everyone will appreciate your dedication to keeping them focused until the end of the webinar, even if that means cutting off someone who is trying to hijack the conversation or presentation.

» **Use any chat or messaging app you have at your disposal to keep the conversation going in real time.** Most virtual event platforms like Demio, Run the World, and Hopin have a built-in chat function to keep attendees engaged. This is especially useful for when people are asking questions.

>> **Give each speaker their own, separate introduction and conclusion.** If there are several speakers, everyone then knows who they're listening to and where attendees should focus their attention.

>> **Leverage the network of your other speakers by creating promotions they can share to their audiences.** Whether by way of custom graphics and posts or email content, most speakers are excited to be a part of your event, so give them the resources to share it as well with their audiences.

>> **Avoid any temptation to start early.** Doing so will only annoy your audience and possibly cause them to leave before you've even started!

>> **Create an engaging presentation that's not too scripted.** The idea here is to give your presenters some room to interact with members of their audience.

>> **Respect the time zone.** Determine in which time zone your audience is primarily based and cater the start and end times to that zone.

>> **Email preregistered attendees several times beforehand.** Remind them about the day and time that the live event starts as well as any promotional offers they might be interested in at that time. This strategy helps build relationships between attendees and organizers ahead of time, which means that people are much less likely to flake on you.

>> **Encourage interaction, even if no questions are being asked throughout your webinar or online event.** Doing so makes members feel more involved with what you're talking about instead of listening in silence — a silence that can definitely be uncomfortable after a while. Maintain their interest levels by asking them what they think at certain points during the presentation as well.

>> Keep an eye on the audience chat box whenever possible, especially if you have a live moderator who likes to get involved. If you need to take a break for any reason, make sure everyone knows so that they can continue the conversation without feeling lost.

>> After the webinar is over, don't forget to send out an email thanking the members of the audience with a link to the replay if one is available. Doing so not only boosts loyalty but also gives them plenty of social proof that other people enjoyed what they just watched, too, which could bring in even more leads.

>> Lastly, keep your energy levels up during the whole event, even if it's getting late or people aren't engaging with you online as well as you'd expected. Don't give up on engaging them until the very end of your presentation. **Remember:** Any interaction is better than none, so try not to get discouraged by anything (online comments included). Just continue doing what you're supposed to do (sell your product or service, perhaps, or provide interesting information) until the very end.

Knowing the technology

Knowing the goals of your webinar or virtual conference is also important when it comes to choosing a technology platform for hosting your event. Each platform has different features, costs, and audience size limits. As you may have guessed, many options are out there, which can make the choice overwhelming, but that doesn't mean that you should give up hope!

The best way to approach the technology issue is by figuring out what type of webinar or event you want. Is it strictly educational? Will people be able to ask questions via chat boxes throughout the session? Do you want them to try out demos on their own devices at home after they've completed some training before the live portion begins so that they're ready with any issues they might have? These are all conditions you should consider when it comes to choosing a platform.

REMEMBER

If you're hosting a webinar, virtual networking, or online conference, the size and nature of your attendees will dictate how robust an experience they should have. The complexity of your event also influences the platform you need. For example, will you need speed networking, a sponsorship "booth" area, a main stage, and breakout rooms — or just a simple platform for one speaker and questions? Use the format of your event to dictate what you need from your hosting platform.

Respecting people's time

Before any webinar or virtual conference, it's important for everyone involved to be aware of their expectations and agenda so that no one feels let down after participating — this means setting a clear agenda and sticking to it. It's better to build in more time and wrap up early than to run late and run the risk of your audience missing your final sales pitch or an important offer.

In addition to sticking to the schedule, it's crucial that you set — and meet — people's expectations. Don't tell people you'll present them with the secrets to eternal youth and then give them a 90-minute sales pitch about your Bitcoin opportunity instead.

REMEMBER

Make a promise to your audience, and then give them what you promised. It's as simple as that.

Presenting best practices

When you're hosting a webinar or live virtual event, you have to make sure a few things are happening. First, you want to make sure that everyone is aware of the amount of time they have to present or speak, and how much time they need for questions, for example.

Another thing you might want for your event is a uniform look that matches the aesthetic of the event. You can do this by providing all speakers with a particular PowerPoint template and the guidelines on how to use it. If you want a certain number of images or a specific word-to-text ratio on the slides, include all that information in whatever you provide for the presenters.

You can also remind people not to read their slides, to stick to their allotted time, and to practice several times beforehand. This helps ensure that their presentations are to the level you expect for your overall event.

Preparing slides or resources ahead of time

Be sure that all presenters prepare their slides of resources ahead of time. Period. That way, you can minimize surprises, ensure that your speakers are adding value (and not sales pitches), and help maintain a high-quality standard.

If you're hosting a webinar, you need all slide presentations ahead of time so that you can complete a practice run. If you're hosting a recorded live event, you need the copies of the recordings in advance so that you have time to review them, place them into the platform, and then practice for a dry run. You also need details in hand about onsite resources, giveaways, booth information, and sponsor information well in advance of the actual date of the event.

This level of quality control helps ensure that you're offering your audience valuable content — so much so that your attendees will walk away excited that it was worth their time. If all you're offering are a couple of speakers trying to sell and promote from the stage, you'll waste people's time, and they'll feel frustrated and probably never again attend one of your events. (What's worse, they'll probably spread the word that your event was a bust.)

Practicing so that you're prepared

Whether you're doing a live event or using a series of prerecorded videos, complete a practice rehearsal at least once before the big day. This event allows you and your team to get used to the technology and troubleshoot any potential issues that may arise on the day of the webinar or event. It's better to identify these kinds of problems during the practice run instead of letting them happen during the real thing!

REMEMBER

It should never be just you practicing as the host; it has to be a dry run of the entire event from start to finish. If you're using prerecorded videos or if you have multiple people presenting live, make sure that they're available to participate in a dry run to practice it.

Use this time to run through all the details. Double-check that everybody's audio and Internet connections work well, that everybody is using a microphone, that their sound quality is good, and that their video backgrounds are appropriate. You want to go through and check off all those different items that can potentially crop up on the day of the event and then come up with a plan for dealing with them.

In addition, you want your speakers and presenters to feel comfortable presenting, knowing that you have a good handle on all the many details and that you're leaving nothing to chance.

TIP

If your presenters are confident in your ability to host a great event, they'll be more likely to promote the event, to be excited about the event, and to show up as their best presenting selves.

If it's a webinar and it's just you, that's great. Practice all the different potential functions of the technology and your presentation so that you're familiar with the platform, the order of things, your script, and your presentation. Practice until it flows naturally for you. Though it won't eliminate the chance of anything going wrong, it helps minimize any potential mistakes, technical problems, and challenges.

REMEMBER

The goal is to minimize surprises, issues, and challenges that can go wrong during the virtual event. Mistakes and technical issues *will* happen.

The key is to practice and be ready to roll with them. The more you're prepared, the more you can adjust and then respond. Have a backup plan ready for what you'll do if anything goes awry.

Reading slides is for amateurs

When presenters read the slides, there's no extra context or insight that can be gained by attendees. It signals to them that they can just read the slides themselves and not have to spend that time there, at your event. It's a common complaint from attendees in any type of presentation.

Practice helps ensure that you and your presenters aren't just reading the slides. If you find yourself or your presenters reading away, ask them (or yourself) to put less text on the slide, or find out whether the slide is even necessary. The slides should be there to move the presentation along and provide a visual cue to you and to your audience members.

The Etiquette of Engaging the Audience

No one wants to listen to people talk on and on while they're just sitting there taking notes. It doesn't do anyone any good, and it's a surefire way to lose your audience. They'll become distracted and then start multitasking or hopping off your event or your webinar. So, you want to make sure that you and your presenters are providing valuable and engaging information.

TIP

One way to grab the attention of your audience is to tell stories that pull people in and tap into their emotions. You can create curiosity, ask questions, take polls, and even use contests to keep attendees engaged. (One strategy we like is to ask people to listen for the key phrase that would enter them into a specific offer. Another is to ask them to share their favorite take-aways on Twitter using the event hashtag (or share on Instagram) for a chance to win a prize).

The art of the Q&A session

One way to keep attendees engaged is to include a question-and-answer session during your presentation. Whether you're hosting a webinar or managing a pre-recorded or live event, you will likely want to include a live Q&A session with your presenters.

Q&A sessions can add a lot of engagement and value for the audience. It gives them the opportunity to learn how to apply the information in the session, clarify any confusion, and continue learning from the speaker.

TIP

People appreciate a live Q&A versus using a prerecorded session, because it allows them to ask their own questions. Consider allotting time for a live Q&A session at the end of your webinar or event.

If you're holding a Q&A session, you should make sure you have all the details taken care of to set up the audience and speakers for success. This means having backup questions ready to go for the speakers, in case questions don't come up right away. You can have questions ready to go by polling the audience about what they want to learn or by having them drop questions in the chat about what they learned and how they might apply the information.

When creating questions, you can also come up with ones based on the presentation topic or the speaker's background, and by targeting whatever they're working on now that's relevant to the target audience.

Another way to help encourage questions from the audience is to narrow the topic for them. Rather than ask, "Does anyone have any questions?" you can ask, "Does anyone have any questions about email marketing best practices?" or "Do you have any questions regarding CBD and cannabis marketing best practices?"

REMEMBER By adding more context and a better framing of the question, you can help draw people's curiosity into wanting to participate in the Q&A.

Post-event tips

Here's the thing: Once your webinar or virtual event is over, do take a moment to celebrate, but keep in mind that your work as a host is not done. Many event hosts miss this opportunity to continue building on the relationship and trust they have created. But not you! You know that there's a lot of opportunity you can take advantage of after you wrap up an event.

Following up with attendees (delivering on promises)

It starts with following up with attendees and delivering on any promises that were made during the event. If you promised resources or copies of the recording(s) or made any offers, this means it's time to deliver them immediately after the event.

The key is to follow up with attendees in a way that is meaningful and that continues to add value for them, helping to grow the relationship and deepen the connection you've made over the course of the event.

TIP For virtual events that might last longer than a few hours, you might consider creating a Facebook group or another opportunity for virtual networking during the event. Whether you offer a virtual happy hour or a speed networking opportunity, by encouraging connections and camaraderie, you can generate more excitement among attendees and help them build a community — with your event at the center of it. Suddenly, your event becomes something bigger in their mind, a catalyst for their business and community. It's a bigger deal.

All of this helps ensure that your audience is engaged and paying attention. Build on the experience of the event, leveraging what they learned so that you can build an emotional connection with attendees. It also shows them that you're serious about your goals and that you're not just using them to fill the seats for only that event and then dropping them. It shows your audience that you want to help them by adding value and a wealth of experiences they can live on, beyond the duration of the event.

Following up with people who missed the event

For the people who missed the event, make the recordings available for them. Many people sign up for events knowing that they can't attend, because they plan to watch the recordings later. Another way to help encourage them to watch the recordings is to charge for them, and/or make them available for a limited time.

REMEMBER

Leaving the recordings available for only a limited amount of time creates a sense of urgency. It signals to your audience that what you're doing is relevant and important — and that they've missed something big by not being there. Remind them of what they missed and use highlights to create FOMO around the event, to use the current vernacular. (FOMO is the *fear of missing out*.)

The Etiquette of Attending a Webinar or an Online Event

So, you've signed up for a webinar or an online event. Whatever the reason behind your decision, signing up is only the first step. To keep things on track, be sure to put the event on your calendar, and include the access information for the event if it's already available. Block the time and set reminders so that you don't miss it!

REMEMBER

Be sure to be prepared as a participant! Keep in mind your goals for attending, what you want to take-away from the event and why you're attending. Then make sure your login and equipment are working in advance. You don't want to be bugging the host to help you log in with 5 minutes to showtime — they are focusing on getting their whole event started.

Not sharing your login/registration information

If you've signed up or registered for a webinar or an online event, whether it was paid or free, don't share your login or registration information. Instead, have your friends, family, or colleagues sign up for their own access to the event.

There are a few reasons you should not share your own login. One is that companies and business owners put a lot of time and effort into creating these events. Despite this time and effort, often they ask for little more than your contact information, particularly for webinars. Even if they're charging for the event, a ton of work still goes into planning, creating, and delivering on the promises and the value you will receive as an attendee.

Another reason is that when you log in, you're logging in as yourself. So, if you're commenting or attending, you don't want other people commenting as you. It creates confusion, especially because networking can be a big part of online events. You'll lose out on making potential connections and confuse people if someone else is logging in as you with your registration information.

Asking questions in the chat box

If you're attending a webinar or a live event and you have the option to actively participate in the chat, use it to show up. There's nothing presenters like more than having an active chat going on while they're presenting, knowing that people are engaged and appreciate their content. It gives presenters immediate feedback into the value of their topic, such as whether it was confusing or clear, valuable or trivial, or created more questions or answered them. It also helps them create better content.

REMEMBER

For presenters and event hosts, any signals that an active chat sends are vitally important and appreciated. So be sure to ask questions and leave comments in the chat box!

Introducing yourself to others

Don't be afraid to introduce yourself to others. One of the things that a lot of people can do is make truly great connections. The fact is, you're attending this event or this webinar or virtual conference because there was something there that interested you. You can assume that the others in the audience have the same interest or need the same knowledge and might prove to be valuable connections.

TIP

If you're attending a multiple-day event, you'll likely see the same people throughout the event — speak up and introduce yourself! They might be someone who knows somebody who can either partner with you or become a new client, or they can end up being a resource and a support for your business or for your role. Don't hesitate to meet them and embrace that camaraderie.

Chatting with other attendees is easy — perhaps too easy. Keep in mind that the other attendees want to pay attention to the presenter and may get distracted by the chat. So, keep your chat content focused on the presentation topic and when (or if) you introduce yourself, keep it short and relevant to the topic at hand.

If it's your first time chatting online, make sure to introduce yourself before jumping into conversation. This way, people know who they're talking with and what expertise you bring!

REMEMBER

Keep in mind when chatting and introducing yourself that multiple conversations at a time are often happening in the chat. If everyone is introducing themselves at one time, it can cause confusion or overwhelm other attendees, so you might need to reintroduce yourself a few times.

Not hogging the conversation

There's nothing worse than going into an online event and having one person be the know-it-all or take up all the conversation and the chat box during networking events. So don't hog the conversation or be greedy with the chat. Instead, share the spotlight and remember why you're there — to make connections and to learn. Other attendees might have insights that can help you, or they might even be your perfect client or your newest perfect job opportunity. You don't want to annoy them by being the know-it-all person who left no room in the chat or on the microphone for them or for anyone else.

Not spamming

Don't spam. Seriously, just don't do it. There's nothing worse than going into someone else's well organized webinar or virtual event that they spent months planning, only to see somebody trying to sell or promote their services without any context or without telling people who they are.

REMEMBER

If you want to promote your product or your company or your business or your job, you need to create your own event. Don't try to spam everybody.

Staying engaged with the content

When you're attending a live event or a webinar, you want to stay engaged with the content and the presenters. You set aside the time to attend and the event host took the time to present their information, so it's worth it to stay engaged so that you can reach the goals you set by signing up in the first place. Learn as much as you can and — when you have a free moment — use that time to connect with others.

Ask questions, comment on any good points the speakers might have made, highlight valuable information, and take notes. In doing so, you can stay engaged and focused on the event — and on getting everything out of it you had hoped for.

TIP

Know your goals for signing up in the first place. Write down what you hope to get out of the event. Then make sure your schedule is clear and that your surroundings have minimal distractions to help you maintain your concentration.

REMEMBER

If there's a hashtag for the event, share it in your Instagram stories or on Twitter or anywhere on social media. Give that event some love if you walk away having learned from the speaker. Other people in your network want to know what resources they can trust. Speakers want to know that others consider their information to be valuable. This also sends a signal to the host that the event was worthwhile and that they should repeat it later.

Asking questions during Q&A time

If you're really into passivity, one thing you can do during the Q&A is sit and watch the poor speaker start squirming awkwardly because none of the attendees asks any questions.

Don't be that person. The speakers took the time to develop the presentation for you with content they thought would be beneficial, so help them know whether it is.

Showing up during the Q&A and asking questions sends signals that you found the information valuable. Ask questions! If there are topics they mentioned, processes they used, or data points you're curious about, ask them questions. How can you apply what you learned? What was relevant to you? Speakers love being asked questions, and you have this rare opportunity to learn from the experts themselves.

Take advantage of it.

Downloading any resources right away

If the event host invites you to submit an email address or provides a URL so that you can receive documents or any other supplemental materials, be sure to do so promptly. If resources are provided, access them immediately. The presenters and the hosts owe you nothing beyond making available to you the information they promised. They can make it available for 60 minutes or 60 days, but if it's information you want, make sure you grab it while it's available!

5

Mobile Mien

Recognize the importance of context when messaging

Play well in public with your phone

Use SMS and direct messaging apps correctly

» **Considering your recipient**

» **Recognizing the benefits of being brief**

Chapter **16**

Context in Messaging and SMS

Considering that many people now spend more time texting than talking on the phone, it's important to be aware of proper text messaging etiquette. Just like when you're speaking to someone face-to-face, there are certain things you shouldn't do when texting. If you do, you could wind up offending the other person or coming across as rude. Text messaging is a useful way to communicate with friends and family, but you should follow some etiquette rules.

Texting: The Better Way to Communicate

Texting and messaging are two of the most powerful communication tools you have. If done correctly, texting can improve social connections, assist individuals in dealing with painful situations, and bridge intergenerational gaps.

Texting can help improve social connections in many ways. For one, texting allows you to stay connected with people you may not see regularly. You might go months without seeing your friends, but you can still feel in touch because of texting. If your significant other is traveling for work, you can send short messages as reminders of your love and affection. You may not get together with friends as often as you might like, but text messages keep you engaged and make you feel part of the group.

Texting can also help you communicate with people you would usually be too shy to talk to in person. For example, if you're getting to know someone you're attracted to, communicating via text messages can take away a lot of the initial pressure.

You can also use texting to relay important, time-sensitive information. This information can include medical test results, appointment reminders, or breaking news. These text reminders are beneficial for both individuals and businesses to stay organized.

Texting is an easy way to communicate with someone who is busy or unavailable. You don't need to disrupt their schedule when you have a quick question or want to relay information. Texting allows you to do it with no inconvenience. You can also send photos, videos, links, and other attachments quickly and easily with no hassle, making texting an ideal communication tool for staying in touch, organizing outings, and receiving daily reminders.

REMEMBER

When it's hard to open up, starting a conversation via text can benefit your emotional and mental health. Studies have shown that text messaging helps people become more open with their feelings. It's beneficial when discussing complex topics where speaking face-to-face may hinder the expression of emotions. Thinking through and expressing what you're feeling via written text is a great way to communicate more clearly. You may find that you're open to being more vulnerable when using texting.

Texting allows you to communicate more effectively when speaking aloud might be inappropriate. For example, if you're in a meeting and need to ask a question quickly, sending a text is the discreet way to do it. Or, whenever you lack the time for a whole conversation but need some information, send a text. Just be sure not to get caught up in a full-on text conversation when you should be fully present in your current situation.

Nowadays, people rely on text messaging for a variety of reasons. For example, you might use text messaging to

>> Check-in with friends and family

>> Make plans with friends

>> Obtain directions or advice from a friend

>> Send a quick hello or goodbye message

>> Communicate when you can't talk on the phone

Text messaging provides a quick and convenient way to communicate with friends and family. Before texting showed up, you would need to call someone to ask for simple things that today don't need a call. Text messaging allows people to keep in touch in ways that, in the past, weren't possible. Although texting has a reputation for being short and impersonal, it does help you stay connected. It can deepen relationships and open doors to possibilities in your life.

Because text messages are usually read right away, they make for an excellent form of communication when immediate responses are necessary. Most people check and respond to text messages faster than any other form of communication. Rather than wait for an email response, you can trust that your text message will be received and you will generally get a prompt response — which is especially helpful when making plans with someone or coordinating an event.

In a world where people are busier than ever, text messages offer a way for people to stay connected without having to take the time out of their day to have a conversation. These quick and sometimes meaningful messages can help deepen connections with others. You can send short-and-sweet notes that show you're thinking of the person, and they can do the same for you. It may be a more casual form of communication, but text messaging has proven to be one of the best ways to stay in touch with those we can't see every day.

Texting isn't just for personal use, either. Companies are using text messages to cut costs and help shorten the sales cycle. Because text message marketing is inexpensive and sees such high open-and-engagement rates, it's easy to see why more and more companies are using it. From marketing to informational notifications, text messaging can be a powerful tool for businesses of all sizes.

TECHNICAL STUFF

An *open* rate is a marketing metric that measure the percentage rate at which emails, messages, and text messages are opened by their recipients. An *engagement* rate tracks how engaged your audiences is in terms of clicks, responses, and taking action.

TIP

Text messages lend themselves especially well to lead generation. Marketers can send out promotional offers via SMS to anyone who has opted in via an online form or API integration. As a result, businesses can see a higher conversion rate from SMS campaigns when compared to email or social media.

Besides marketing, companies use texting for a variety of other purposes within businesses. For example, they can be used as a communication tool for internal notifications and alerts. This can help reduce the need for employees to check multiple channels throughout the day, which means that critical updates are sent out quickly and efficiently. Companies are also using text messages for alerts related to IT security, such as data loss prevention.

In the non-profit space, text messaging is used to get more donations with Text to Donate campaigns or to keep donors updated on announcements and events.

Text messaging is even appropriate for customer service representatives (CSRs). During the sales process, reps can send customers helpful tips or recommended products that will help move them along. Additionally, CSRs can use text messages to follow up on outstanding requests or provide better support. When used correctly, text messaging can be a powerful tool for businesses of all sizes.

REMEMBER

Be sure to obtain consent from your recipients before sending them any marketing messages. Also, make sure your messages are short and to the point — people are more likely to read a text message that is fewer than 200 characters long. Finally, always include the option to unsubscribe from your messages when in doubt. You can add unsubscribe features in the message itself or via a link in the body of the message.

Overall, text messaging is a great way to keep in touch with people when you can't talk on the phone. Just be sure to use common sense and etiquette when sending or receiving texts.

Putting Yourself in the Recipient's Shoes

You might not think it necessary to use proper text etiquette, but if you consider that someone is taking the time out of their day to read your message and that text messages are easily misinterpreted, you'll probably start to see the importance of being polite. After all, just because there's a screen between you and the person you're texting doesn't mean they can't see your bad habits!

The first step in practicing good text etiquette is to put yourself in the recipient's shoes. This means thinking about how they might interpret your message. For example, if you're asking a question, use a question mark so that the recipient knows you're expecting a response. If you're making a request, be specific and polite. For example, "Could you please pick up some milk on your way home?" is better than "Pick up milk!" Though brevity is essential, you also need to convey the right tone when you text. Just like when you're speaking to someone face-to-face, you should try to imagine what the other person might be thinking or how they might react to your message.

Also, consider the individual you're texting. Although texting and private messaging have become the preferred way to communicate across most generations, each generation uses text differently. Millennials generally enjoy long text messaging strings back and forth, whereas Boomers prefer short-and-sweet text messages to answer questions quickly. Older generations are unlikely to want to have a full back-and-forth conversation over text message — they would much rather speak on the phone. So, it's always advantageous to consider whom you're texting and then adjust your communication style accordingly.

The next step in practicing good text etiquette is to be aware of your tone. Just like when you're speaking to someone, your tone can be easily misinterpreted when texting. Avoid sarcasm or irony in your messages, because they're often lost in translation. (I tell you more about tone a bit later.)

When you're texting or having a conversation via text, always try to ask yourself, "What if I were the other person? Would I feel offended by this message?" If you think the topic is too sensitive or might easily upset the recipient, it may be best to hold off on a text. Instead, you might consider giving them a call or writing them a longer email.

REMEMBER

There is a medium for just about every kind of communication out there, so it's just as important to know when text is best as it is to know how to do it the right way. Sometimes, an email, a call, or a face-to-face conversation is the way to go.

Considering the Context

Another rule of etiquette to remember is to think about the context before you text. Because it establishes what you're talking about and whom you're sending the message to, context is crucial in text messaging. You can convey context via time, location, topic, tone of the message, relationship with the recipient, or even punctuation. In other words, consider what you're texting about and who will receive it. For example, you might not want to text someone about a personal topic if you don't know them that well. And you should never send a text message when you're angry — it's better to wait until you've calmed down before sending anything.

TIP

There is a definitely a time and a place for text messaging — text messaging is more convenient for communicating short messages and thoughts. Nevertheless, it may not be the ideal platform for deeper talks, sensitive topics, or situations where the recipient might misinterpret a message's tone. Again, it all comes down to your relationship with the person you're texting.

REMEMBER

Different occasions call for varying levels of formality. For example, you wouldn't want to text someone about a family emergency at 2 A.M., even though it would be appropriate during regular waking hours. Calling is always better than texting in high-stress situations such as emergencies because the tone of your voice can relay information that a text message cannot.

Text messaging etiquette also includes knowing your relationship with the recipient of your message. It's important to understand what kind of relationship you and your recipient have and what level of conversation they usually engage in before deciding whom you should text, how often, and the tone of your text.

Another consideration with context is understanding that your text recipient may not know the backstory of what you're sharing. That means sending a message that doesn't convey the backstory or context can confuse the recipient. Forwarding a message or screen shot you received that may have upset you but not explaining why you're delivering the message can put the recipient in an awkward situation. Never assume that your recipient knows the full context of your messages. Make messages easy to understand, and if further explanation is needed to establish context, be sure to provide it, to make the text string easier to follow.

Noting the Importance of Tone When Texting

Have you ever been in a situation where you're texting someone and you're unsure how to respond because the tone of their text is ambiguous? In a world where communication often takes place via text, it's essential to be aware of your tone when typing out your messages.

When it comes to text messaging, you should know what *tone* means. The *tone* is how the words sound when you say them. If you want to be sure that someone understands what you're saying, make sure they know your tone. The tone is essential in text messaging because it can often be misinterpreted. As we mention earlier in this chapter, sarcasm and irony are often lost in translation and can easily offend the recipient if they're not aware of your tone. So, even though you may be joking, the other person may not see it that way and might take offense. Not everyone has the same text tone or language, so knowing how certain words and phrases are perceived is important.

One way to make sure your tone is correctly interpreted is by using emoticons and emojis. These symbols help to convey the style of your message and help you avoid any misunderstandings. When used correctly, they can help explain how you're feeling or what your intended message is. However, just beware that some people don't use or understand emoticons, so they should never be the main strategy you rely on to convey your tone.

REMEMBER

It's important to use emojis and emoticons with caution when you don't know the person well. They come across as too informal in specific contexts and can be considered unprofessional if misused or overused.

The punctuation you use can also help convey your tone. For example, using capital letters and exclamation points can help express that you're angry or excited about what you're saying. Using periods can help convey that you're being serious. Younger generations, however, see the final period (one at the end of your message) as rude because it means that you're being short with them or too final in your discussion.

REMEMBER

USING ALL CAPS IS THE SAME AS YELLING, and it's considered horribly rude. If you're typing while you're angry, try to use all caps and exclamation points in moderation.

It's also important to be mindful of your tone when responding to someone else's text. If their message is sad and you reply with a joke, it may not be the best thing to do, because it can come across as insensitive.

Tone can also be conveyed by the promptness the two parties use when communicating. If someone types back slowly, they might not be interested in continuing the conversation or understanding what you're saying. On the other hand, if someone types back quickly, it might mean that they're excited about the conversation or in a hurry.

REMEMBER

When it comes to text messaging, always be aware of your tone when typing out your messages. Not everyone has the same text tone or language, so knowing how certain words and phrases are perceived is important. Even though we can't hear the tone of someone's voice when we're texting, it's still possible to convey how we're feeling through our words. Just make sure your text tone is clear to the recipient, to avoid any misunderstandings.

Being Brief but Clear

Texting is a great way to communicate when you need to be brief. You can send short messages that don't require a lot of response, which is perfect when you're in a hurry or trying to avoid distractions. But just because it's easy to be brief doesn't mean you should sacrifice clarity. Remember that the person on the other end can't see your facial expressions or hear the tone of your voice, so it's essential to be as straightforward as possible.

Here are a few tips for being brief but clear when text messaging:

>> **Use proper grammar and spelling.** The use of proper grammar and spelling may seem like a no-brainer, but it's important to remember that poor grammar and spelling can be confusing and frustrating. Don't rely on autocorrect to fix your spelling for you — doing so has been known to create some *awkward* mistakes. If you make a mistake, let the other person know about the error and then retype your message correctly.

>> **Give context clues when necessary.** If your texts are part of a conversation where previous messages have been sent, be sure to include the relevant information in your reply. Providing this needed context helps keep the conversation flowing and avoids confusion.

>> **Use abbreviations sparingly.** Though it's acceptable to use abbreviations for common phrases (*See you later* can be shortened to *CUL8R* and *Laugh out loud* is commonly abbreviated to *LOL*), using too many abbreviations can be confusing. Try to use abbreviations sparingly and only when they make sense in the context of your conversation. Though texting may encourage the use of abbreviations or acronyms, your recipient must know precisely what you're saying. When abbreviations aren't appropriate, take a quick second to spell out your whole thought so that there's no confusion. Unless you're messaging someone who regularly uses and understands text shorthand, it's best to use them sparingly or avoid them altogether.

>> **Use short, simple sentences.** When possible, try to stick to one or two clauses per sentence. Shorter text strings make your message easier to read and understand. Text messages that hold a single thought at a time also allow your recipient the opportunity to respond to a single idea or topic. So, rather than say

"Where should we meet? Are you still at work?"

try this:

"Up for grabbing dinner later?"

Once the recipient responds to the first question, it's acceptable to ask the next question.

Once the recipient responds to the first question, it's acceptable to ask the next question.

>> **Use emoticons judiciously.** Though emoticons are helpful for adding some color to your texts and are even helpful in conveying tonality, don't go overboard! You want to use them sparingly so that they remain effective and meaningful. If you're sending five or more in a row, you might want to reconsider your message. The overuse of emojis and emoticons can also be confusing and frustrating, so use them wisely.

Avoiding Miscommunication with Others

Avoiding miscommunication via text messaging may take some practice until it becomes second nature, but the benefits of an accurate and clear message far outweigh any perceived effort. When communicating via text message with someone you're unfamiliar with or have never met in person, it's important to be on your best behavior. Many people read into the tone of a text message and can often be offended by something not meant to be hurtful.

To avoid misunderstandings, always remember to be clear and concise and to use proper grammar. If you're unsure about the tone of your text message, it's best to err on the side of caution and refrain from sending it. Until you have had a chance to clarify things in person, remember that there's a big difference between what you mean and what the other person may infer.

Knowing your audience is also vital. If you're close friends with the person you're texting, you can be less formal and more playful. However, if you're messaging someone for the first time or someone you don't know well, it's always best to err on the side of caution and maintain a more formal or professional tone.

Being More Mindful of What You're Typing

Being more mindful of what you're typing when texting helps you avoid miscommunication and unnecessary drama. Sometimes messages can be misinterpreted when they're sent in a text. Because text lacks many of the social signals that are supplied when people speak face-to-face — such as tone of voice, laughter, and body language — it's essential to take the time to think about what you want to say before hitting Send.

Longer-form written communications benefit from having longer written-out thoughts, helping to convey an idea more clearly. However, text messaging is short and generally contains slang and abbreviations. With shorter messages comes the greater chance of misunderstandings or misinterpretations of intention.

One approach for avoiding these misunderstandings is to stop and consider anything you're saying that might be misconstrued. Stopping and rereading your message before pressing Send might help clear up any possible confusion. If you've gotten into the habit of sending messages without thinking, this method might feel cumbersome at first — but it becomes easier with time and practice.

REMEMBER

Taking a pause when sending messages is even more critical when you're angry. It's easy to take a bad situation and make it far worse by sending text messages while angry. If you're feeling angry, take a break from your phone and wait until you've calmed down before sending anything. This break helps to ensure that your messages are clear and free of emotion-based typos and misinterpretations.

When it comes to a sensitive issue or subject matter that can be easily misunderstood, take special care when constructing your messages and pause for a minute to reassess what you're writing. Using emojis to deliver your message can be beneficial if you believe you're on delicate ground. And, as always, if the topic is better communicated via other means, choose the medium that best fits the situation. Sometimes, text is not the best way to go.

REMEMBER

Being mindful of your words isn't just about avoiding drama — it can also prevent you from hurting someone's feelings or even misrepresenting yourself. As with face-to-face communication, some things are better left unsaid when messaging someone.

Chapter **17**

No One Wants to Hear Your Phone

We've all been there — you're in a meeting or out to dinner with friends and you can't help but check your phone every few minutes. Though it's easy to get caught up in the world of phone notifications, it's important to remember that using your phone in public can be seen as rude. In this chapter, we explain the proper etiquette for using your phone around others and offer some tips for breaking the habit of constant phone-checking. Are you ready to put down your phone and focus on the present? Let's get started!

Following Etiquette When Using Your Phone in Public

There is absolutely nothing wrong with using your phone in public. However, it can be pretty bothersome to others if you don't follow certain rules. Rule 1: If you're in a public space, you need to respect your people. This means keeping your phone calls to a minimum, keeping your voice volume low when you talk on the phone, and silencing the ringer and notifications to avoid annoying the people around you.

The world is becoming more and more digitized with technology. More people own a smartphone, which means that more people can check every email, text notification, and social media post that comes their way. This leads to phones being used at nearly every opportunity — in line at the grocery store, for example, or waiting for an appointment. Though it's perfectly acceptable to use your phone in these situations, there are a few things you can do to be courteous of the people around you or the people who are with you. The next several sections fill you in on the details.

Deciding when to pick up (and when to put down) your phone

It isn't easy to imagine life before cellphones. Today, we use our phones for everything from communicating via text to messaging to making calls to browsing the Internet and, in some cases, running an entire business from the palm of our hands. But when you're using your phone around people, it's essential to remember that the sound of notifications or your conversations in a public space can be distracting and downright annoying.

The way you use your phone in public has a lot to do with what others think of you. Some people consider it rude, depending on the situation and how you do it. The difference between being perceived as respectful and not is often just one little detail — like putting your phone on Silent or looking up from it when talking to others. If you're meeting someone for business, *put away your phone* — otherwise, you might look unprofessional. When riding public transit or sitting in a cafe, respect that you're in a shared space and adjust your phone use accordingly. Whether at dinner with a loved one or ordering coffee from a barista, put your phone away and focus on the present. Being respectful and considerate of those around you shows that they're worth your time.

Is it ever okay to use your phone in public? In most cases, people enjoy some time without being interrupted by technology when they have a chance to socialize. And generally, the public doesn't care to hear your conversations or the clicking of your keyboard. But there are a few times when it's acceptable — and even expected — to use your phone in public. For example, if you're waiting in line, it's perfectly fine to use your phone to kill time. You can also check your phone if you're expecting an important call. Just make sure that, if you do use your phone in public, it's set to Vibrate mode or Silent mode and refrain from using the speakerphone or FaceTime or another video calling feature without headphones while in public spaces.

Your use of your phone in public is not just about the people you're with but also about the other people in the public space. Remember that they can hear and see what you're doing, so inappropriately using your phone can reflect poorly on you and serve to disrespect your fellow humans.

REMEMBER

Though texting has a significant number of benefits, it's also worth noting that sometimes it would be considered not only rude but also dangerous to text. For instance, texting while driving should be avoided at all costs. It's not only illegal but also incredibly dangerous. According to the National Highway Traffic Safety Administration (NHTSA), texting while driving is six times more dangerous than driving under the influence of alcohol.

Walking and texting can also be considered a no-no. Not only is it dangerous but other people may also get irritated by you bumping into them. Additionally, if you're traveling in an area where you face a potential danger, it's best always to be fully alert to your surroundings and not be distracted by your phone. Anytime you're distracted in a way that may be dangerous to you or the people around you, it's best to put away your phone.

Keeping the conversation going (and keeping your phone in your pocket)

Don't let your phone get in the way of enjoying time with friends or family! When you spend too much time on your phone, it sends the message that you would rather spend time alone than with the person you're with. This can hurt their feelings and make them feel like you don't care about them.

It's inappropriate to text while someone is talking with you. When you're face-to-face with someone, it's an excellent time to turn off your notifications and put your phone away. When gathering with friends, having a meal with your family, or having fun on a date, you should put away your phone and be present in the moment. If you have to check your phone or you're expecting an important call, be sure to apologize to the person you're with before responding to a text or picking up a call. Keep these occurrences to a minimum to avoid upsetting the person with whom you're speaking. Nothing makes a person feel less important faster than you interrupting the conversation to answer your phone. In general, it's okay to check your phone intermittently if you have to, but do try to keep your attention on the people you're with.

Turning off notifications to avoid distractions

Notifications are useful for keeping you in the know, but they can also be distracting. Notifications influence your ability to focus on tasks and drain your energy and create unnecessary stress. It's best to limit or completely turn off notifications to focus on your work and reduce distractions.

The benefits of turning off notifications go further than just showing consideration for others around you. Constant notifications can be bad for your mental health, making you feel like you're always "on" and making it hard to disconnect from the online noise and distraction. Completely removing or silencing notifications from the apps on your phones can significantly improve your focus and reduce stress. This is especially true with social media platform notifications, which foster an addictive response to the apps.

All phones have settings for limiting notifications, blocking calls, and scheduling times for Do Not Disturb (described after the following step list). You can do this in a few ways.

On an iPhone:

1. **Go to Settings.**

2. **Select Notifications.**

3. **Select the app you want manage.**

4. **Toggle the Allow Notifications option.**

   If on, select your notification style or set Allow Notifications to off. (You can also turn off vibrations and sound alerts.)

On an Android phone:

1. **Go to Settings.**

2. **Tap Notifications.**

3. **Select an app and turn off the Allow Notifications switch.**

   Feel free to pick and choose which apps you want to receive notifications from, but it's best to shut off the sound for all notifications, especially while you're in public spaces.

Outside of managing your notifications, there are other ways to reduce annoying phone noises while out in public or when you need to focus. If you're out with friends, in an important business meeting, or on a date, consider setting up Do Not Disturb on your phone. This feature blocks all calls and notifications from sounding on your phone when it's set. Most people already have Do Not Disturb set up for when they're sleeping, but you can set up different Do Not Disturb schedules for specific times of day or days of the week. You can even create notifications or exceptions for specific people. For example, when you're in a meeting, you might want to block all notifications except for calls from your boss. Or, if you're on a date but want to be sure you don't miss any calls from your babysitter, you can create an exception to have your phone ring from that specific person. Having these settings in place allows you to confidently put down your phone, knowing that you won't miss essential calls.

REMEMBER

Treat your companion and yourself with more respect and manage your notifications to benefit everyone.

Realizing that the world doesn't need to see or hear your conversation

Before taking a call, consider what the people around you are doing. It's essential to remember that others around you probably don't want to hear or see your conversation in public spaces. Keep in mind that if you're in a public area, you cannot expect the people around you to give you privacy or leave that space because you want to talk on the phone. If people are trying to work, having conversations with friends, or enjoying a meal, talking on the phone can be downright disruptive.

REMEMBER

People can see and hear you when you're on your phone in public, so act accordingly. Be considerate of those around you by keeping your voice down and not having long, drawn-out conversations.

If you must take a call in public, try not to have deeply personal conversations on the phone or even on video calls where people can see you. For example, you might not want to have a conversation about your medical history in a busy public place. Use headphones to help keep the sound at a minimum, and make sure the topic you're discussing and the language you're using is considered safe for all ears. Profanity and emotional outbursts are not things you want to be seen or heard by other people.

If you're ever in doubt whether something is appropriate to say or discuss on your phone, it's okay to politely let the person on the other end of the line know that you're in a public space so that they're aware that not all topics are best discussed aloud.

TIP

Whenever possible, take phone calls outside of public spaces or into an area that's more private. You should avoid taking calls in confined spaces, restaurants, theaters, and other places where silence or lower volumes are expected.

Though having phone conversations in public isn't always avoidable, there are ways to make it less disruptive for those around you. Follow these general tips and be conscious of your surroundings, and you'll be sure to have a more pleasant phone experience when out and about.

Keeping other phone uses in mind

Phone etiquette while in public goes further than just managing your calls and text messages. The way you use your phones or even tablets in public spaces is also important.

Music, movies, and games can be fun to pass the time or unwind, but never forget that others might not want to hear your entertainment or see the brightness of your screen. When watching movies on your phone or tablet, try not to use the speaker function. Instead, opt for headphones. Also, be sure that the games and movies on your screen are appropriate for any eyes that may see what you're watching. The last thing you want to do is watch an R-rated movie while a small child looks on from an airplane seat or table behind you.

If you enjoy your music loud, be sure that the sound isn't leaking into the public space, even with headphones on. You may enjoy your music; others may not. Keep the volume at a level that doesn't interfere with others.

Also, if you're in a dark space, like an airplane at night, dim the screen to an appropriate brightness. If you're in a theatre, don't even think of keeping your screen up; shut it off altogether. As they say in the movie industry, "Silence is golden," but darkness is also golden when the people around you are trying to enjoy a show. Respect the people around you by knowing why people are gathered in that space. A movie theater, live play production, or fancy restaurant aren't appropriate places for your phone, even if they're set to Silent or you're using headphones.

Another critical consideration is the keyboard sounds your phone makes. If you're in public, make sure your keyboard is also set to Silent. The people around you don't need to hear the click-click-clicking of you typing a text to a friend or searching for directions on Google. A quick fix for turning off the clicking sound of your keyword is to put your phone on Vibrate. But you can also control the sounds in your phone's settings.

TAKING VIDEO AND PHOTOS WITHOUT PERMISSION

Though taking pictures and videos of people without their permission might not seem like a big deal, it can be pretty intrusive and even embarrassing for the person being photographed or filmed.

Keep a few guidelines in mind if you want to take a picture or video of someone. First, always ask for permission before filming or photographing someone, especially minors who aren't your own. Many people get upset when they discover that the photos or videos you have of them were taken without their permission.

Always assume that someone does *not* want to be photographed or filmed. Don't take pictures at sensitive times, like during personal conversations, medical treatments, funerals, weddings, or other special occasions where people are trying to make emotional connections. This is especially true if a professional photographer has been hired to document the occasion, because your use of flash photography or trying to capture the proper angle can mess up the efforts of the professional. And let me tell you, you don't want to be the one who messed up the professional photos of a bride's wedding! If you're taking pictures at parties, events, or even concerts, always check the rules set by the venue or organizer. Often, shooting videos and taking photos are off-limits at large public venues. When in doubt, ask.

If you're taking photos for business use, there may be some legal risks you need to consider. For this reason, it's even more important that you not only ask permission but also obtain written consent, by having people sign a photo release. Make sure you keep for your records a copy of the document signed by the person. It may seem cumbersome, especially if you have a lot of people in your video or photo shoot, but having this documentation can save you from legal troubles down the line. In addition, never take photos or videos of children without the consent of their parent. Some parents have become upset when their child's photo turned up on a company website without their being notified and asking for permission first.

Dealing with the Poor Etiquette of Others

Nothing is more annoying than having your meal or an intimate meeting of friends interrupted by someone nearby talking loudly on their phone. Phone use has become such second nature that people often don't consider how they might be disrupting others when they make or receive a call in public.

It's no secret that people often use their phones in public settings, but what should you do if someone is using their phone and it's causing a disturbance?

The way you handle a situation like this one depends significantly on your relationship or lack thereof with the etiquette offender. When the offender is a friend or an acquaintance, it might be best to remind them of the situation tactfully. For example, you might say, "I'm sorry to interrupt, but would you mind taking your call elsewhere?" Or, if the person is somebody close to you that you're meeting with and they take a call or are constantly texting on their phone, you can wait until they're done and explain to them how it makes you feel when they use their phone right in front of you. Often, our loved ones don't know how we feel until we tell them.

If the offender is a stranger, the way you handle the situation is quite different. The first thing you might attempt is to ignore the offense and hope they finish their call quickly. If they carry on with the disruptive behavior, asking them politely to stop can sometimes work (although it depends on the individual). When you approach a stranger about their behavior, be as kind and empathetic as possible. Make sure to say please and thank you. Politeness goes a long way in defusing confrontations. Often, the person doesn't realize that they're being a disturbance or they just haven't thought about their actions.

If, after you have asked politely, the person doesn't stop, your next step should be to move away from them. Moving farther away lessens the distraction for you and helps create some distance, and hopefully, the person gets the hint. If the problem persists, it might be time to seek assistance from an outside authority or employee.

REMEMBER Never take any action that might lead to an altercation no matter what you do. Remaining calm and collected is the key to handling these types of situations.

Sometimes, when you're in public and someone is breaking the phone etiquette rules, there isn't much you can do. In these instances, take a deep breath and shrug it off. You'll feel better knowing that you were the bigger person and didn't resort to poor phone etiquette yourself.

Remember that, like most things in life, you learn from your mistakes and grow from your experiences. Everyone can start now, by learning to be more aware of those around them when using a cellphone in public places.

Knowing When It's Time to Take a Break from Your Smartphone

It's easy to get lost in the virtual world of electronics, but there are many benefits to taking a break. People spend most of their waking hours staring at screens — scrolling social media on the phone, working on a computer, watching TV — you name it. But all those hours spent staring at screens have been shown to have some severe consequences. Studies show that spending too much time on the computer or in front of a screen can lead to mental fatigue, eyestrain, neck pain, and carpal tunnel syndrome — and that's just for starters. What's more, spending lots of time hunched over a screen leaves you with poor posture and increases your chance of developing chronic back problems later in life. Add to that the mental health issues that can arise from the pressures of being present on social networks and it's easy to see how one can really suffer. So, what can you do?

Every once in a while, you have to take a break. Don't worry — it doesn't mean that you have to pack up your electronics and head into the wilderness to live off the grid. It just means that you need to set some boundaries for yourself regarding screen time. Here are some helpful tips on how to take a break:

>> **Set time limits.** Decide how long you're going to spend on your electronics each day and stick to it. It's also a good idea to take a break every 30 to 60 minutes. Just as you shouldn't spend all day doing just one task, make sure you aren't looking at the screen for hours on end, either. Use the built-in time limit settings in your phone or download an app that will keep tabs on your usage and prevent overuse.

>> **Turn your phone's display to grayscale.** You might be surprised to learn that removing all colors from the screen is a more effective deterrent than you think. Apps, games, and social media platforms are designed specifically to keep you logged in and active. They do this via colors, notifications, and sounds. By turning your phone to grayscale, you'll find these platforms less interesting and thus less addictive. An added benefit of grayscale is that it's easier on your eyes, making this a great way to cut back on time on your electronics. You can even set timers to turn on grayscale mode at specific times of the day or after a certain amount of usage time has been used.

>> **Turn off app notifications.** This is a truly helpful way to decrease the frequency of your picking up your phone. You don't need to know whenever someone liked your post or commented on your photo. If you can, try disabling all notifications for social media and other apps on your phone. This way, you can check in on them when you have time rather than be continually interrupted.

Disconnecting from the Internet altogether might not be possible or desirable for you, but there are ways to reduce your online presence. One way is to delete the app from your phone. If you don't have the app, you can't check it. This is a drastic measure, but if you find yourself compulsively checking an app, it might be worth it. This is especially helpful if your use of a specific app or platform is causing you mental duress. If you're dealing with negative emotions, trolls, or overall exhaustion, these are all signs it's time to delete some apps.

TIP

Have some perspective. Take a walk, go to dinner, or leave your pocket or at home altogether. Believe it or not, not so long ago, people didn't always have to be connected to technology. And with the right amount of self-control and the help of your phone settings, you can enjoy a nice balance in your life.

Telecommuting and the Phone Etiquette That Comes Along with It

Telecommuting is becoming more and more popular in today's world. The advantages of working from home include not having to spend time commuting, the opportunity to set your own hours, and increased productivity. However, with these benefits come some phone etiquette rules that should be followed when speaking on the phone while you or your employees are at home. It is easy for personal life and work lifelines to be blurred when telecommuting — though telecommuting affords you more flexibility on where and when you work. There are many issues to take into consideration.

Your first order of business should be an office setup. Though you can work from anywhere, your employer probably prefers that you have a designated workplace. It should not only be free from distractions but also include the necessary equipment to continue working. Without an office, you may find yourself having trouble concentrating, dealing with unnecessary and noisy distractions, or giving in to temptations for procrastination. Your home office should include a desk or table that can be seen by anyone who walks into the room. This serves as an immediate reminder that you are working and aren't available for idle chitchat.

Set up in a quiet place where you won't be interrupted. You should have a dedicated phone line for work calls so that you can use the proper etiquette when answering work-related calls, and your personal lines and business lines do not mix. The line should be as free as possible from noise, and it is off limits for anyone but yourself.

To be successful at telecommuting, you need to know some telephone etiquette rules. The first rule of thumb is that if someone calls you at your office or home on a work-related matter, answer the phone only during working hours. You might be tempted to give in, but the important thing is that if you're not working, don't act like it. Setting proper expectations for when you can be reached, and personal boundaries for when you should be working, will help you avoid blurring the lines too frequently.

When you answer the phone, eliminate any distractions and noise. Close your office door and turn off any noise or distractions. You want to make sure it's just you and the person on the other end of the phone. If you're in a public space, such as a co-working space or shared office, use an appropriate volume when you speak, so as not to distract other workers.

REMEMBER

Never take a work call in the bathroom. Also, you should limit personal phone calls to lunch or break times and respect your colleagues' time by not calling or texting outside of working hours.

If you have employees telecommuting, establish some ground rules for phone etiquette. Just as you would expect them to be respectful of your time, you should be respectful of theirs. So, make sure to call or text only at appropriate work hours in the day. Ensure that they know any policies you have in place for taking calls during work hours and answer any questions they might have. You set the tone and the rules for your company, so you set a good example.

Telecommuting can be a great way to have more flexibility in your work schedule, but with that flexibility comes some responsibility. By following these simple phone etiquette rules, you can ensure that your work-life balance remains intact, and you can continue to be successful at telecommuting.

Chapter **18**

When and How to Use Text Messaging SMS

S MS etiquette is all about timing and appropriateness. When used correctly, SMS can be a powerful communication tool. It allows you to find fast answers and have short communication strings with someone you need to share with. But when misused, it can lead to annoyed friends and blocked numbers. In this chapter, we help you use SMS in the most effective way possible so that you can take advantage of all that this technology has to offer — without causing any harm or misunderstandings.

One-to-One Text Messaging

Texting someone for the first time can be a daunting experience. What do you say? How do you introduce yourself? And what should you avoid at all costs? We help you explore ways to navigate the intricate maze of one-to-one text messaging.

Introducing yourself properly

The first time you text-message someone you just met or aren't close to in real life, it's imperative that you begin the conversation with a proper introduction. Start by sending a simple, friendly greeting that includes your name and a little context on where they know you from or what you're texting them about. Remember that the recipient may not have your name stored in their phone and thus may not know who is on the other side of the text message.

Examples: "Hi, this is Jen! We met at the picnic yesterday?" or "Hello, this is John, Mary's dad. Our children are in kindergarten together."

Try to avoid assuming that the receiver knows who you are right off the bat. Avoid initial text messages such as this one: "Hey, how are you?" A vague greeting can be off-putting when someone doesn't recognize the number. Be clear from the start — no one wants to have to ask "Who dis?"

Secondly, it's helpful if you state the purpose of your text message. This ensures that the receiver knows what you're referring to and doesn't mistake a simple text message for something it is not. Plus, it sets the right tone immediately. Examples: "Hi, this is Samantha. Do you still have my jacket?" or "Hi, Jan. This is Bob. Did you drop off those files at Jim's office?"

Notice in these examples the texter introduced themselves, gave context, and got right to the point. It's also important to keep the initial text message short. You're not yet on a level where you can have a long conversation with someone using only text messages, so it's essential to convey your information at a reasonable length during this initial encounter. In other words, don't just do a word-dump in the first text message when this is your first time corresponding with this individual over SMS text message.

And last but not least, be sure to send the first text message on a positive note. Politely thanking the other person or letting them know you're looking forward to connecting more often are great ways to close the text conversation on the first go-round. Closing out your conversation with a pleasant tone leaves the receiver eager to continue texting with you further in the future.

REMEMBER

Do not cut off communication abruptly after your first text exchange. Instead, build on it with several follow-up messages before it ends.

It's easy to write off an initial text message as unimportant and not give it your full attention. Try not to do this. The receiver will note how you treat their initial communication, and that perception will carry over into any future interactions. In other words, you can leave a great first impression by simply conveying a little information and being courteous.

Responding in a timely manner

Text messages, unlike phone calls, allow you to send and receive responses at your convenience. This isn't inherently bad, but it can lead to misunderstandings and frustration if not done correctly.

People use text messaging on their phones when they're on the go, studying for an exam, and even while they're busy multitasking other activities. Quick responses are best when it comes to SMS communication. Avoid making the other person feel that their messages aren't as important to you. Respond to them immediately, even if it's just a quick acknowledgment of their message. Understandably, you can't always engage in a back-and-forth manner, but a simple acknowledgment can go a long way. It can be as simple as saying, "I'm sorry, I'm in the middle of something. I'll get back to you soon" or "I can't text much right now. Can I call you when I'm done?" Both are good ways to assure the person that you have received their initial text message and cannot respond at this time.

REMEMBER

Though you aren't obligated to respond right away to every message sent to you, if it's important, try to get back to the sender as soon as possible. And, at the very least, acknowledge the message when it comes in so that you don't leave the sender hanging. Also keep in mind that if you choose to ignore the text for now, you may forget to respond later, when you have more time. This has been known to put a strain on relationships and can come off as downright rude. That's why you should at least let the other person know you'll get back to them soon. People are understanding as long as you're straightforward with them. Otherwise, they may think you're *ghosting* them — ignoring them intentionally, in other words.

To text or not to text

Although there is definitely a time and a place for using SMS text messaging as a communication vehicle, it's equally true that sometimes it can be considered rude or even dangerous to text. For example, if you're driving and trying to text someone, that's pretty much the epitome of being unsafe. If you're crossing a street, walking around other people, or otherwise distracted by your phone, people around you have every right to be annoyed. In some instances, you might be having dinner or drinks with someone on a date and you're tempted to text in the middle of it. This is a big no-no because it shows a lack of respect for the person you're with.

There are also times when the medium of SMS text messaging isn't necessarily the best way to communicate. If you need to convey a lengthy and important message, for example, it would be best to do so in a voice call or email. On the other hand, if you're looking to make plans for a last-minute outing with friends or want to convey something in smaller bits of information, text messaging can be an effective way to keep your messages brief.

Texting when you're angry or upset about something should also be avoided, unless you're prepared to handle the consequences of saying something you can't take back or a message that may be misinterpreted. We recommend that, if you find yourself tempted to text while angry, just step away for a while, breathe, and formulate a more appropriate message. Once a text is sent, it can no longer be taken back; its information is out in the world after it leaves your device.

REMEMBER

Your text messages can come back to haunt you or be misinterpreted if they're sent in haste or anger. If you wouldn't be okay with what you've said becoming public knowledge, it's best not to say it via text message.

Texting can be used to express feelings healthily, but only if you think about what you send and when. Knowing when to communicate via text message and when not to allows you to have more effective conversations with your friends, family members, teachers, or anyone else who may be in your daily life. Just remember the golden rule of texting: Think before you text, compose yourself accordingly, and all will be well!

At certain times of the day, you should avoid texting people. If it's very early in the morning or very late at night, don't send that text. Outside of sleep hours, it would help if you also considered the schedule of the person you're texting before hitting Send. If they're at work or traveling, you may want to wait. If you have to send a text during hours that are likely busy, keep your message concise.

Using emojis and photos correctly

Emojis are a fun and popular way to bring emotion and context to a text message conversation. When used correctly, emojis can help make your chats more lively and expressive. Emojis express everything from love to anger, and from happiness to sadness. However, if you aren't careful about what you choose (or how many of them to choose!), emojis can turn a simple conversation into an indecipherable mess of smiley faces and random objects that say nothing about what you're trying to convey.

REMEMBER

If you want to add an emoji, make sure it means something and adds something useful to the conversation before clicking the Send button! If you don't do your due diligence, your conversation partner will likely get confused or frustrated when they cannot decipher what exactly is going on in your text message because of all the random emojis added.

Emojis are best used when there's already context in a conversation or you're trying to add emotion to an otherwise dull, text-only conversation. The best way to use emojis is to keep them simple and add only those that make sense with your text message conversation. Don't let emojis take over your messages — instead, use them as a bonus for expressing yourself.

Photos are another great way to bring life to a text message conversation or chat. Whether it's an image of your new puppy or a funny meme, photos are always an excellent way to add life to any text message conversation. However, like emojis, photos can quickly take over the entire discussion if you aren't careful with what you send and how often you send them.

A general rule of thumb for photos is to use them sparingly and only in specific situations. Share with a friend an image of an outfit you're thinking about buying when asking their opinion. Or share a picture of an issue you may be having with your rental when texting your landlord. Both are great use cases for photos. No matter how you use these visuals, remember that there are no takebacks, so don't send any photos you may later regret.

It's a Party in Your Phone

Group texting is a form of communication that connects more than two people simultaneously. In this type of communication, the message is sent from one person to several phone numbers at a time, using text messaging or other multimedia sharing services. Group texting is a popular form of mobile communication because it allows users to communicate more efficiently and effectively with each other simultaneously.

Group texting is now fast becoming one of the most common methods of communication. Group texts are also beneficial because they allow people to communicate about an event, such as a birthday party or funeral, even if you have friends who live in different cities or countries. The message can be sent with accurate location information, reaching all the people you're trying to connect with. Although there are many benefits, if done incorrectly, group texting can become annoying fast.

Knowing when to use group texting

Group texting is a wonderful way to stay in touch with your best friends, plan events for a small gathering of people, or send important information to the people who need to stay in the know without having to contact them individually. However, there is a time and a place for group text messaging. Though group texting can be a time-saver and a great way to stay in touch, it can also be a burden. One fundamental way to keep group texting on a positive note is to know the purpose of your group text and then stay on track.

When deciding whether to use group texting, ask yourself why you're sending this message. If what you're sharing can be said more concisely in a face-to-face conversation or via other technology such as email or phone call, consider the alternative means of communication. If none of these alternatives seems appealing or possible, group texting might be your best bet.

If, after assessing the benefits of group texts, you decide that this is the best way to contact your friends, you should keep a few things in mind before pressing Send. First off, ask yourself what the purpose of your group text is. Do you want immediate answers, or can everyone take their time to get back to you? Group texts often come with a sense of urgency, making them seem like the best fast-paced way to stay in touch with your friends. However, when there is no need for immediacy, it might be better to send an email or make a phone call. This way, if urgency does come up, you can be sure that your friends will be the first to know.

TIP
When sending a group text message, try using an informal greeting, such as "Hi, everyone" rather than "Hello" or another formal greeting. The use of *everyone* in this context is an indication that you want to hear from everyone with a single message. You can also include a brief description of what the group text is about so that your friends know what they agree to by replying. Finally, make sure that you only add people to a group chat who know each other, and stay within proper waking hours when texting.

As for how many people should be included in a group text, keep your group small — the fewer, the better when it comes to group text messaging. Adding too many people in a single message can be confusing and overwhelming. Try not to exceed ten people, and sometimes even that number can be too many. If you want to send out messages to more people, consider using email or a platform that is better suited for group messaging, where people have more control over the group. Messenger or Slack is a better option in this case.

REMEMBER
If you can stay on topic, keep your group small, and respect each other's time, you will be off to a great start with group texting!

Adding people to a group text

The first thing you need to do when starting a group text is to ask whether it's okay to add someone to said group. Group texting can be annoying and unwanted, so there is no reason to add someone without asking. Understand that although most messaging apps allow participants to leave or mute group conversations, the same isn't true for SMS texting on the phone. Most phone carriers lack the option to quickly opt out of any unwanted group text.

Keep the number of participants to a reasonable number. If you have too many members in your group chat, the notifications can become overwhelming, making the conversation harder to follow. If you ask people to join your group chat, it's best to have just enough people to make the discussion manageable. Again, if you find that you need to add more people, it may be time to switch to a new communication platform that's easier for users to manage.

Replying to a group text

Once you've established a group, be sure to keep the messages short and within the intended use of the group. If you started a group text to keep family members in the know about the health and wellness of another family member, don't begin texting about weekend plans or telling jokes. Remember that the point of a group text is to communicate efficiently about a specific topic. Because all recipients in the group are receiving text notifications, unnecessary chatter or off-topic text messaging can quickly grow tiresome and annoying.

All group members should be considerate of one another when sending messages and avoid disrupting others' sleep schedules. When participating in a group text, you should stay on topic and take all side conversations to separate text strings. If you're starting to have a back-and-forth chat with a single group member, it's good etiquette to move that conversation out of the group chat to avoid annoying other members. It's also courteous to refrain from texting in the middle of the night or early in the morning.

When participating in the group text conversation, be mindful that all recipients in the group receive a notification for every message you send. If you have a lot to share, consider sending a link or consolidating your thoughts into one message. Be mindful that notifications happen when you like or heart a message. This is not to say that liking or hearting a message is terrible, but keep in mind that group settings are already heavy with notifications, so the more you can help limit the amount of notifications sent to other members, the better.

Avoiding SMS missteps

Sending SMS messages can be a great way to stay in touch with friends and family, but there are a few things to avoid if you want to keep the conversation flowing smoothly. In this section, we give you eight of the *worst* bad habits that could be holding you back every day.

Not introducing yourself

When messaging someone new or participating in a group message, don't assume that everyone knows who you are. Failing to properly introduce yourself or giving the proper context can leave the receiver of your message in an awkward position. Avoid having the other person guess who you are. Unless you're already an established contact to the recipient, it's always best to introduce yourself before diving into a whole SMS conversation.

Excessive use of emojis and pictures

Though emojis and photos can be helpful when expressing tone in messages and showing an idea or a topic of importance, don't overuse them.

Excessive use of emojis and pictures can take away from the message you're trying to convey. Keep your messages simple so that it's easy for the other person to understand. Overuse of emojis can clutter the message string, making it hard to read and understand.

Adding one or two emojis to express emotion or give tonality is useful, but excessive use can take away from the message. If you're trying to express how you feel, focus on the words that describe your feeling. This way, it's easier for the other person to understand what you're trying to convey without using too many emojis.

When you do send emojis, keep them within your message and not as stand-alone messages. One heart or smiley face emoji standing alone is one thing, but excessively posting emoji after emoji is notification overload.

REMEMBER

Every message equals a notification, so don't send emojis or photos for the sake of sending. Make sure you have an excellent reason to include them.

The photos you send take up valuable space on the receiver's phone. For someone with limited space, it may be more difficult to save your message. So, be sure to use photo images and larger file shares sparingly. Also, remember that larger files take longer to receive, so sending many images means that the receiver may not receive them for a while, depending on their download speed or phone reception.

Not keeping an eye on tone

It's no secret that text messaging can be rife with misunderstandings. After all, we humans are deprived of the nonverbal cues that we rely on in face-to-face conversations to help us understand the tone of what someone is saying. This problem is only exacerbated when SMS messages are sent in a hurry and can contain abbreviations and emoticons that are open to interpretation.

Tone can be difficult to decipher in written form, so it's best not to assume tone when text messaging. You never know what someone intended for their message to say. Try not to take offense or read too much into the tone that isn't there. Jokes, sarcasm, and emotion don't come across well in text messaging, so be careful what you write and how you read things. Instead, ensure that your messages are clear and easy to understand by shortening the text or using emojis sparingly if necessary to help show tonality.

One big challenge that we humans face when it comes to interpreting tone is believing that our own natural tone colors our message. But if your friend takes offense because they misinterpreted your humorous intentions as sarcasm, you might be puzzled by their reaction. After all, you were only kidding! However, as frustrating as it can be, you have to remember that your friend may be reading a very different tone into your words than the one you intended. To keep the confusion to a minimum, keep the following in mind:

>> **Be aware of context and the possible tone of your words and the words of the people you're texting with.** A joke can quickly turn serious, if not communicated in a way that reflects that tone. Sarcasm often can't be read in nonverbal texts, so keep that to a minimum.

>> **When you're first getting to know someone, don't use text messages for emotionally charged conversations until you determine how they typically respond face-to-face.** If your new friend gets upset with you over an offhand remark that was meant as humor, this could be a sign that some of your messages are being interpreted as more serious than you intended.

>> **Be straightforward with people about how you want them to communicate with you.** If you're frequently upset by how people are texting, let them know clearly that they need to adjust their style so that it works for you.

>> **When in doubt, apologize and clarify what you meant if there is a misinterpretation.** It isn't worth it to dig in your heels over text.

Indulging in lengthy texts

SMS stands for Short Message Service, which means that a text message should be kept short. So why would you send a lengthy text message?

There are several reasons to avoid sending long text messages. It can be annoying and tedious for someone to read a long text message, preventing them from replying promptly. When it comes to texting, brevity is the key. If your text message takes longer than 30 seconds to read, it may be best to pick up the phone and call or send a longer, more detailed email to your intended recipient.

Text messages that are too long can come off as desperate or too serious. Plus, a long text message generally has many points that a recipient may find hard to respond to via text. If you have many points to make and you must text, go ahead and break down each issue into its own text message and give the receiver a chance to respond.

To be sure, having a more extended text exchange is sometimes acceptable, but if this becomes the norm or your messages go from short to much longer in a single conversation, consider switching gears. Not all types of conversational topics should be discussed over text messaging. Sometimes, a different kind of communication medium is needed. Emails, phone calls, or even voice messaging may better express longer thoughts and topics. If you decide that you need to switch to email or another form of written communication, let the recipient know so that they can follow along. If you plan to call, ask first. Not everyone likes to talk on the phone. Just because someone is willing to have a text exchange doesn't mean that they want to have a conversation over the phone.

REMEMBER

Keeping your texts shorter than the standard 140 characters (which is standard on Twitter) helps you stay on target and save time.

SMS that should have been a call

Have you ever had a text message exchange that started to grow longer and more involved and, finally, you decided to pick up the phone and call? It happens more often than you think, and for a good reason. Sometimes a phone call *is* warranted.

So, if you find that your text exchange is getting too long and you're starting to think it just might be better to call, just pick up the phone. If things are getting out of hand because of a misunderstanding, pick up the phone. And, if you have emotionally charged information to share or need to have a conversation where tonality is vital, a phone call is the answer.

Blowing up someone's phone

Blowing up someone's phone is defined as the act of sending a text or series of texts excessively at such a high frequency that the receiver might believe it to be an electronic attack. Though it may be tempting to text someone who hasn't responded to you continually, it's best to walk away and wait for a response.

It's never appropriate to text someone's phone so often that the notifications seem endless. This can be annoying, overwhelming, and even harassing. If you want to get in touch with someone, try calling them or sending a message through another channel.

REMEMBER

People may have other commitments going on, and answering a text message may not be a priority for them at that time. Blowing up someone's phone with nonstop messaging only shows that you're too self-absorbed to check in with the other person when they're possibly busy. If someone isn't responding, it's okay to take a breather and wait for them to recheck their phone before sending more messages.

If you're getting blown up by someone's texts, your first reaction may be to respond with anger. Though it's understandable to feel annoyed, consider that the person blowing you up may be unaware that they're doing so. Try to stay calm, and explain how their texts overwhelm or distract you from your other responsibilities. Let them know you will get back to them when you have some time. Let them know before you do, to give them a chance to stop. If they're unwilling to stop blowing up your phone and it becomes a problem, consider blocking their number either temporarily or permanently.

REMEMBER

Blowing up someone's phone can be a form of cyberbullying, stalking, or harassment. If the constant messaging becomes threatening, it may be necessary to contact the authorities. Though you should never blow up someone else's phone, it's important not to suffer through an electronic attack, either. If someone is constantly blowing up your phone, take the necessary precautions to protect yourself, and block them, if necessary.

Not cleaning up your voice-to-text

Voice-to-text technology was designed to convert speech into written words. It has become more and more necessary with the rise of texting, emailing, social media, and so on. Voice-to-text is important because it can save time by your not having to type everything out.

Despite its being a fantastic tool that helps you type at the speed of speaking, it still has flaws. When texting using voice-to-text, it's best to double-check what was typed and edit if necessary. It only takes a quick skim through what was written to ensure that you don't make a big mistake. The voice-to-text assistant can easily misinterpret what you're saying and write all kinds of random messages. If these errors are caught early enough, they can be fixed before sending off the message. But if not, it can cause all sorts of misunderstandings that could end up being embarrassing or even damaging, in some cases. So don't just send without a quick skim.

TIP

If you cannot check your voice-to-text messages (while driving, for example), just let the recipient know from the start that you're using voice-to-text and that they may see some typos. Setting these expectations up-front reduces some of the misinterpretation and frustration.

Knowing What Not to Send in an SMS Text Message

In this day and age, you should be aware of the different ways you can communicate with people. Text messaging has become a popular form of communication, and for many reasons. One reason is that it allows for quick responses without your having to wait on hold or spend time composing a reply in your head before answering.

Another helpful aspect of text messages is that they're usually short and to the point. All this is good, but it doesn't mean that there are no rules when texting someone.

Not sending unsolicited content

Never send unsolicited content in a text message. Don't send messages, images, or memes that would be considered offensive, sensitive, or triggering. It's important to note that what you might find funny or appropriate in a conversation over text wouldn't be okay when sent unsolicited. It can also trigger someone and cause them distress and anxiety.

REMEMBER

Whatever you send in an SMS text message can be saved and shared with others. So often, people forget that that the quick content they send will stand as a permanent record of their thoughts. Keep that in mind before you click Send.

Sending unsolicited content via SMS text messaging is also a big no-no for businesses. A business must initiate any contact you have with potential customers or else it's spam. Sending unsolicited messages to potential customers and clients is harmful and can turn someone off from your company. Whether you've sent a message or the person has the option of ignoring the message, it still shows up in their inbox. It becomes another unwanted strain on your relationship with that person. It sets the wrong first impression, and depending on how you acquired their phone number, it could be illegal.

Keeping your messages spam-free

Sending spam via SMS is, without a doubt, the worst thing someone can do when using text messaging. It not only overloads someone's phone but also clutters their inbox and could potentially get your business blacklisted from doing business via text messaging in the future or, worse, fined by the Federal Communications Commission (FCC).

Sending spam also shows the recipient that you're not mindful of your relationship with them and don't respect their time. It can make them less inclined to communicate with you in return in a respectful way. Overall, spam leaves a horrible lasting impression.

If you don't want your business to get blacklisted, or if you don't want other people to think of your messages as spam, there are ways you can send out messages and communicate with customers without looking like a scammer. Here's what you should keep in mind:

>> **Do not send marketing and promotional messages without permission.** Before you send out a message, you should ensure that the recipient has opted in to receive messages from your company. If they haven't, don't send them anything!

>> **Never buy lists of phone numbers to message.** It goes without saying that you're not likely to get an initial opt-in from total strangers who know nothing about your business yet show up on a list you bought from somewhere. Follow the laws of the country your recipient lives in. Some countries, such as Canada, require that if you're sending SMS messages to cell numbers, they should be opted-in numbers. This is the only acceptable way to get text message recipients' phone numbers.

>> **Follow FTC requirements.** The FTC has said that each SMS text needs to contain an opt-out mechanism that lets the recipient unsubscribe from all future messages at any time. You also need to ensure that you have an easy way for the recipient to unsubscribe at any time. Ensure that your message and unsubscribe mechanism comply with the law in each country where you're sending messages.

>> **If a customer replies *STOP* (or any other word that means *stop*), the best thing you can do is honor their request and immediately unsubscribe them from any future messages.**

REMEMBER

People are worried about being spammed when they receive text messages, so you need to make sure you can be trusted. If you want to send out promotional text messages regularly, you have to allow customers to opt out at any time,

>> **Make sure your text messages are relevant, timely, and personalized.** Avoid sending content that your recipients would not deem helpful or valuable. If you send out relevant and engaging messages, the customer won't see your messages as spam.

>> **Follow up after receiving a new lead or contacting someone for the first time.** Establishing a relationship can help build trust and rapport with potential customers; it should be done early on.

>> **Keep your messaging in check.** There's no need for you to send messages all the time: Sending messages too often isn't only annoying — it can also make you look like a spammer. Try to avoid sending text messages multiple times in one day. (In fact, keeping them to once a week is probably a good strategy.)

>> **Thank your customers for communicating with you.** Don't forget to thank your customers when they send a message back to you or reply to one of your promotional messages. This shows that you care about them and appreciate their business.

>> **Don't use language that is misleading or vague.** Another thing you need to watch out for when sending text messages is making sure you aren't trying to deceive your customers in any way. This includes misleading them about who the message is from, what it pertains to, why they receive it, and how they can opt out.

REMEMBER

Spam is in the eyes of the beholder. If someone says your messages are spam, they are, so always take the proper precautions to ensure a good text exchange between you and your leads.

Chapter **19**

Pleasant Direct Messaging

Texting (SMS) and messaging (MMS) are similar and can be used similarly in many use cases; however, the two have vastly different purposes. SMS stands for Short Message Service, which allows the user to send and receive text messages from their mobile device. MMS Stands for Multimedia Messaging Service, which can be used for sending and receiving photos, audio files, video files, and other large files.

Messaging apps are different from SMS in that they can act as an application on your phone to send messages (voice, text) to friends or family both domestically and internationally.

Exploring the Differences: Messaging App versus SMS

Instant messaging is a real-time online chat feature enabled through a software application. Some of the most popular messaging platforms are Facebook Messenger, WhatsApp, Telegram, and WeChat. Both WhatsApp and Messenger are owned by Meta (formerly Facebook) and are consistently at the top of the charts for most users.

Multimedia messaging apps are similar to SMS in that they allow users to communicate using instant text-based messaging but offer in addition a multitude of other functions. Messaging apps typically include chat rooms for group conversations; stickers, emoticons, and GIFs for more fun interactions; voice and video calling; and even games with other users.

Messaging apps are typically used internationally between friends to keep in touch while abroad or to communicate better (or cheaper) than via SMS. Messaging apps are also widely used domestically and internationally to communicate with large groups of people simultaneously through group messaging because sometimes it's much easier to type out a message and send it than to send multiple separate text messages. Messaging apps also usually allow for easier file transfer and photo sharing, which is why they (rather than SMS) are typically used between friends to communicate. Another benefit of messaging apps over SMS is the control the user has over their notifications, their participation in group chats, and their ability to block others who step out of line.

REMEMBER

Though messaging apps can be used on desktops, tablets, and smartphones, all participants must have the same messaging app to send or receive messages — unlike SMS, which can be sent to anyone with a phone. In addition, you must have access to Wi-Fi or cellular data to use messaging apps.

Overall, messaging is far more powerful and has many more features than SMS, making it a better option for communicating domestically and internationally. Messaging apps are also free and are free of charges that SMS and phone carriers impose on users.

Comparing Messaging and Email

Email sends messages over an open, usually public, network using standardized formats for text and multimedia messages. *Messaging* apps are similar to email in that they allow the user to send and receive messages to friends and family via an Internet connection. However, messaging apps are typically used only between people who have signed up for the app, who are on the same network, or who use a VPN.

Though messaging is being adopted by Internet users rapidly, some people still prefer the familiarity of email. It's an older system that's been around for a few decades, so it tends to be more widely used in professional culture. When users *do* choose messaging apps over email, it's usually because such apps are usually faster and more secure, allow you to chat on multiple devices (tablet/laptop), and let you send larger files (MMS). Email offers no *real-time* communication — the ability to chat in groups of people simultaneously — and lacks features such as voice and video messaging.

Given the lay of the land, most users prefer messaging apps over email because they're fast, secure, and accessible on multiple devices with group chat, and they allow for full multimedia support. This is not to say that an app like Messenger will (or should) replace email. Email isn't going anywhere anytime soon — it still has an important role in how people communicate, both personally and professionally. Don't assume that messaging apps will replace email. Instead, recognize that these two communication mediums are different in many ways and should be used in the proper circumstances.

If you're using these two mediums for business, understand that messaging and email are important when communicating with customers. Email is useful for sending out marketing messaging, longer-form communications, and customer service status reports. Messaging, on the other hand, works well for customer service, answering time-sensitive questions, and providing updates on new products or services. Another benefit of using messaging apps is the ability to integrate chat automation technology and artificial intelligence to help handle up to 80 percent of your incoming messages. This is a huge advantage for companies of all sizes because you're assured that many aspects of your company's interaction with leads and clients can be taken care of initially via chat automation; only when the automation is unable to help is there a handoff to a human agent. Creating this type of seamless experience for the end-user saves a company valuable time and money.

REMEMBER

Don't use messaging as you would use email. Messaging is for two-way engagement, not one-way blasts. Messaging is also more conversational and less formal. You should avoid sending large blocks of text or communications that aren't meant to be part of a two-way discussion.

Messaging and email can also complement each other in a business setting. Messaging is helpful for lead generation and lead qualification. Email is helpful for taking over the lead and doing marketing campaigns over time to warm the lead up and ultimately convert them into customers.

Knowing When to Use Messaging

There are more messaging app users than social media users, and this number will continue to grow. It has never been more important to have a presence on messaging apps if you plan to communicate with your customers or potential customers. If your company receives inquiries by messaging, you need to seriously consider adding messaging marketing (also known as chat marketing) to your marketing mix.

When you choose to ignore messages, you're essentially saying you don't care. If you aren't responding, you're chasing business away. Fortunately, certain technologies can help you manage these messages. Chat automation and artificial intelligence have come a long way. These technologies are becoming the go-to way for companies to manage messages at scale.

Chatbot-building tools like ManyChat can help you build chat automations so that you can respond to messages automatically. Such tools support chatbots on Messenger, Instagram, and WhatsApp, with more and more platforms added all the time. Sticking with ManyChat, we can say that this particular tool has an easy-to-use interface for you to create chatbots without having to know how to code. Social networks like Facebook also support native chat automation for business pages. If you want to create simple chatbot automation on your Facebook business page, go to Settings on your business page, choose Messaging from the menu on the left, and then explore everything Facebook has to offer. You can set up Away messages, FAQ automation, and other helpful automation. These tools will buy you time to respond to customers and can often answer a question automatically before you get to it.

You can also find industry-specific chat automation tools — for example, tools such as Tap The Table for restaurants and real estate companies. Tap the Table is a full-service chat automation platform built to meet the needs of these industries. Companies can use this tool to make sales from comments on social media posts. It can also take food orders, make calculations, and qualify people so they are perfectly matched with the products or services they need or want — all without a human agent. This automation saves a company loads of time and resources and allows human agents to focus on more important tasks.

TIP

Before you discount the concept of automation, consider that well-built chat automation can help companies cut costs by 30 percent. Plus, satisfaction rates are at or above human agents when used in customer service settings. The key is to do it right and make sure you have a human handover when needed.

When should you use messaging apps in your business? Always. The benefits of utilizing chat messaging for your business far outweigh avoiding it. Not using messaging can be costing you customers and hurting the bottom line.

Now that that's taken care of, the next question is obvious: What about using messaging for personal use?

We're glad you asked. One of the main benefits of using messaging over SMS or email has to do with the controls that messaging offers. It's far easier to control group notifications, remove yourself from chats, and mute conversations. You can even delete messages after they're sent! Furthermore, most messaging apps offer higher-security options such as encrypted messaging. This makes it an excellent tool for managing discussions with friends and family.

Another benefit of messaging apps is the ability to have real-time voice and video discussions. Whether you're sending video or voice messages or you're talking live, these tools make it easy to stay in touch. This is particularly helpful for families living long distances away from each other; you get to catch up in real-time and stay better connected to friends and family — no matter the distance.

Evaluating the More Popular Messaging Apps

With so many messaging apps to choose from, it can be hard to know which one is the best for your needs. Let's dive deeper into some of the most popular messaging apps available.

Facebook Messenger

First up is Facebook Messenger, one of the world's most popular messaging apps. More than 1.3 billion people use Messenger, sharing more than 17 billion photos and 400 million voice and video chats every month.

REMEMBER

As long as you and your recipient have Messenger, you can freely communicate via chat, voice, or video on desktop or mobile devices — all at no cost. Popular features include photo sharing, group chat, video chat, and even sending and receiving payment instantly.

Facebook Messenger's video chat feature is made even more popular by Facebook Portal. This video chat device allows you to use Messenger's video chat feature, among other unique features, like voice commands and built-in interactive augmented reality (AR) games and virtual storybooks. Now people worldwide can chat face-to-face with friends and loved ones with ease.

Messenger is also a popular tool for businesses wanting to take advantage of its robust platform. On Messenger each month, people and businesses exchange 20 billion messages. Messenger has even launched business tools like Messenger for Business, which helps companies not only connect more easily with current customers but also attract new ones. Integrating seamlessly with e-commerce shops, chat automation, custom apps, Facebook advertising, scheduling tools, and more, Messenger has quickly become an essential asset to all types of businesses.

WhatsApp

WhatsApp is the world's second most popular messaging app. With more than 1 billion global users, 1 billion videos, 4.5 billion photos, and 80 million GIFs shared per day, WhatsApp provides a safe and secure way to reach people worldwide. Using end-to-end encryption, people can chat via text, audio, photos, and videos — knowing that their communication is safe. Only you and the person you're communicating with can read or listen to your messaging; nobody in between, not even WhatsApp, can access your conversation or history.

As long as you and your recipient have WhatsApp installed on their phone, you can securely share messages, pictures, videos, audio notes, and even locations for free. WhatsApp is popular among users who like to do group chats, where you can share and message up to 256 people at a time. You can also further customize your group with a name, colors, and personalized notifications, to name a few.

In addition to chatting, WhatsApp also has a voice and video calling feature that works via the Internet and Wi-Fi connections. These features allow you to chat with friends worldwide without costing you a cent in data charges, making WhatsApp widely popular among people who travel internationally or who have friends and family in other countries.

WhatsApp is available on all major mobile platforms, making it widely accessible. As a bonus, WhatsApp has an extremely user-friendly interface that makes it easy to learn and use.

Businesses can also use WhatsApp to help them connect with their customers worldwide. By adding a WhatsApp Business account to a phone or tablet, users can see messages from team members and send messages right back for free. You can choose from multiple business profiles and add a profile picture to make it even easier for clients to recognize your brand when they chat. In addition, businesses can use WhatsApp Business to answer FAQs, send transactional messages like password-reset links and receipts, share images and videos, and more. With such a high percentage of people around the world using the app to connect with their friends and loved ones, it's fantastic that you can also join in on the conversation via business messaging as well!

Telegram

Telegram Messenger is a popular messaging app for smartphones, tablets, and computers. It reportedly has more than 550 million monthly active users and is considered one of the top ten most active social media networks globally. Like the other apps mentioned in this section, Telegram supports sending text messages, photos, videos, files of any type (documents, zip archives, and so on), and creating groups for up to 200,000 people! It also has an open API that allows developers to create custom tools with Telegram.

Telegram is a cloud-based mobile and desktop messaging app focusing on security and speed, which makes it popular among users who want control over having their messages stored on their phones and those who enjoy group chats. In addition, Telegram supports secret chats that allow users to set an expiration time for all messages sent within the chat. If you're looking for a secure messaging experience, Telegram is the way to go.

With so many users worldwide sending messages via Telegram, businesses can use it as another channel to reach their audiences and generate more revenue opportunities. Telegram has a growing list of tools that companies can use to engage with their customers, such as polls, support bots, or real-time customer service chatbots. With an open API, developers have made some fantastic tools that you can tap into when using Telegram for business.

What's more, Telegram supports sending messages to multiple users at a time and broadcasting messages to an unlimited number of subscribers. If you're looking for a way to streamline your customer service efforts, Telegram might be the mobile messaging app for you.

Slack

The revolutionary messaging app Slack brings together all your communication in one place. Although many people believe that the term *slack* means "lazy" or "slacking," its name stands for Searchable Log of All Conversation and Knowledge. Slack has revolutionized how business teams communicate with each other. With over 10 million people using Slack daily and 43 percent of Fortune 100 businesses paying to use the service, companies adopt it mainly to stay connected with employees and clients.

Slack is available on all major mobile and desktop operating systems and also has a web version. This allows you to message your team from anywhere using any device, staying organized and up-to-date on customer conversations.

Slack not only provides users with messaging capabilities but also features integrations that allow for tool and bot communication that can be specific to your industry. For example, Slack has been used by those working in education as tools that can be integrated into the platform that helps teachers and parents communicate with one another about students' progress.

The same goes for those working in finance or HR: If you work in a tight-knit organization where your team needs to stay up-to-date on each other's work, Slack is the best app to use.

Slack even supports over 4,000 different third-party applications, so businesses can get more out of their experience by connecting it with other services they may already be using. This includes Google Drive, Stripe, Twitter, Zendesk, and countless others that you might be using.

As a cloud-based mobile and desktop messaging app focusing on speed, security, and flexibility, Slack has become quite popular among users who have to communicate across different platforms. It features group and direct messaging tools that allow you to chat one-on-one with a colleague or get an entire group of people on the same page quickly.

In addition, Slack allows those taking part in the conversation to send files from their devices directly into the conversation; you can then see who's attached what kind of file and determine whether it needs reviewing or sharing. You can also synchronize your work calendars with Slack to instantly see everyone's availability whenever you're looking to schedule a meeting.

Slack offers some of the best real-time customer service tools available on the market. As more and more businesses turn to chatbots to provide instant resolutions for their customers, Slack is perfect for creating these bots. It comes with a robust API that allows you to create your own integration or use prebuilt Slack apps that offer bot-building functionality.

Slack is also significant for real-time collaboration. You can create a channel in your company's Slack team so that everyone working on the same project can communicate with one another in one place. This includes attachments, images, and videos files to help keep your work organized and up-to-date because you'll always know where everything is.

WARNING

Slack creates a lot of notifications and noise, so you may want to disable some of the notification features on your device if you're constantly getting notified by Slack.

TECHNICAL STUFF

One of the most significant benefits of using Slack for business correspondence focuses on compliance and security. Slack delivers enterprise-grade protection at every layer, adhering to multiple compliance certifications, including SOC 2, SOC 3, ISO/IEC 27001, and more. Slack is GDPR-compliant and can be configured for HIPAA and FINRA compliance. It's also FedRAMP Moderate authorized.

On top of security and compliance, Slack's features give its users the ability to configure which employees have access to which files and conversations so that you can ensure that your most sensitive data is protected. This gives you control over how information gets shared across your team.

Messaging apps such as Slack may be one of the best ways for teams to stay in touch, but it's up to IT administrators to set proper policies so that they don't get in the way of work.

Following Best Practices for Personal Messaging

There are many benefits to using a messaging app for your personal use. Apps like Messenger and Telegram offer the ability to easily chat with friends and family via private messages or group chats. You can share photos, videos, and articles. You also have better control over your messages because most messaging apps offer notification controls, muting features, and the ability to delete sent messages.

With this increased control of your messages comes the temptation to overmessage. Messaging apps are also riddled with spam, and group chats can just as quickly spiral out of control as SMS group chats. So take heed when using these apps and stay respectful.

Respecting other people's time

Many people are on their phones throughout the day, so they're already being bombarded with messages between work, family, friends, and others. They might not have time to respond to all your messages immediately, so don't expect immediacy in response even if your message shows that it has been read.

REMEMBER

In messaging apps, if the recipient opens the chat window, it shows up as Read. This doesn't necessarily mean that the recipient has had time to read or respond to your message thoroughly. So, patience is key.

If someone doesn't reply to one of your messages, take it as a cue that they're busy — and don't message them again until a reasonable amount of time has passed. Don't be offended if someone doesn't respond to you immediately or if someone doesn't want to chat with you for long periods. It's possible that the user is in the middle of an important task and can't get distracted easily.

One thing people tend to forget is that messaging can be a big distraction for others. It can be tough to stay focused at work when you're hearing the constant "Ping!" from a messaging app. Try to avoid personal messaging during work hours or sleep hours.

Not treating messaging apps as though they're Google

Messaging apps aren't search engines, and your contacts aren't the human equivalent of Google. Before asking questions, make sure the answer isn't one that could have been easily found by doing a simple Internet search. Often, people are in such a hurry to find answers that they turn to platforms like Messenger or social media groups to ask questions — questions they expect to get answered immediately. It's important to remember that the people you chat with are busy, so you should try to avoid unnecessarily bothering them with things that you can solve yourself.

Avoiding the overmessaging temptation

Don't overmessage others. There's a fine line between getting attention and annoying someone by constantly messaging them or spamming a group chat with useless messages. It's easy to fall into the trap of being needy when keeping in touch with friends from school and with family members.

REMEMBER

People are busy with their own lives and obligations, so don't expect them to drop everything and chat with you at a moment's notice. Avoiding the overmessaging temptation and sending messages only when necessary keeps your contacts happy and not overwhelmed by incoming messages.

Be selective about whom you message — if people don't respond to your attempts to get in touch, take the hint and stop messaging them for a while. Wait until you have something important to tell them before resuming communication.

If someone doesn't want to chat with you at a particular time, don't take it personally; their life might just be *busy* at that moment. If you think the person is avoiding your messages or if people don't respond to messages in a group chat, take it as a cue that you might have been messaging them too often.

REMEMBER

Messaging is a wonderful way to stay in touch with the people you care about, but you also need to respect others' time and personal lives. Don't bombard them with messages when you know that they are busy or have no time to chat.

Including the context from the get-go

Like any other form of communication, starting off a conversation (especially a group chat) with context is important. This gives the other participants a chance to see whether they can contribute, and it saves them from having to reply to a bunch of messages that don't seem relevant. Here are a few examples of what to include in the initial messages:

>> **Context about who you are and why you're messaging this group.** This helps especially if you're messaging a group whose members don't know each other well. You don't necessarily have to introduce yourself if you already know everyone, but if the group has new people in it, this is a good move.

>> **The reason for your message.** "Found a great deal online, does anyone want to go in on this?" or "I am planning a surprise party for our friend Tom, so I started this chat to see who is in?" Having a purpose behind the messages shows people what you're trying to get out of the conversation and how they can contribute. If there's no purpose behind your messages, people might feel like you're just spamming them and ignoring their requests for context.

>> **If you're adding a new member to a group, be sure to catch them up by adding a summary of the conversation so far.** This is especially true if it's a long chain or group chat. This helps everyone stay on track and avoid having to scroll through countless messages to figure out what's going on.

Even in 1-to-1 messaging, you should give context. You never just want to message someone single lines like "Hi" with nothing else, because it leaves no opening for a conversation and can make things awkward right off the bat. Also consider that scammers will try to use messaging apps for phishing scams, so messaging app users are wary of incoming messages that are too vague or have no context.

REMEMBER

Context helps others understand the intention of the conversation so that they can be more comfortable chatting with you. Leaving out context can confuse people and make them feel like they may be missing something.

Using Messenger in this way can enhance your overall experience on the app and make sure that the people you message are happy to help you.

Keeping Messaging Professional

Instant messaging apps have revolutionized business communication by making it easier than ever to communicate with coworkers and clients virtually. With more and more consumers utilizing messaging apps and reaching out to businesses over chat, companies must follow suit and create ways to meet customers where they are. Though there are definitely some kinks left to work out, organizations should at least start implementing best practices for utilizing these tools properly and professionally.

Staying professional at all times when using messaging apps

Though there are many benefits to using messaging apps for business, you mustn't go about using them in the wrong way. Whether you're using messaging to correspond with employees or coworkers or to communicate with leads and customers, it's crucial always to be professional.

As an individual using messaging apps for professional use, be sure you're respectful of the people you're sending messages to. One clear way to do that is to keep business correspondence during business hours. This is especially important if you're in management and are sending messages to employees. It isn't fair to pressure your employees to respond outside of business hours. If it can wait, you should wait. If you have to send a message, include context that they don't have to respond until the next day or during business hours.

For all messaging app interactions to go smoothly and in the most professional manner possible, include context and be respectful of where others are in their day and what they're doing. It's also important to clearly define the purpose of your conversation before you start messaging others. This helps them know what to expect and makes them more likely to respond positively. It also keeps the communication clear and concise on both ends.

REMEMBER

You're representing your company when using instant messaging apps. Though it's important to be personal with the people you message, there's a time and place for everything. When in doubt, keep things professional by including purpose and context and not overstepping boundaries.

TIP

Never ignore your customers when they message you — if you have a business, you must respond promptly to messages from your customers or potential customers. Most people expect a response to messages they send in real-time. Letting your customer messages sit without responding can be detrimental to your brand and even affect future business. To ensure that you don't leave customers hanging, set up chat automation (also known as *chatbots*) to respond to customers with your automated responses, or direct them to specific team members. (Chat automation is relatively easy to build and can include AI to help respond to customer inquiries.)

Skipping the unsolicited spam or sales pitches

If you're an individual using messaging apps for business or marketing, you mustn't spam conversations with unsolicited sales pitches or spam in general. If someone doesn't ask for an advertisement, they probably don't want one. Not only can such unsolicited messages be annoying, but they can also be overwhelming and off-putting in a conversation.

One of the biggest pet peeves social media users have is when someone sends them unsolicited spam. If you're looking to grow an audience or keep the one you have, it's essential to be respectful of your audience. Don't send them unsolicited sales pitches. Full stop. This is especially important if you recently became social media connections ("Friends") or if someone was asking a question in a social media group and you decided to send them a sales pitch. It doesn't matter how much you think your product or service would help out the poster; you should never send unsolicited sales pitches unless the person asked for it. If you see an opportunity to help someone, ask them first if it would be okay for you to send them a message.

Messaging apps are meant to be personal, so sending unsolicited messages with links to your website or products is not only spammy but impersonal as well. If you're looking to grow an audience, you must first become genuine friends with social media connections before offering them something on your website.

There's a time and place for everything. Not everyone wants to be interrupted by unsolicited messages about your product or service. It's essential only to send messages when requested and not just because you think it would be a good message to send.

REMEMBER

The first message you send to someone is their first impression of you. Make sure you make a great first impression by being friendly, respectful, and not salesy.

Being sure to respond promptly

Messaging apps are taking over as one of the top ways people communicate with each other and with businesses. Messaging is easy and quick. As a business, you simply must have a strategy for responding promptly to customers who message you.

One study found 40 percent of consumers expect brands to respond within the first hour of reaching out on social media, and 79 percent expect a response in the first 24 hours. Similar studies have found similar reports. The bottom line is that your customers expect a response to their message as soon as possible.

But how can you stay on track on the various platforms and respond promptly? One thing you can do is have a collection of responses ready for common questions and concerns. Save these canned responses to your phone or desktop (wherever you tend to respond to most messages). If you become overwhelmed by messages or want to hand over the burden of messaging, consider hiring a dedicated customer service rep or implementing chat automation.

A chat automation (also known as a *chatbot*) is an excellent way to help businesses respond promptly to customers. A chatbot can help you not only save time and money but also take on some of the burdens of responding to messages so that you or your customer service reps can focus on more complex issues. Additionally, chatbots can be set up to respond to specific questions or concerns immediately so that customers don't have to wait for a human representative to respond. This helps businesses keep up with customer expectations for response times and ensure no unanswered messages.

Chatbots have come a long way since their introduction into the mainstream, and they show no signs of slowing down. Innovative companies are learning to make them a part of their overall customer funnel, seeing where they fit and where they don't. All in all, chatbots and other automated messaging tools can help businesses respond to customers quickly and efficiently so that you, as a businessperson, can focus on more important tasks.

Checking messages throughout the day so that nothing slips through the cracks

When using chat messaging apps for professional use, especially when dealing with customers or when corresponding with coworkers, managers, and employees, it can be hard to stay connected without becoming overwhelmed. Notifications can become a distraction, and messages can slip through the cracks. One way to manage the obstacles of professional messaging is to limit your notifications and create a consistent habit of checking your various platforms at specific times during the day.

Be sure to set the expectation with coworkers, or anyone else you message, that you check your messages at these specific times, and let them know when they can expect to hear back from you. If you work in an office setting and need to respond to customers or clients by a specific time, set that expectation with them. No one likes having their message go unanswered for days on end.

When setting a schedule for checking messages, we suggest that you choose three points during the day. This strategy ensures that no messages get lost in the shuffle. One of the best times to check messages is first thing in the morning, when you first arrive at work. This strategy allows you to not only get a jump-start on the day and respond promptly to any emergencies but also helps ease your transition from home life to work life.

Another great time is after lunch. This allows you to ease back into your workday after a break for lunch, catch up on the messages that may have come in since the morning check-in, and respond to anyone who needs your attention.

The last suggested check-in time is in midafternoon, about an hour before you clock out for the day. This gives you the best chance at responding to any messages that need your attention before you leave for the day.

REMEMBER

If you're using a Messaging app that offers the feature, be sure to put up an Away message when you're unavailable. This helps keep messages and notifications from being overwhelming and helps set expectations with others messaging you.

Managing Group Messaging

If you're like most people, you're probably using a messaging app to communicate with friends, family, or coworkers. Think of group messaging as a digital water cooler. It's a place to catch up with friends, gossip about the latest news, or simply shoot the breeze. But before you dive headfirst into this online hangout, it's important to be aware of the etiquette that goes along with it. The next few sections spell out ways you can ensure that your group messaging experience is enjoyable for everyone involved.

Adding people to a group chat

It can be overwhelming when you first start a group chat, because other people may not want to join immediately. It isn't easy to know how to reach out and ask someone to come to the group chat. There are various ways of asking someone to join your group message, but here we give you some general guidelines for inviting others into one of your chats.

Tips for group chat owners

Before you start a group chat, you should know what you want out of this digital hangout. What is the purpose of your chat? There are group chats for all kinds of reasons. Some people have a chat for family, some have chats for friends who are spread out in different locations, and some have group chats to plan events and gatherings. Sometimes the groups are formed temporarily, and sometimes those chats evolve over months and years. As the group owner, it's up to you to decide what kinds of conversations should be had in your chat.

The first thing you should do when inviting someone to one of your chats is to give them an idea of why they're being asked to join. Send a quick one-to-one message to those you want to invite and see whether it's cool to add them to the chat and let them know what the group's purpose is all about. Once that's clear, you can determine whether someone is a good fit for your chat.

Once the group chat is created, make a post introducing everyone to the purpose of the chat. Let them know why you have gathered them together. This helps with transparency and clarity.

Respect others' time and try not to overpost. Initially, it's normal for a group chat to "blow up" with interaction, but you should not expect this level of engagement at all times.

Make sure you have reviewed the group settings and named your chat to give it context. Also, make sure your admin settings are set to how you want the group to function. Things like allowing or disallowing other members to add people as well as setting up your notifications are key settings.

Tips for members

Okay, so you've been invited into a group chat — now what? One of the first things you should do when you're added to a group chat is to go to the group settings and set up your notification preferences. This way, you won't be overwhelmed. Feel free to introduce yourself or say hello after you're added to the group. You should avoid adding new members without asking permission from the admin of the group or even the entire group. Some people in the group may feel uncomfortable if new people are added. It's essential to respect the feelings of the other members of the group.

Respecting the intention of the group

As a member of a group chat, you should keep the initial intention of the group in mind at all times. Sometimes, the group was created simply to keep in touch with friends and family. If that is the case, you'll have more flexibility when it comes to topic choices and discussion. But if there's a clearly defined purpose, like planning an event or business project, stay on topic. New members shouldn't take over this function of the group or try to make too much noise if the group isn't intended for that kind of banter.

Going too far off course in the discussion can be frustrating for other members and make it hard for group chat admins to bring the conversation back on track. Also, you should not try to use the chat to vent negative feelings about others in the group. This can be hurtful and disruptive.

REMEMBER

If you have an off-topic question or discussion point, it's best to create a separate chat for that purpose.

Respecting other people's time

Staying on topic is important, but keep in mind as well that any message you send will notify everyone in the group. You should not only try to stay on topic but also avoid creating unnecessary noise. Constant message blocks that could have been consolidated, excessive GIFs or emojis that don't fit the room's vibe, and nonessential messages should be kept to a minimum.

Be mindful of your audience — several platforms have a feature that allows you to mute or block certain people from messaging you or seeing you when you're online. So, if someone is being inappropriate or annoying, don't hesitate to use these features to help them out.

One thing that group "chatters" complain about most is when people engage in one-to-one conversations inside of a group. So, if you have something to ask one member of the group that doesn't bring value or pertain to the other members, don't post it in the group. It's considered inconsiderate and rude. Side conversations create an unnecessary distraction to other members and can be easily avoided by taking 1:1 conversations out of the group.

REMEMBER

Group messaging is about group engagement. It's easy to take side conversations to the side, so go ahead and do that so that no one else is bothered.

Notification overload: Managing the noise

If you've ever been invited into a conversation with lots of people or have been added to a larger chat room, you might have experienced the frustration of receiving too many notifications. Active group chats can quickly become chaotic and confusing. These distractions are not good for your mental health or your productivity. But minimizing the noise doesn't mean you can't participate in group chats!

The first thing you can do is turn off the notifications for that specific app on your phone and desktop. This action turns off all notifications for that app. If it's only that particular group chat you're trying to mute and not all your messages, you can go into the chat settings for your specific group chat and mute or manage messages there. Messaging apps like Facebook, for example, have the capability to go into the group settings and mute message notifications, mute call notifications, or mute all notifications. Additionally, you can completely ignore a group, block specific group members, or altogether leave a group.

This is why messaging apps are far superior in group chats than traditional SMS text message groups. You have so much more control over your involvement and notifications from the group chat and the freedom to use tools that can even save your sanity and improve productivity.

REMEMBER

As a member of the group, you need to respect the time and productivity of the other members. Avoid unnecessary discussions and distractions, especially if the group purpose isn't casual or for keeping in touch.

Knowing when to leave a group

There are many reasons you may want to leave a group. You may have been added accidentally, the group has become overwhelming, or you've had dealings with a specific group member. If any of these situations applies to you, it's entirely okay to leave a message group at any time.

However, if you feel like you need to continue being a part of the group or you sense that the impulse to leave might be emotionally charged, your first move should be to temporarily mute the group. This gives you time away from the group discussion and notifications but doesn't remove you from the group altogether. After you take some time away, you may find that you want to remain in the group chat, after all, and it's far better to unmute the group than to have to go to an admin and ask to be let in.

However, if the time has come for you to leave for whatever reason, do so. The beauty of messaging apps is that you can easily leave a group at any time.

REMEMBER

You don't need to announce your departure unless you feel it's necessary to avoid hurt feelings or a hit to your reputation. Still, generally speaking, it's seen as unnecessary and rude to announce your departure from a group chat.

Don't take offense if people leave

There are many reasons people choose to leave a group chat. Sometimes it's because the notifications are too much and sometimes because the topic is no longer important to them. Some people simply don't like being in a group chat, and it has nothing to do with the people who are involved in the group. If someone does leave the group you're in, don't take offense.

It's okay to leave a group. But it isn't okay to bad-mouth or make fun of those who decide to depart. Often, the reasons someone has for leaving a group chat have nothing to do with you, and it isn't because of anything you did. Bad-mouthing others isn't acceptable and should stop immediately.

Leaving a group can be a difficult decision, especially if you're close to the people in the group. It's important to remember that there are many reasons that someone might choose to leave a group, and it isn't always personal.

6

The Part of Tens

> » Being aware of your language
>
> » Being careful with humor and sarcasm
>
> » Citing your sources
>
> » Minding your grammar, spelling, and punctuation
>
> » Using email properly
>
> » Respecting others' privacy
>
> » Fact-checking before reposting
>
> » Sharing with discretion
>
> » Being forgiving

Chapter **20**

Ten Good Manners to Follow

The old saying "You have to give respect to get respect" is trite for a good reason — it's always true in human relations. It's especially true online because it's easy to think you can get away with typing anything online because people can't see your face.

Even if you think you can manage to behave yourself when people look at your face on a webcam but are free to behave differently when they can't, people are usually smart enough to read your true intentions in what you say — and they will react accordingly. That can lead to lost connections and lost opportunities. So it's always important to act like an adult — no matter when and how you communicate with others.

Sometimes people need reminders, so here are ten good manners to follow so that you can keep your connections strong and build new ones.

Respecting Others

Respecting others is the first and most important good manner to remember. It's easy to say disrespectful and even hurtful things to someone when you're not face-to-face (especially when you don't know that someone).

It's important to remember that others you communicate with online are real people and are affected by what you say and write. You likely wouldn't say something mean or disrespectful to someone's face in person, because you would see their emotional reaction (and perhaps get an unfortunate physical reaction).

Think of the reaction you or someone you care about would have if someone else says what you're thinking to say. Would you still say it?

REMEMBER

Even if someone is being hurtful or disrespectful to you, you don't have to behave that way.

Watching Your Language

Without the contexts of emotional and nonverbal communication online, written text can *easily* be misunderstood. For example, have you ever sent a text or an email message to someone with some of the text in ALL CAPS to make a point?

The recipients likely responded by demanding to know why you were yelling at them — right there, you've experienced being misunderstood. Other people may react badly if you use strong language, all caps, or multiple exclamation marks, and/or profanity in your message, especially if recipients have young children and don't want their kids to read that message and then ask the parent uncomfortable questions.

TIP

Whenever you plan on sending a message to someone, let it sit for at least a few minutes, walk away, come back, and read it to yourself. If you find that you have an emotional reaction to some of the text, edit that text before you send it. That can save you a lot of grief.

Using Humor and Sarcasm with Care

Being funny is a natural part of seeing your personality shine through. If you're typing something humorous, you may also be tempted to add emoticons to show that you're being humorous (a smiley face) or sarcastic (a winking face). Or you may want to share an animated GIF file with something you think is funny.

However, you need to be aware of people you're talking with in either a Zoom meeting or a discussion group. You'll find that something seemingly funny to one audience is hurtful and disrespectful to others. Emoticons don't protect you from negative energy if you type something that one or more people find less than amusing.

Giving Credit When Credit Is Due

Whenever you share an idea with someone else, cite your sources. It's easy to ignore this advice, because you want to be seen as knowledgeable, to make yourself feel better and have others think highly of you. Of course, if you're proven to be wrong, you'll be called out on it. You may decide to double down on your assertion, but that won't stop people from seeing you as an egotist who should be ignored.

Cite the source of your information. It may lead to a discussion about the information, and you may discover that the source isn't completely true. If that's the case, others won't see you as someone who's rude but instead as someone who is genuinely looking for answers.

Dotting Your I's and Crossing Your T's

Online communication is largely a written medium. Even in an online conversation, you still have the ability to chat online. But you should be aware of both your audience and your communication medium when you decide how to type.

For example, in text messages, you may want to use text abbreviations such as *lmao*, *gr8*, or *rofl* with your friends because you know that they'll accept them. If you're in a professional situation, such as participating in a company online discussion group, or you just want to be taken seriously as someone who's educated and worth talking to, ditch the trendy abbreviations and follow proper writing style.

When you have a lot of grammatical errors or you use text in the wrong style for the situation, don't be surprised when few, if any, people engage with you.

TIP

After you compose a post, read it again to catch any errors you find in the spelling and determine whether you can rewrite a passage to make things clearer. Taking a minute to read what you wrote can catch a lot of unforced errors.

Being a Proper Emailer

Email is still a vital communication medium, especially in professional settings. Following good manners with email ensures that others don't refer to you as that person who complicates their lives by clogging their inboxes.

You may think that it's important for everyone to know your response to an email because the person you're replying to sent their email to a large group of people. But everyone may not want to read your reply. Just click or tap Reply, not Reply All, and respond to the person one-on-one.

You may think that attaching multiple large image files will help you make your point, but it can also cause an email server to slow down or crash or result in the server not even sending your email with the image file attachments. If you need to send large files, consider putting the files in the appropriate location on the company intranet, or use an online file sharing service that offers free space, like Dropbox.

REMEMBER

If you reply to a message, delete all but the most recent correspondence from the sender. When that doesn't happen, more messages in the thread pile up, and suddenly the messages becomes long and cumbersome. That can be a pain when you have to look in the message thread for something — or have to print the message. However, if you have a thread that has crucial information in it that people need to know, then consider removing just the non-crucial parts. You can also start a new message with a subject line that refers to the topic and tell recipients that you're starting a new thread.

Keeping Other People's Private Information Private

Treat others' privacy as you would your own. Don't assume that if you have someone else's contact information, it's okay to share with others. (And keep in mind the old saying about what *assume* means.)

Be careful with information, including private conversations, locations, pictures, and especially passwords. Giving away personal info without using the appropriate amount of caution can put that other person or even people you don't know in online or physical danger.

TIP

Talk with the sender of an email before forwarding that email to someone else. It may even be a good idea to talk about a standing rule about how to forward email with that sender and/or an entire group.

If you're sending email to someone else and you want to copy someone, blind-carbon-copy (bcc) them rather than carbon-copy (cc) them. The people you're copying may not want the recipient to know their contact information, especially if the copied people don't know the recipient.

When you upload photos and/or videos of other people, either in a public forum or to your own friends on a social media platform, be sure to get their permission. This is especially true if you're sharing a photo of someone else's kids or relatives.

WARNING

If you tag people on Facebook or Instagram, others can access pictures of those people on their profiles unless they have changed their settings to ensure that their profiles are private.

Keeping Your Facts Straight

Plenty of misinformation is on the web, and you may unintentionally spread it by passing along information that you think looks good. However, if you don't fact-check what you post from another source, others will check up on it. If they find out that you're wrong and you're posting bad information, people will decide that they shouldn't be wasting their time on you.

There are ways to find the right information. You can ask someone you know who you think may have the answers or knows someone who does. Search for the information on Google — and check the information to make sure that it's accurate, attributed to a person correctly, and up-to-date.

You can also visit a fact-checking site like Snopes to see whether it has any information, because, if you're sharing misinformation, it's likely that it has spread far and wide and so a fact checking site has researched the issue. (You're right — that jingle is "The More You Know.")

REMEMBER

Viruses and other malware can be contained in online invitations asking you to send a pertinent piece of information to ten of your friends and then asking them to do the same. Phishing also happens when people post information on social media feeds asking questions that seem harmless, like who your favorite teachers were in school. This is a common question for security questions that posters like to ask to entice people to respond. Then the posters use that information to try to access your account.

That cure for cancer might sound pretty impressive, but it just causes upset if it's a hoax. And urban myths add to the noise of the Internet and waste people's time. If you aren't sure of the facts, do the necessary due diligence to make sure that what you're intending to post as factual is in fact true.

Refraining from Oversharing

It should go without saying that you don't post or share inappropriate material, even privately. But we've seen news reports over time about how people continue to share even their private videos and pictures to others and somehow believe that won't be shared with the world.

Also consider that your boss, your kids, your relatives, and your friends keep an eye on your social media profile. If you don't want your relatives asking you uncomfortable questions, or your boss requesting that you come into their office, don't make inappropriate posts. Data on the Internet is never truly private, and what's on the Internet stays there *forever.*

What's more, be careful about what you say during phone conversations in public places. Everyone can see and hear you, and you don't know who may be watching to see whether you're distracted so that they can steal info or may be listening to try to get some information they can use to hurt you and/or the company you work for or own.

WARNING

You and others can unwittingly share information that thieves can look at to get your information. For example, a common access security question is your mother's maiden name, and if your mother shares that information in her social media posts that also appear on your feed, then you should alert her to this threat. If your social media profile is public, and you decide to post pictures showing things like your home address or that you're on vacation far away, thieves can see these posts and put 2 and 2 together.

Knowing That to Err Is Human, and to Forgive, Divine

Not everyone knows the rules. Some people can't write well. They're not as careful as one should be about sharing information, because they don't see anyone else in front of them helping to guide them about appropriate behavior. Computer-mediated communication is different from communicating face-to-face, where you have more verbal and nonverbal cues.

So be forgiving and be patient. And then lend them this book or encourage them to buy their own copy!

REMEMBER

If a friend or colleague has posted something that you know is questionable, false, or insensitive, consider sending them a private message or talking with them in person privately to tell them why you found their post problematic and ask if they would consider reposting it. Don't bring up the issue publicly and shame them. Your friend or colleague may even thank you for talking about your concerns on the q.t.

IN THIS CHAPTER

» Using ALL CAPS

» Failing to proofread

» Thinking you're the only one who deserves attention

» Behaving or texting inappropriately

» Arguing with or flaming people

» Failing to respect others' privacy

» Spamming others

» Ignoring others

» Holding loud cellphone conversations

» Texting while in a conversation

Chapter **21**

Ten Bad Behaviors to Avoid

I f you're the type of person who needs to convince your brain to do something by reading about all the negative stuff you should avoid rather than the positive things you should do, this is the chapter for you.

When you avoid the ten bad behaviors that we list in this chapter, you minimize any bad energy or karma or just plain old stress that would come your way from people upset with you and your behavior.

Capping Everything

It can be difficult, sometimes, to put that special emphasis on something you really want to say in text form. Or maybe it's just too hard to use the Shift key — too much work. Instead, it's easy to just press the Caps Lock key and then type a few words to ensure that your feelings come across properly, or just to type an entire message that way because it's much easier on you.

Then you may wonder why people are asking you why you're shouting at them. Or that people aren't getting back to you in response to your messages, only to find out through the grapevine that people find your use of all caps annoying.

You can be even more annoying by telling folks that this is just the way you are and that they will just have to get used to it.

Leaving Your Mistakes for All to See

Do you never worry that what you're typing is what you really intended to say? After all, your writing skills are good enough and people can understand what they're reading even if you make typos, right? And if you type on a smartphone, people know all about autocorrect errors and will be able to figure out what you're saying?

Oh, yes, and people know that when you use acronyms, they'll immediately understand what you're saying. For example, when you use *LOL*, they know you mean Lots of Love — until you find out that everyone wonders what's wrong with you when you're responding to messages with Laughing Out Loud.

Putting Yourself at the Center of Everything

If you think you're the only one who's worthy of attention, it's perfectly fine to talk over people in a Zoom meeting, just as you would in a face-to-face meeting — right? Especially if you're the host of the meeting, because that makes you the most important person. All you need to do is mute everyone.

And, if someone has an opinion you personally disagree with and find harmful, you can just mute them or interrupt them as soon as they start talking so that they can't express themselves. You've saved the day!

Or so you think — until people stop attending your online meetings, give terse responses, or ignore your messages or avoid you in person. If you engage in your behavior at work and you have a manager, soon you'll have an uncomfortable conversation with your superior. Feeling heroic now?

Being Inappropriate No Matter the Occasion

People know what you're talking about when you make jokes, because everyone feels the same way as you do, don't they? People know that you're joking around when you make fun of a co-worker or a whole class of people. They won't take it seriously. And, if you swear or make inappropriate gestures in an online meeting? Adults are used to that stuff, right?

Sure, until you get an immediate and intense response from people who feel distressed and upset, which makes you defensive and angry. Now you're in a heated argument that drains your energy.

An argument also puts you at risk. If you engage in inappropriate behavior in an online meeting, there are plenty of witnesses. And, when you write inappropriate comments in an email or text, people have evidence they can use to move against you.

If you double down on your comments that others find inappropriate, don't be surprised if people shun you. If you make these comments or engage in these behaviors at work, look at it this way — soon you'll have plenty of time to make these comments as often as you like without having to get up every morning, go to work, and make money.

TIP

Oh, and if you own a business, you'll enjoy the fun of draining company money and your time battling one or more lawsuits from angry employees.

Being Argumentative

The term *flame war* goes all the way back to the time of bulletin board systems (BBSs), which were the main online communications medium from the late 1970s until the mid-1990s, when the Internet quickly replaced BBSs as the online communications medium of choice. (For those not in the know, *flaming* is a heated exchange that goes back and forth between two or more parties where insults are liberally hurled.)

And if someone says something to you online or in a virtual meeting, it's natural to get your emotions involved, right? It's exciting because now you're highly engaged with someone you think is wrong. And it's okay to insult the other person or group of people because you're defending yourself and you want to "own" that person or group.

If you're on social media, how long do you think you can keep up arguments and flame wars and not be banned?

If you're in an email argument at work with one or more coworkers, how long until the coworker(s) you insulted report you to your boss?

If you're in a heated argument with a subordinate in your business, you're just acting like Steve Jobs, right? That subordinate won't leave and take all their knowledge with them, because they're just as committed as you are and they'll be motivated! Right?

How long do you think it'll be until you get burned?

REMEMBER

Social networks are more attuned than ever to stopping bad behavior. Workers have more options these days for working elsewhere and starting their own business — and especially since the COVID-19 pandemic. Employers want to keep the good employees who want to stay — and not put their businesses at risk of legal trouble.

Invading Others' Privacy

Do you think that whoever connects with you online has given you the right to share their information whenever and wherever you want?

Don't be surprised if you find that when you share people's information, they don't like it. If you share someone else's contact information with others without their permission, you may get rebuked or, in the case of doing so while on the job, you may be reported to your supervisor.

If you're an employer and you share employee information with others, the situation is murkier. You may want to seek legal advice about the ground rules before you do that, and then share that information with your employees so that everyone is on the same page.

WARNING

Sharing information about people without their consent, especially private information, may also fall within the definition of *doxing,* which is publishing others' information with malicious intent. (Or what someone thinks is malicious.) Laws in some countries, and areas within countries, prohibit doxing. For example, the state of California includes doxing in its cyberharassment laws. So, unless you think you look good in orange, this is another reason to respect everyone's privacy online.

Being a Spammer

If you want to attract the attention of someone, why not bombard them with repeated messages demanding that they connect with you? That's especially tempting on social media if you need to get hold of a company or an individual.

That is also one definition of spam. Yes, you thought it was bad just to send email messages to others promoting yourself or your business when the other party hasn't (or parties haven't) asked for it. But you can also be a spammer just as easily on social media platforms and on messaging systems.

It doesn't take long until your repeated messages are construed as harassment, and it takes even less time for someone to take action if you're trying to get someone to go out with you or, worse, sending sexually explicit text messages and/or photos.

With email and text messaging, people can take legal action in the United States against you under the Controlling the Assault of Non-Solicited Pornography And Marketing Act of 2003 (affectionately known as the CAN-SPAM Act). Other countries have spam laws, too, so if you're outside the US or want to spam people in other countries, don't assume that you're safe.

REMEMBER

Users on social media can block others easily, but social media also makes it easy for people to complain about users on a platform, for a variety of reasons, including harassment. What's more, social networks have strict anti-spam policies. For example, Twitter thinks of spam as "platform manipulation" that could lead to your account being banned. If you like being on social media, it's a good idea to follow their rules, yes?

Leaving Others in the Lurch

On social media, people can easily approach you for direct help. For example, someone you don't know can send you InMail on LinkedIn asking for a specific service that the person thinks you offer. If your company doesn't perform that particular task, you can take a little time to find out who does it in your area and provide that information. (Yes, this happened to Eric recently, and he was happy to help.)

You may receive no immediate benefit beyond feeling like you earned some brownie points, receiving good karma, or just plain feeling good, but consider that you may be building your credibility as a trusted source. When you help others who ask for it, you're playing the long game.

Also consider that social networks keep track of how long it takes you to respond to a message. For example, Facebook publishes your response time in your response so other people can see how helpful you are.

REMEMBER

If someone in your office asks you directly for help in an online meeting, by email, or even by text, it should go without saying to help that person as much as you can. Helping others makes you look good and won't get you in trouble as either an unhelpful employee or an uncaring boss.

Talking as Loudly as Possible on Your Cellphone

When you're talking loudly on the phone, everyone can easily hear you and you can easily annoy everyone. Doing so can also be dangerous. If you're in the dairy aisle and gabbing about the other items you still need to buy at the store, the worst that can happen is that other shoppers may just grab their provisions and move away from you as soon as possible. But if you're talking about sensitive company information or a private matter with another person while in public, you never know who may be listening. Someone may be interested in staying close to you and finding out more about you or the person you're talking to.

You make a nefarious person's job even easier if you talk using a speaker on your smartphone, because then someone else can hear both sides of the conversation. And, if you're holding your phone away from you, someone nearby can more easily sneak a glance at your screen and find out, for example, the name of the caller or their phone number. That person may then remember that name or number and look it up on social media or search online for other information, like a physical address.

WARNING

So, you may ask, what might really happen? Think about how someone you talked to would feel if they were suddenly being harassed by someone they don't know. Or determine how you would feel if your company secrets were being leaked by someone and the leaders (at the very least) were demanding to know who the leaker is. Get the idea?

Texting While Talking with Others (The Wrong Kind of Multitasking)

You can *easily* become bored in an online meeting, especially when the topic under discussion doesn't involve you. So, it's easy to look at your phone to see what's going on and start texting other people. No one else will notice, right?

If everyone has their cameras on during the meeting, people will notice that you're looking down at your phone just as they would if you were doing it in an in-person meeting.

REMEMBER

You can do something on your phone if there is a pertinent question to be answered during the meeting, such as to confirm how many packages were shipped during the previous month. But be transparent about it by announcing what you're going to do. When you're done talking with or texting the other person, put the phone back down.

Even if you're talking with one person in an online conversation, repeatedly looking down and avoiding eye contact is considered rude. No one looks at people constantly throughout a conversation, but if you think that texting one person while you're talking with another person is acceptable, I'll leave to your imagination any images of what can happen.

Index

A

abbreviations, in text messaging, 254

acceptable-use policy (AUP), 173

accessibility, virtual meetings and, 190

acronyms, using, 57

actions

  on agendas for virtual meetings, 208

  planning after going viral, 120–121

adding

  people to group chats, 298–299

  people to group texts, 274–275

adults, digital etiquette and, 52–54

age

  about, 51–52

  common rules, 59–62

  variations in etiquette for different, 52–59

agendas

  creating for virtual meetings, 207–208

  for online events, 234

  sticking to, in virtual meetings, 227

  for webinars, 234

Android phones, Do Not Disturb feature on, 260

anger, in personal emails, 161

"anonymous" function (Facebook), 86

apologizing, during crises, 124–125

argumentative, being, 316

attendance, of virtual meetings, 193, 215–223

attendees

  on agendas for virtual meetings, 207

  creating connections in virtual meetings, 209–211

  following up with of webinars and online events, 240

  following up with who couldn't attend webinars and online events, 241

  for online events, 235

  for virtual meetings, 204–206

  for webinars, 235

attribution, 96

audience

  being mindful of your, 67–68

  etiquette for engaging in webinars and online events, 239–241

  knowing your, 230–231

  negative comments and, 107

  negative reviews and, 107

  respect for in livestreams, 155

audio, muting in virtual meetings, 225

authenticity, as an option after going viral, 118

avoiding

  bad behaviors, 313–319

  bad reviews, 112–113

  burnout from virtual meetings, 199–200

  common mistakes in social media groups, 135–137

  embarrassment in livestreams, 153–154

  miscommunication, 255

  mistakes with text messages, 275–279

  negative reviews, 112–113

  overmessaging, 292–293

  plagiarism, 122–123

  taking over in webinars and online events, 243

B

background noise, eliminating, 60–61

banning spam, 31–33

Barcellos, Anthony (instructor), 56, 57

behaviors to avoid, 313–319

benefits, of actively participating in livestreams, 156

best practices, for direct messaging, 291–294

blocking, 84–85

blogs, sharing livestreams on, 148

blowing up phones, 278–279

boundaries

  establishing, 119

  maintaining, 41–48

breaks, on agendas for virtual meetings, 208

About the Authors

Eric Butow is the owner of Butow Communications Group (BCG) in Jackson, California. BCG offers web development, online marketing, and technical writing services for businesses of all sizes. The author of 41 computing and user experience books, Eric's most recent books include *Instagram For Business For Dummies,* 2nd Edition, *Ultimate Guide to Social Media Marketing* (Entrepreneur Press), and *MCA Microsoft Office Specialist Complete Study Guide* (Sybex). Eric also holds bachelor's and master's degrees in communication from California State University, Fresno, where his master's thesis focused on computer-mediated communication. When he's not working or writing books, you can find Eric enjoying time with his friends, walking around the historic Gold Rush town of Jackson, and helping his mother manage her infant and toddler daycare business.

Kendra Losee is an award-winning marketing strategist with more than 20 years of strategic digital marketing experience and leadership at digital agencies and universities. She is the founder of Mota Marketing, a boutique marketing agency, and is an adjunct social media professor at several universities around San Diego. An expert in the areas of digital marketing, social media, and omnichannel marketing strategies, Kendra has won numerous marketing awards and was named Higher Education Marketer of the Year by the American Marketing Association in 2011. A firm believer in the power of education, Kendra loves teaching students and entrepreneurs. She received her BA in Communications from the University of California, San Diego and her EMBA from Purdue University. In her free time, you can find her exploring dog beaches with her furry sidekick, Westley, or with her outrigger canoe team somewhere off the coast of Southern California.

Kelly Noble Mirabella is an internationally sought-after digital marketing trainer and consultant. She is the creator of Baby Got Bot and the owner of Stellar Media Marketing. Kelly has had an action-packed 14-year career in digital marketing, which can be attributed to her vast knowledge of not only digital marketing but also her experience running a successful bootstrapped business. Over the past 14 years, Kelly has helped teach and mentor digital marketers, Realtors, entrepreneurs, and professionals across various industries to not only use the digital marketing tools and platforms available today but also in the starting and running of new entrepreneurial adventures. Kelly's depth of knowledge is well known in the industry, and some have even joked that she is a digital marketing encyclopedia.

Dedication

To my family and friends, who keep inspiring me.

— Eric Butow

To my family, friends, and students who continually support, inspire, and motivate me to be a better person, achieve my goals, and help others do the same. And to my coffee maker, which kept me caffeinated throughout.

— Kendra Losee

To my husband, Jeff, who has listened, encouraged, and helped me achieve all my dreams and more. And to my spirited girls, who are my inspiration.

— Kelly Noble Mirabella

Authors' Acknowledgments

I'd like to thank my coauthors, Kendra Losee and Kelly Noble Mirabella, for being such wonderful coauthors and great people to work with. I want to thank our amazing technical editor, Rebecca Bollwitt. My thanks, as always, to the intrepid Matt Wagner, who served as the agent on this book. I also want to thank all the pros at Wiley who made this book possible, especially Steve Hayes and Paul Levesque. And I also thank you for buying this book and working to make yourself a better human being.

— Eric Butow

Thank you to my amazing coauthors, Kelly Noble Mirabella and Eric Butow, who made the writing of this book a truly enjoyable experience. I'd also like to thank Yvi Heimann for her role in helping this book become a reality. And to the team at Wiley, including the fantastic Steve Hayes and Paul Levesque, thank you for your hard work on this book, and for your vision in recognizing the need for this book! Thank you to my family and friends for your ongoing support and encouragement. Finally, thanks to you for purchasing this book and taking the steps toward making the digital world a kinder, more empathetic place.

— Kendra Losee

I would like to say a huge thank-you to my talented coauthors, Kendra Losee and Eric Butow. Also to Yvi Heiman who was the door opener for this project and to all the women and men who made this book happen. To my family and friends who encourage, support, and keep me inspired. And of course, to the team at Wiley, including the talented and much appreciated Steve Hayes and Paul Levesque, who make us look good. Finally, thank you to all who purchase this book and practice the fine art of caring about other people with empathy and respect. The digital landscape might be changing, but we can still be kind.

— Kelly Noble Mirabella

Publisher's Acknowledgments

Acquisitions Editor: Steve Hayes

Senior Project Editor: Paul Levesque

Copy Editor: Becky Whitney

Tech Editor: Rebecca Bollwitt

Production Editor: SaiKarthick Kumarasamy

Cover Image: © pressmaster/Adobe Stock Photos